working
SPANISH
for
HOMEOWNERS

Gail Stein and
Paulette Waiser

1807
WILEY
2007

Wiley Publishing, Inc.

Published by Wiley, Hoboken, NJ
Published simultaneously in Canada

Library of Congress Cataloging-in-Publication Data:
Stein, Gail.
Working Spanish for homeowners / Gail Stein and Paulette Waiser.
         p. cm.
     ISBN-13: 978-0-470-14562-3
     ISBN-10: 0-470-14562-5
     1. Spanish language—Conversation and phrase books (for homeowners)
I. Waiser, Paulette, 1951– II. Title.
PC4120.H66S74 2008
468.3'421—dc22
                                          2007028134

Printed in the United States of America

10 9 8 7 6 5 4 3 2 1

Book design by Melissa Auciello-Brogan
Book production by Wiley Publishing, Inc. Composition Services
Wiley Bicentennial Logo: Richard J. Pacifico

This book is dedicated to my husband, Douglas, for his love and patience; to my wonderful children, Eric, Michael, and Katherine, for their encouragement and support; and to my mother, Sara Bernstein, and in memory of my father, Jack Bernstein, for always being there for me.
—Gail Stein

This book is dedicated to my husband, Samuel, for his patience and support; to my wonderful children, Melissa and Justin, whose encouragement and determination were steadfast and enabled me to persevere; and to my parents, Gene and Sam Meisner, whose love inspired me to pursue my goals.
—Paulette Waiser

Acknowledgments

Many thanks to Roxane Cerda, our acquisitions editor, who was so helpful in getting this book off the ground; to Elizabeth Kuball, our project editor and copy editor, whose excellent editing skills and suggestions made this book a reality; to Wigberto Rivera, whose technical expertise and input were invaluable; and to Christina Stambaugh, Kristie Rees, and all the other people at John Wiley & Sons, for their patience and help.

Contents

1

Pronunciation Guide

Spanish sounds are relatively easy to master because they resemble the sounds of English, and because Spanish letters and letter combinations are generally pronounced phonetically (unlike English letters and letter combinations, which may be pronounced in a variety of ways—car versus cat; **tough** versus thr**ough**). When speaking Spanish, if you stress the wrong syllable or mispronounce a word, don't worry—you'll still be understood and your efforts will be appreciated.

Stress and Accents

Here are the rules for stress in Spanish:

1. If the word ends in a vowel *(a, e, i, o, u)*, *n*, or *s*, stress the next-to-the-last syllable:

ventana (window)	*behm-__tah__-nah*
joven (young)	*__hoh__ behn*
espejos (mirrors)	*ehs-__peh__-hohs*

2. If the word ends in a consonant other than *n* or *s*, stress the last syllable:

pared (wall)	*pah-__rehd__*
comedor (dining room)	*koh-meh-__dohr__*

3. Any exceptions to the preceding rules have accent marks to help you place the stress correctly:

buró (nightstand)	*boo-__roh__*
lámpara (lamp)	*__lahm__-pah-rah*

Here are the three accent marks in Spanish:

* ´: This accent goes above a vowel to indicate that the syllable is stressed.
    ático (attic)   *ah-tee-koh*
    inglés (English)   *een-glehs*

* ˜: The tilde goes above an *n* to produce the *ny* sound in un**i**on:
    baño (bathroom)   *bah-nyoh*
    bañera (bathtub)   *bah-nyeh-rah*

* ¨: The umlaut is used on the letter *u* in *diphthongs* (combinations of vowels) to show that each vowel is pronounced separately:
    nicaragüense (Nicaraguan)   *nee-kah-rah-goo-ehn-seh*

Vowels

The sound of each Spanish vowel consistently remains the same and is pronounced the way it is written.

Vowels

Vowel	Sound	Example	Pronunciation
a	ah	**mesa** (table)	*meh-sah*
e	eh	**estufa** (stove)	*ehs-too-fah*
i	ee	**piso** (floor)	*pee-soh*
o	oh	**techo** (roof)	*teh-choh*
u	oo	**ducha** (shower)	*doo-chah*

Diphthongs

A diphthong is generally (but not always) a combination of one weak vowel (*i* or *u*) and one strong vowel (*a, e,* or *o*) that appear in the same syllable.

Diphthongs

Diphthong	Sound	Example	Pronunciation
ai	ah-ee	**aire** (air)	*ah-ee-reh*
au	ah-oo	**auto** (auto)	*ah-oo-toh*
ay	ah-ee	**hay** (there is/are)	*ah-ee*
ei	eh-ee	**veinte** (twenty)	*beh-een-teh*
eo	eh-oh	**video** (VCR)	*bee-deh-oh*
eu	eh-oo	**euro** (euro)	*eh-oo-roh*
ia	ee-ah	**limpiar** (to clean)	*leem-pee-ahr*
ie	ee-eh	**siete** (seven)	*see-eh-teh*
io	ee-oh	**patio** (patio)	*pah-tee-oh*
iu	ee-oo	**ciudad** (city)	*see-oo-dahd*
oi	oh-ee	**oigo** (I hear)	*oh-ee-goh*
ua	oo-ah	**cuarto** (room)	*koo-ahr-toh*
ue	oo-eh	**dueño** (owner)	*doo-eh-nyoh*
ui	oo-ee	**cuidar** (to care for)	*koo-ee-dahr*
uo	oo-oh	**cuota** (quota)	*koo-oh-tah*

Consonants

Most Spanish consonants are pronounced in the same way as they are pronounced in English.

Consonants

Consonant	Sound	Example	Pronunciation
b (beh)	b	**balcón** (balcony)	*bahl-kohn*
c (seh)+ e or i	s	**césped** (lawn)	*sehs-pehd*
c (seh)+ a, o, u	k	**cocina** (kitchen)	*koh-see-nah*
ch (cheh)	ch	**chimenea** (fireplace)	*chee-meh-neh-ah*
d (deh)	d	**desayuno** (breakfast)	*deh-sah-yoo-noh*
f (eh-feh)	f	**fecha** (date)	*feh-chah*

continued

Consonant	Sound	Example	Pronunciation
g (heh)+ e or i	h	**gente** (people)	*hehn-teh*
g (heh)+ a, o, u	g	**garaje** (garaje)	*gah-rah-heh*
h (ah-cheh)	silent	**horno** (oven)	*ohr-noh*
j (hoh-tah)	h	**julio** (July)	*hoo-lee-oh*
k (kah)	k	**kilo** (kilo)	*kee-loh*
l (eh-leh)	l	**lávabo** (sink)	*lah-bah-boh*
ll (eh-yeh)	y	**silla** (chair)	*see-yah*
m (eh-meh)	m	**muebles** (furniture)	*moo-eh-blehs*
n (eh-neh)	n	**no** (no)	*noh*
ñ (eh-nyeh)	ny	**niño** (child)	*nee-nyoh*
p (peh)	p	**pasillo** (hall)	*pah-see-yoh*
q (koo)	k	**quince** (fifteen)	*keen-seh*
r (eh-reh) (within a word, rolled a little)	r	**televisor** (TV set)	*teh-leh-bee-sohr*
r (eh-rreh) (r at the beginning of a word, rolled a lot)	rr	**reloj** (clock)	*rreh-loh*
rr (eh-rreh) (rolled a lot)	rr	**terraza** (terrace)	*teh-rrah-sah*
s (eh-seh)	s	**sala** (room)	*sah-lah*
t (teh)	t	**tienda** (store)	*tee-ehn-dah*
v (beh)	soft b	**veinte** (twenty)	*beh-een-teh*
w (doh-bleh beh)	w	**western** (western)	*wehs-tehrn*
x (eh-kees)	ks	**excusa** (excuse)	*ehks-koo-sah*
y (ee gree-eh-gah)	y	**yo** (I)	*ee-oh*
z (seh-tah)	s	**zapato** (shoe)	*sah-pah-toh*

The Basics

Polite Expressions

Please.
Por favor.
pohr fah-bohr

Thank you (very much).
(Muchas) Gracias.
(moo-chahs) grah-see-ahs

Thanks a million.
Un millón de gracias.
oon mee-yohn deh grah-see-ahs

You're welcome.
De nada.
deh nah-dah

Bless you!
¡Salud!
sah-lood

Excuse me. (Use if you bumped into or disturbed someone.)
Perdón.
pehr-dohn

Excuse me. (Use if you are leaving a group or passing through a crowd.)
Con permiso.
kohn pehr-mee-soh

Excuse me. (Use if you want someone's attention.)
Con permiso.
kohn pehr-mee-soh

I'm (very) sorry.
Lo siento (mucho).
loh see-ehn-toh (moo-choh)

Don't worry.
No se preocupe.
noh seh preh-oh-koo-peh

Have a nice day!
¡Que le vaya bien!
keh leh bah-yah bee-ehn

Cardinal Numbers

Cardinal numbers are used for counting.

Number	Spanish	Pronunciation
0	**cero**	*seh-roh*
1	**uno**	*oo-noh*
2	**dos**	*dohs*
3	**tres**	*trehs*
4	**cuatro**	*koo-ah-troh*
5	**cinco**	*seen-koh*
6	**seis**	*seh-ees*
7	**siete**	*see-eh-teh*
8	**ocho**	*oh-choh*
9	**nueve**	*noo-eh-beh*
10	**diez**	*dee-ehs*
11	**once**	*ohn-seh*
12	**doce**	*doh-seh*
13	**trece**	*treh-seh*
14	**catorce**	*kah-tohr-seh*

Number	Spanish	Pronunciation
15	quince	keen-seh
16	dieciséis (diez y seis)	dee-ehs-ee-seh-ees
17	diecisiete (diez y siete)	dee-ehs-ee-see-eh-teh
18	dieciocho (diez y ocho)	dee-ehs-ee-oh-choh
19	diecinueve (diez y nueve)	dee-ehs-ee-noo-eh-beh
20	veinte	beh-een-teh
21	veintiuno (veinte y uno)	beh-een-ee-oo-noh
22	veintidós (veinte y dos)	beh-een-ee-dohs
23	veintitrés (veinte y tres)	beh-een-ee-trehs
24	veinticuatro (veinte y cuatro)	beh-een-ee-koo-ah-troh
25	veinticinco (veinte y cinco)	beh-een-ee-seen-koh
26	veintiséis (veinte y seis)	beh-een-ee-seh-ees
27	veintisiete (veinte y siete)	beh-een-ee-see-eh-teh
28	veintiocho (veinte y ocho)	beh-een-ee-oh-choh
29	veintinueve (veinte y nueve)	beh-een-ee-noo-eh-beh
30	treinta	treh-een-tah

From 30 on, compound numbers are always written separately:

31	treinta y uno	treh-een-tah ee oo-noh
40	cuarenta	koo-ah-rehn-tah
45	cuarenta y cinco	koo-ah-rehn-tah ee seen-koh
50	cincuenta	seen-koo-ehn-tah
60	sesenta	seh-sehn-tah
70	setenta	seh-tehn-tah
80	ochenta	oh-chehn-tah
90	noventa	noh-behn-tah
100	ciento (cien)	see-ehn-toh (see-ehn)
101	ciento uno	see-ehn-toh oo-noh
200	doscientos	doh-see-ehn-tohs
500	quinientos	kee-nee-ehn-tohs
1000	mil	meel
2000	dos mil	dohs meel
100.000	cien mil	see-ehn meel
1.000.000	un millón	oon mee-yohn
2.000.000	dos millones	dohs mee-yoh-nehs
1.000.000.000	mil millones	meel mee-yoh-nehs
2.000.000.000	dos mil millones	dos meel mee-yoh-nehs

When you want to use Spanish cardinal numbers, remember to do the following:

* Use **uno** only when counting. **Uno** becomes **un** before a masculine noun and **una** before a feminine noun:

uno, dos, tres . . .	one, two, three . . .
un muchacho y una muchacha	a boy and a girl
treinta y un días	thirty-one days
veintiuna horas	twenty-one hours

* Use the conjunction *y* (and) only for numbers between 16 and 99. Note, however, that compound numbers between 21 and 29 are frequently written as one word (see the table earlier):

setenta y dos	seventy-two

but

ciento setenta y dos	one hundred seventy-two

* Show agreement with a feminine noun in compounds of **ciento** (for example, **doscientos, trescientos**):

doscientos kilos	two hundred kilos
trescientas libras	three hundred pounds

* Use **cien** before nouns and before the numbers **mil** and **millones**. Before all other numbers, use **ciento**:

cien copias	one hundred copies
cien mil dólares	one hundred thousand dollars
cien millones de personas	one hundred million people
ciento dos grados	one hundred and two degrees

* Use **un** before **millón** but not before **cien/ciento** or **mil**. When a noun follows **millón**, put **de** between **millón** and the noun:

cien razones	one hundred reasons
ciento ochenta días	one hundred eighty days
mil euros	one thousand euros
un millón de ideas	a million ideas

When reading Spanish numbers, keep in mind that the Spanish-speaking world writes numbers differently from the way Americans do. The number 1 has a little hook on top, which makes it look like a 7. So, to distinguish a 1 from a 7, a line is put through the 7, to look like this: 7.

In numerals and decimals, Spanish uses commas where English uses periods, and vice versa:

English	Spanish
6,000	6.000
0.95	0,95
$14.25	$14,25

Ordinal Numbers

Ordinal numbers allow you to express numbers in a series.

Ordinal	Spanish	Pronunciation
1st	**primero**	*pree-meh-roh*
2nd	**segundo**	*seh-goon-doh*
3rd	**tercero**	*tehr-seh-roh*
4th	**cuarto**	*koo-ahr-toh*
5th	**quinto**	*keen-toh*
6th	**sexto**	*sehks-toh*
7th	**séptimo**	*sehp-tee-moh*
8th	**octavo**	*ohk-tah-boh*
9th	**noveno**	*noh-beh-noh*
10th	**décimo**	*deh-see-moh*

When you want to use Spanish ordinal numbers, remember to do the following:

* Use Spanish ordinal numbers only through the tenth. After that, cardinal numbers are used:

el sexto piso	the sixth floor
el siglo veintiuno	the twenty-first century

* Change the final *o* of the masculine form to *a* for agreement with a feminine noun:

el segundo mes	the second month
la cuarta vez	the fourth time

- Drop the final *o* before a masculine singular noun when using **primero** and **tercero**:

  el primer minuto   the first minute
  el tercer día   the third day
  but
  el siglo tercero   the third century

- Use **primero** in dates to express the first of a month:

  el primero de julio   July 1st

Time

To ask for the time say:

What time is it?
¿Qué hora es?
keh oh-rah ehs

To express the time say:

It is one o'clock.
Es la una.
ehs lah oo-nah

It is two (three) o'clock.
Son las dos (tres).
sohn lahs dohs (trehs)

To ask the time of a certain activity or event say:

At what time. . . ?
¿A qué hora. . . ?
ah keh oh-rah

To answer, use **a** + **la** (singular) or **las** (plural) + a cardinal number:

at one o'clock
a la una
ah lah oo-nah

at ten o'clock
a las diez
ah lahs dee-ehs

The table that follows gives the times in Spanish before and after the hour:

Time	Spanish	Pronunciation
1:00	**la una**	*lah oo-nah*
2:05	**las dos y cinco**	*lahs dohs ee seen-koh*
3:10	**las tres y diez**	*lahs trehs ee dee-ehs*
4:15	**las cuatro y cuarto** or **las cuatro y quince**	*lahs koo-ah-troh ee koo-ahr-toh* or *lahs koo-ah-troh ee keen-seh*
5:20	**las cinco y veinte**	*lahs seen-koh ee beh-een-teh*
6:25	**las seis y veinticinco**	*lahs seh-ees ee beh-een-tee-seen-koh*
7:30	**las siete y media**	*lahs see-eh-teh ee meh-dee-ah*
7:35	**las ocho menos veinticinco**	*lahs oh-choh meh-nohs beh-een-tee-seen-koh*
8:40	**las nueve menos veinte**	*lahs noo-eh-beh meh-nohs beh-een-teh*
9:45	**las diez menos cuarto**	*lahs dee-ehs meh-nohs koo-ahr-toh*
10:50	**las once menos diez**	*lahs ohn-seh meh-nohs dee-ehs*
11:55	**las doce menos cinco**	*lahs doh-seh meh-nohs seen-koh*
noon	**el mediodía**	*ehl meh-dee-oh-dee-ah*
midnight	**la medianoche**	*lah meh-dee-ah-noh-cheh*

When time is of the essence, remember the following:

* To express time after the hour (before half past) use **y** and the number of minutes:

  At 7:05   **A las siete y cinco.**   *ah lahs see-eh-teh ee seen-koh*

* To express time before the next hour (after half past) use the number of the next hour + **menos** + the number of minutes:

  At 2:50.   **A las tres menos diez.**   *ah lahs trehs meh-nohs dee-ehs*

* You may hear the verb **faltar** (to be needed) + minutes + **para** + the next hour to express the time before the hour:

  It's 4:59.   **Falta un minuto para las cuatro.**   *fahl-tah oon mee-noo-toh pah-rah lahs koo-ah-troh*

  It's 9:40.   **Faltan veinte minutos para las diez.**   *fahl-tahn bee-een-teh mee-noo-tohs pah-rah lahs dee-ehs*

* Time may also be expressed by giving the hour and the number of minutes following it:

It is 2:20.	**Son las dos y veinte.**	*sohn lahs dohs ee beh-een-teh*
At 2:45.	**A las dos y cuarenta y cinco.**	*ah lahs dohs ee koo-ah-rehn-tah ee seen-koh*

Time-Related Vocabulary

English	Spanish	Pronunciation
a half-hour	**media hora**	*meh-dee-ah oh-rah*
a minute	**un minuto**	*oon mee-noo-toh*
a quarter of an hour	**un cuarto de hora**	*oon koo-ahr-toh deh oh-rah*
a second	**un segundo**	*oon seh-goon-doh*
after 3:00	**después de las tres**	*dehs-poo-ehs deh lahs trehs*
ago	**hace [time] que**	*ah-seh [time] keh*
an hour	**una hora**	*oo-nah oh-rah*
at about 2:00	**a eso de las dos**	*ah eh-soh deh lahs dohs*
at exactly 9:00	**a las nueve en punto**	*ah lahs noo-eh-beh ehn poon-toh*
before 8:00	**antes de las ocho**	*ahn-tehs deh lahs oh-choh*
early	**temprano**	*tehm-prah-noh*
eve	**la víspera**	*lah bees-peh-rah*
frequently	**frecuentemente**	*freh-koo-ehn-teh-mehn-teh*
from time to time	**a veces**	*ah beh-sehs*
immediately	**inmediatamente/ en seguida**	*een-meh-dee-ah-tah-mehn-teh/ehn seh-gee-dah*
in a while	**dentro de un rato**	*dehn-troh deh oon rrah-toh*
in an hour	**en una hora**	*ehn oo-nah oh-rah*
in the afternoon	**por la tarde**	*pohr lah tahr-deh*
in the evening	**por la noche**	*pohr lah noh-cheh*
in the morning	**por la mañana**	*pohr lah mah-nyah-nah*
in the very early morning	**por la madrugada**	*pohr lah mah-droo-gah-dah*

English	Spanish	Pronunciation
late (in arriving)	**tarde**	*tahr-deh*
later	**más tarde**	*mahs tahr-deh*
often	**a menudo**	*ah meh-noo-doh*
on time	**a tiempo**	*ah tee-ehm-poh*
per hour	**por hora**	*pohr oh-rah*
sharp	**en punto**	*ehn poon-toh*
since 10:00	**desde las diez**	*dehs-deh lahs dee-ehs*
Since what time?	**¿Desde qué hora?**	*dehs-deh keh oh-rah*
two hours ago	**hace dos horas**	*ah-seh dohs oh-rahs*
until 1:00	**hasta la una**	*ahs-tah lah oo-nah*

Days

What day is it today?
¿Qué día es hoy?
keh dee-ah ehs oh-ee

Today is Thursday.
Hoy es jueves.
oh-ee ehs hoo-eh-behs

What is today's date?
¿Cuál es la fecha de hoy?
koo-ahl ehs lah feh-chah deh oh-ee

Today is May 3rd.
Hoy es el tres de mayo.
oh-ee ehs ehl trehs deh mah-yoh

The days of the week in Spanish are not capitalized.

English	Spanish	Pronunciation
Monday	**lunes**	*loo-nehs*
Tuesday	**martes**	*mahr-tehs*
Wednesday	**miércoles**	*mee-ehr-koh-lehs*
Thursday	**jueves**	*hoo-eh-behs*
Friday	**viernes**	*bee-ehr-nehs*
Saturday	**sábado**	*sah-bah-doh*
Sunday	**domingo**	*doh-meen-goh*

To express "on a particular day," use the masculine, singular definite article **el** + singular day of the week:

I would like you to work on Monday.
Me gustaría que trabajara el lunes.
meh goos-tah-ree-ah keh trah-bah-hah-rah ehl loo-nehs

To express "on" when speaking about the day in a general sense, use the masculine, plural definite article **los** + plural day of the week:

I would like you to work on Mondays.
Me gustaría que trabajara los lunes.
meh goos-tah-ree-ah keh trah-bah-hah-rah lohs loo-nehs

Months

English	Spanish	Pronunciation
January	**enero**	*eh-neh-roh*
February	**febrero**	*feh-breh-roh*
March	**marzo**	*mahr-soh*
April	**abril**	*ah-breel*
May	**mayo**	*mah-yoh*
June	**junio**	*hoo-nee-oh*
July	**julio**	*hoo-lee-oh*
August	**agosto**	*ah-gohs-toh*
September	**septiembre**	*sehp-tee-ehm-breh*
October	**octubre**	*ohk-too-breh*
November	**noviembre**	*noh-bee-ehm-breh*
December	**diciembre**	*dee-see-ehm-breh*

To express "in" a particular month, use **en**:

We generally celebrate Easter in April.
Generalmente celebramos la Pascua en abril.
heh-neh-rahl-mehn-teh seh-leh-brah-mohs lah pahs-koo-ah ehn ah-breel

Dates

What is today's date?
¿Cuál es la fecha de hoy?
koo-ahl ehs lah feh-chah deh oh-ee

To answer, use the following formula:

Est + day + **(el)** + cardinal number (use **primero** only for the first day of each month) + **de** + month + **de** + year

It's (Tuesday) February 2nd (2008).
Hoy es (martes) el dos de febrero (de dos mil ocho).
oo-ee ehs (mahr-tehs) ehl dohs deh feh-breh-roh (deh dohs meel oh-choh)

When expressing a date in Spanish, remember that, although English dates are generally expressed in hundreds, Spanish years are expressed in thousands and hundreds:

1992 (nineteen [hundred] ninety-two)
mil novecientos noventa y dos
meel noh-beh-see-ehn-tohs noh-behn-tah ee dohs

If you have to read or write a date in Spanish, remember that the numerals are written with the day before the month. So January 12, 2009, would be written **el 12 de enero de 2009** or **12/1/09**.

Words and Expressions Pertaining to Dates

English	Spanish	Pronunciation
a day	**un día**	*oon dee-ah*
a week	**una semana**	*oo-nah seh-mah-nah*
a month	**un mes**	*oon mehs*
a year	**un año**	*oon ah-nyoh*
a week from today	**de hoy en una semana**	*deh oh-ee ehn oo-nah seh-mah-nah*
always	**siempre**	*see-ehm-preh*
ago	**hace**	*ah-seh*
day after tomorrow	**pasado mañana**	*pah-sah-doh mah-nyah-nah*
day before yesterday	**anteayer**	*ahn-teh-ah-yehr*
during	**durante**	*doo-rahn-teh*
from	**desde**	*dehs-deh*
in	**en**	*ehn*
last (in a series)	**último (última)**	*ool-tee-moh (ool-tee-mah)*
last (most recent)	**pasado (pasada)**	*pah-sah-doh (pah-sah-dah)*

continued

English	Spanish	Pronunciation
next	**próximo (próxima)**	*prohk-see-moh* (*prohk-see-mah*)
never	**nunca**	*noon-kah*
sometimes	**a veces**	*ah beh-sehs*
today	**hoy**	*oh-ee*
tomorrow	**mañana**	*mah-nyah-nah*
tomorrow afternoon	**mañana por la tarde**	*mah-nyah-nah pohr lah tahr-deh*
tomorrow morning	**mañana por la mañana**	*mah-nyah-nah pohr lah mah-nyah-nah*
tomorrow night	**mañana por la noche**	*mah-nyah-nah pohr lah noh-cheh*
two weeks from tomorrow	**de mañana en dos semanas**	*deh mah-nyah-nah ehn dohs seh-mah-nahs*
until	**hasta**	*ahs-tah*
yesterday	**ayer**	*ah-yehr*

The Seasons

winter	**el invierno**	*ehl een-bee-ehr-noh*
spring	**la primavera**	*lah pree-mah-beh-rah*
summer	**el verano**	*ehl beh-rah-noh*
autumn/fall	**el otoño**	*ehl oh-toh-nyoh*

We go on vacation in the winter.
Vamos de vacaciones en el invierno.
bah-mohs deh bah-kah-see-oh-nehs ehn ehl een-bee-ehr-noh

Holidays

New Year's Day
el Día del Año Nuevo
ehl dee-ah dehl ah-nyoh noo-eh-boh

Martin Luther King Day
el Natalicio de Martin Luther King
ehl nah-tah-lee-see-oh deh Martin Luther King

Presidents' Week
la Semana de los Presidentes
lah seh-mah-nah deh lohs preh-see-dehn-tehs

Valentine's Day
el Día de San Valentín
ehl dee-ah deh sahn bah-lehn-teen

Easter
Pascua
pahs-koo-ah

Mother's Day
el Día de las Madres
ehl dee-ah deh lahs mah-drehs

Memorial Day
el Día de los Caídos
ehl dee-ah deh lohs kah-ee-dohs

Father's Day
el Día de los Padres
ehl dee-ah deh lohs pah-drehs

Independence Day
el Día de la Independencia
ehl dee-ah deh lah een-deh-pehn-dehn-see-ah

Labor Day
el Día del Trabajo
ehl dee-ah dehl trah-bah-hoh

Columbus Day
el Día de la Raza
ehl dee-ah deh lah rrah-sah

Halloween
la Víspera de Todos los Santos
lah bees-peh-rah deh toh-dohs lohs sahn-tohs

Election Day
el Día de las Elecciones
ehl dee-ah deh lahs eh-lehk-see-oh-nehs

Veterans Day
el Día del Armisticio
ehl dee-ah dehl ahr-mees-tee-see-oh

Thanksgiving
el Día de Acción de Gracias
ehl dee-ah deh ahk-see-ohn deh grah-see-ahs

Christmas Eve
la Nochebuena
lah noh-cheh-boo-eh-nah

Christmas
la Navidad
lah nah-bee-dahd

New Year's Eve
la Víspera del Año Nuevo
lah bees-peh-rah dehl ah-nyoh noo-eh-boh

You have off for Christmas.
Usted tiene libre el día de Navidad.
oo-stehd tee-eh-neh lee-breh ehl dee-ah deh nah-bee-dahd

The Weather

It's bad weather.
Hace mal tiempo.
ah-seh mahl tee-ehm-poh

It's cloudy.
Está nublado.
ehs-tah noo-blah-doh

It's cold.
Hace frío.
ah-seh free-oh

It's cool.
Hace fresco.
ah-seh frehs-koh

It's foggy.
Hay niebla (neblina).
ah-ee nee-eh-blah (neh-blee-nah)

It's hot.
Hace calor.
ah-seh kah-lohr

It's humid.
Está húmedo.
ehs-tah oo-meh-doh

It's thundering.
Está tronando.
ehs-tah troh-nahn-doh

It's thundering.
Truena.
troo-eh-nah

There's lightning.
Hay relámpagos.
ah-ee rreh-lahm-pah-gohs

It's nice weather.
Hace buen tiempo.
ah-seh boo-ehn tee-em-poh

It's overcast.
Está nublado.
ehs-tah noo-blah-doh

It's pouring.
Llueve torrencialmente.
yoo-eh-beh toh-rrehn-see-ahl-mehn-teh

It's raining.
Llueve.
yoo-eh-beh

It's raining.
Está lloviendo.
ehs-tah yoh-bee-ehn-doh

It's showery.
Está lluvioso.
ehs-tah yoo-bee-oh-soh

It's drizzling.
Está lloviznando.
ehs-tah yoh-bees-nahn-doh

It's snowing.
Nieva.
nee-eh-bah

It's snowing.
Está nevando.
ehs-tah neh-bahn-doh

It's sunny.
Hace sol.
ah-seh sohl

It's sunny.
Está soleado.
ehs-tah soh-leh-ah-doh

It's windy.
Hace viento.
ah-seh bee-ehn-toh

There's a hurricane.
Hay un huracán.
ah-ee oon oo-rah-kahn

There's a tornado.
Hay un tornado.
ah-ee oon tohr-nah-doh

There are showers.
Hay lloviznas.
ah-ee yoh-bees-nahs

There are gale winds.
Hay un vendaval.
ah-ee oon behn-dah-bahl

There's hail.
Hay granizo.
ah-ee grah-nee-soh

There's a storm.
Hay una tormenta (tempestad).
ah-ee oo-nah tohr-mehn-tah (tehm-pehs-tahd)

Family Members

Let me introduce you to my _____.
Quiero presentarle a mi _____.
kee-eh-roh preh-sehn-tahr-leh ah mee _____

aunt	**tía**	*tee-ah*
brother	**hermano**	*ehr-mah-noh*
cousin	**primo (prima)**	*pree-moh (pree-mah)*
father	**padre**	*pah-dreh*
godfather	**padrino**	*pah-dree-noh*
godmother	**madrina**	*mah-dree-nah*
grandfather	**abuelo**	*ah-boo-eh-loh*
grandmother	**abuela**	*ah-boo-eh-lah*
mother	**madre**	*mah-dreh*
sister	**hermana**	*ehr-mah-nah*
stepbrother	**hermanastro**	*ehr-mah-nahs-troh*
stepfather	**padrastro**	*pah-drahs-troh*
stepsister	**hermanastra**	*ehr-mah-nahs-trah*
stepmother	**madrastra**	*mah-drahs-trah*
uncle	**tío**	*tee-oh*

Question Words

How?
¿Cómo?
koh-moh

When?
¿Cuándo?
koo-ahn-doh

Where?
¿Dónde?
dohn-deh

To where?
¿Adónde?
ah-dohn-deh

From where?
¿De dónde?
deh dohn-deh

What?
¿Qué?
keh

With what?
¿Con qué?
kohn keh

Why?
¿Por qué?
pohr keh

For what purpose?
¿Para qué?
pah-rah keh

Who?
¿Quién?
kee-ehn

Whom?
¿Quiénes?
kee-ehn-ehs

How much (many) _____ ?
¿Cuánto (¿Cuántos, ¿Cuánta, ¿Cuántas) _____?
koo-ahn-toh (koo-ahn-tohs, koo-ahn-tah, koo-ahn-tahs)

How many people are in your family?
¿Cuántas personas hay en su familia?
koo-ahn-tahs pehr-soh-nahs ah-ee ehn soo fah-mee-lee-ah

How much were you paid on your last job?
¿Cuánto le pagaron en su último trabajo?
koo-ahn-toh leh pah-gah-rohn ehn soo ool-tee-moh trah-bah-hoh

How do you spell your name?
¿Cómo se deletrea su nombre?
koh-moh seh deh-leh-treh-ah soo nohm-breh

When can you start?
¿Cuándo puede empezar?
koo-ahn-doh poo-eh-deh ehm-peh-sahr

Until what time?
¿Hasta qué hora?
ahs-tah keh oh-rah

Until what time can you work?
¿Hasta qué hora puede trabajar?
ahs-tah keh oh-rah poo-eh-deh trah-bah-hahr

For when?
¿Para cuándo?
pah-rah koo-ahn-doh

For when do you need this information?
¿Para cuándo necesita esta información?
pah-rah koo-ahn-doh neh-seh-see-tah ehs-tah een-fohr-mah-see-ohn

Where do you live?
¿Dónde vive?
dohn-deh bee-beh

Where would you like to go?
¿Adónde querría ir?
ah-dohn-deh keh-rree-ah eer

Where are you from?
¿De dónde es?
deh dohn-deh ehs

What do you think of this idea?
¿Qué piensa de esta idea?
keh pee-ehn-sah deh ehs-tah ee-deh-ah

What are you cleaning the table with?
¿Con qué está limpiando la mesa?
kohn keh ehs-tah leem-pee-ahn-doh lah meh-sah

Why were you late?
¿Por qué llegó usted tarde?
pohr-keh yeh-goh oo-stehd tahr-deh

Why (for what purpose) are you using a wet sponge?
¿Por qué está usando una esponja mojada?
pohr keh ehs-tah oo-sahn-doh oo-nah ehs-pohn-hah moh-hah-dah

Who is your current employer?
¿Quién es su patrono actualmente?
kee-ehn ehs soo pah-troh-noh ahk-too-ahl-mehn-teh

To whom?
¿A quién (quiénes)?
ah kee-ehn (kee-eh-nehs)

To whom are you referring?
¿A quién se refiere usted?
ah kee-ehn seh rreh-fee-eh-reh oo-stehd

About whom?
¿De quién (quiénes)?
deh kee-ehn (kee-eh-nehs)

About whom are you speaking?
¿De quién (quiénes) habla?
deh kee-ehn (kee-eh-nehs) ah-blah

With whom?
¿Con quién (quiénes)?
kohn kee-ehn (kee-eh-nehs)

With whom would you like to speak?
¿Con quién (quiénes) quisiera hablar?
kohn kee-ehn (kee-eh-nehs) kee-see-eh-rah ah-blahr

Which?/Which one? (Which ones)?
¿Cuál? (¿Cuáles?)
koo-ahl (koo-ah-lehs)

Which one (Which ones) do you prefer?
¿Cuál (¿Cuáles) prefiere?
koo-ahl (koo-ah-lehs) preh-fee-eh-reh

Is/Are there?
¿Hay?
ah-ee

Is there a problem?
¿Hay un problema?
ah-ee oon proh-bleh-mah

The Interview

Beginning the Interview

Good morning.
Buenos días.
boo-eh-nohs dee-ahs

Good afternoon.
Buenas tardes.
boo-eh-nahs tahr-dehs

Good evening.
Buenas noches.
boo-eh-nahs noh-chehs

Hello, I am Mr. (Mrs., Miss, Dr.) _____.
Hola. Yo soy el señor (la señora, la señorita, el doctor, la doctora) _____.
oh-lah yoh soh-ee ehl seh-ñyohr (lah seh-nyoh-rah, lah seh-nyoh-ree-tah, ehl dohk-tohr, la dohk-toh-rah) _____

This is my husband (wife).
Le presento a mi esposo (esposa).
leh preh-sehn-toh ah mee ehs-poh-soh (ehs-poh-sah)

This is my son (daughter).
Le presento a mi hijo (hija).
leh preh-sehn-toh ah mee ee-hoh (ee-hah)

These are my children.
Le presento a mis hijos.
leh preh-sehn-toh ah mees ee-hohs

I am (We are) looking to hire someone to work _____.
Busco (Buscamos) a alguien que pueda trabajar _____.
boos-koh (boos-kah-mohs) ah ahl-gee-ehn keh poo-eh-dah
trah-bah-hahr _____

one day (two days, three days, four days, five days)	**un día (dos días, tres días, cuatro días, cinco días)**	*oon dee-ah (dohs dee-ahs, trehs dee-ahs, koo-ah-troh dee-ahs, seen-koh dee-ahs)*
a week	**una semana**	*oo-nah seh-mah-nah*
daily	**diariamente**	*dee-ah-ree-ah-mehn-teh*
Monday through Friday	**de lunes a viernes**	*deh loo-nehs ah bee-ehr-nehs*
on Mondays (Tuesdays, Wednesdays, Thursdays, Fridays, Saturdays, Sundays)	**los lunes (martes, miércoles, jueves, viernes, sábados, domingos)**	*lohs loo-nehs (mahr-tehs, mee-ehr-koh-lehs, hoo-eh-behs, bee-ehr-nehs, sah-bah-dohs, doh-meen-gohs)*
on weekends	**por los fines de semana**	*pohr lohs fee-nehs deh seh-mah-nah*
as a live-in	**de interno (interna)**	*deh een-tehr-noh (een-tehr-nah)*

I need (We need) someone to start working _____.
Necesito (Necesitamos) que alguien empiece a trabajar _____.
neh-seh-see-toh (neh-seh-see-tah-mohs) keh ahl-gee-ehn ehm-pee-eh-seh ah
trah-bah-hahr _____

immediately	**inmediatamente**	*een-meh-dee-ah-tah-mehn-teh*
tomorrow	**mañana**	*mah-nyah-nah*
the day after tomorrow	**pasado mañana**	*pah-sah-doh mah-nyah-nah*
next week	**la próxima semana**	*lah prohk-see-mah seh-mah-nah*
at the beginning of next month	**al principio del próximo mes**	*ahl preen-see-pee-oh dehl prohk-see-moh mehs*

Personal Information

What is your name?
¿Cómo se llama usted?
koh-moh seh yah-mah oo-stehd

Nice to meet you.
Mucho gusto.
moo-choh goos-toh

Do you speak (understand, read, write) English?
¿Habla (Comprende, Lee, Escribe) usted inglés?
ah-blah (kohm-prehn-deh, lee-eh, ehs-kree-beh) oo-stehd een-glehs

Do you speak any other languages fluently besides Spanish?
¿Habla usted bien otros idiomas además de español?
*ah-blah oo-stehd bee-ehn oh-trohs ee-dee-oh-mahs ah-deh-mahs
deh ehs-pah-nyohl*

Where do you live?
¿Dónde vive usted?
dohn-deh bee-beh oo-stehd

What country are you from?
¿De qué país es usted?
deh keh pah-ees ehs oo-stehd

Are you a citizen of the United States?
¿Es usted ciudadano (ciudadana) de los Estados Unidos?
*ehs oo-stehd see-oo-dah-dah-noh (see-oo-dah-dah-nah) deh lohs ehs-tah-dohs
oo-nee-dos*

Are you a resident of the United States? (Do you have a green card?)
**¿Es usted residente de los Estados Unidos? (¿Tiene una tarjeta
verde?)**
*ehs oo-stehd rreh-see-dehn-teh deh lohs ehs-tah-dohs oo-nee-dohs (tee-eh-neh
oo-nah tahr-heh-tah behr-deh)*

What is your address?
¿Cuál es su dirección?
koo-ahl ehs soo dee-rehk-see-ohn

What is your (cell) phone number?
¿Cuál es su número de teléfono (celular)?
koo-ahl ehs soo noo-meh-roh deh teh-leh-foh-noh (seh-loo-lahr)

Do you have a Social Security card?
¿Tiene una tarjeta de seguro social?
tee-eh-neh oo-nah tahr-heh-tah deh seh-goo-roh soh-see-ahl

How long have you lived in the United States?
¿Cuánto tiempo hace que vive en los Estados Unidos?
koo-ahn-toh tee-ehm-poh ah-seh keh bee-beh ehn lohs ehs-tah-dohs oo-nee-dohs

Have you ever had a problem with the law?
¿Ha tenido problemas con las autoridades?
ah teh-nee-doh proh-bleh-mahs kohn lahs ah-oo-toh-ree-dah-dehs

If yes, when? What was the problem?
¿Sí? ¿Cuándo? ¿Qué fue el problema?
see koo-ahn-doh keh foo-eh ehl proh-bleh-mah

Do you have a driver's license?
¿Tiene licencia de conducir?
tee-eh-neh lee-sehn-see-ah deh kohn-doo-seer

Do you drive?
¿Conduce?
kohn-doo-seh

Do you have a car?
¿Tiene coche?
tee-eh-neh koh-cheh

Do you know how to take public transportation?
¿Sabe usar el transporte público?
sah-beh oo-sahr ehl trahns-pohr-teh poo-blee-koh

Do you have car insurance?
¿Tiene seguro de automóvil?
tee-eh-neh seh-goo-roh deh ah-oo-toh-moh-beel

There is no smoking in this house.
No se fuma en esta casa.
noh seh foo-mah ehn ehs-tah kah-sah

You may not smoke (drink alcohol, use drugs, speak on the phone).
Se prohíbe fumar (beber alcohol, usar drogas, hablar por teléfono).
seh proh-ee-beh foo-mahr (beh-behr ahl-koh-ohl, oo-sahr droh-gahs, ah-blahr pohr teh-leh-foh-noh)

We have a dog (cat, bird).
Tenemos un perro (gato, pájaro).
teh-neh-mohs oon peh-rroh (gah-toh, pah-hah-roh)

Are you afraid of (allergic to) dogs (cats)?
¿Tiene miedo de (alergia a) los perros (los gatos)?
tee-eh-neh mee-eh-doh deh (ah-lehr-hee-ah ah) lohs peh-rrohs (lohs gah-tohs)

Do you have any allergies? To what?
¿Tiene alergias? ¿A qué cosas?
tee-eh-neh ah-lehr-hee-ahs ah keh koh-sahs

Do you have any health-related problems? What are they?
¿Tiene problemas con la salud? ¿Cuáles son?
tee-eh-neh proh-bleh-mahs kohn lah sah-lood koo-ah-lehs sohn

Do you have medical insurance?
¿Tiene seguro médico?
tee-eh-neh seh-goo-roh meh-dee-koh

Experience and References

Have you ever taken care of infants (children, the elderly)?
¿Ha cuidado usted de infantes (niños, personas mayores)?
ah koo-ee-dah-doh oo-stehd deh een-fahn-tehs (nee-nyohs, pehr-soh-nahs mah-yoh-rehs)

Do you know how to cook (iron, sew)?
¿Sabe usted cocinar (planchar, coser)?
sah-beh oo-stehd koh-see-nahr (plahn-chahr, koh-sehr)

What kind of training have you had?
¿Qué clase de entrenamiento ha tenido?
keh klah-seh deh ehn-treh-nah-mee-ehn-toh ah teh-nee-doh

What experience do you have?
¿Qué experiencia tiene?
keh ehks-peh-ree-ehn-see-ah tee-eh-neh

Where have you worked before?
¿Dónde ha trabajado antes?
dohn-deh ah trah-bah-hah-doh ahn-tehs

When did you work there?
¿Cuándo trabajó allá?
koo-ahn-doh trah-bah-hoh ah-yah

Do you still work there?
¿Todavía trabaja allá?
toh-dah-bee-ah trah-bah-hah ah-yah

Why are you leaving?
¿Por qué se va?
pohr keh seh bah

Why did you leave?
¿Por qué se fue?
pohr keh seh foo-eh

What were your duties?
¿Qué responsabilidades tenía usted?
keh rrehs-pohn-sah-bee-lee-dah-dehs teh-nee-ah oo-stehd

Did you have any problems on your last job?
¿Tenía usted problemas en su último trabajo?
teh-nee-ah oo-stehd proh-bleh-mahs ehn soo ool-tee-moh trah-bah-hoh

What were they?
¿Por ejemplo?
pohr eh-hehm-ploh

How many times did you miss work? For what reasons?
¿Cuántas veces faltó al trabajo? ¿Por cuáles razones?
koo-ahn-tahs beh-sehs fahl-toh ahl trah-bah-hoh pohr koo-ah-lehs rrah-soh-nehs

Do you have any work-related (personal) references?
¿Tiene referencias relacionadas al trabajo (personales)?
tee-eh-neh rreh-feh-rehn-see-ahs rreh-lah-see-oh-nah-dahs ahl trah-bah-hoh (pehr-soh-nah-lehs)

May I contact your references? How?
¿Puedo contactar a sus referencias? ¿Cómo?
poo-eh-doh kohn-tahk-tahr ah soos rreh-feh-rehn-see-ahs koh-moh

Especially for Sleep-In Nannies

Good afternoon.
Buenas tardes.
boo-eh-nahs tahr-dehs

Good evening.
Buenas noches.
boo-eh-nahs noh-chehs

Hello, I am Mr. (Mrs., Miss, Dr.) _____.
Hola. Yo soy el señor (la señora, la señorita, el doctor, la doctora) _____.
oh-lah yoh soh-ee ehl seh-nyohr (lah seh-nyoh-rah, lah seh-nyoh-ree-tah, el dohk-tohr, lah dohk-toh-rah) _____

This is my husband (wife).
Le presento a mi esposo (esposa).
leh preh-sehn-toh ah mee ehs-poh-soh (ehs-poh-sah)

These are my children.
Le presento a mis hijos.
leh preh-sehn-toh ah mees ee-hohs

I am (We are) looking to hire someone to work _____.
Busco (Buscamos) a alguien que pueda trabajar _____.
boos-koh (boos-kah-mohs) ah ahl-gee-ehn keh poo-eh-dah trah-bah-hahr _____

What experience do you have in caring for children?
¿Qué experiencia tiene cuidando niños?
keh ehks-peh-ree-ehn-see-ah tee-eh-neh koo-ee-dahn-doh nee-nyohs

What age children have you cared for?
¿Qué edades tenían los niños que usted ha cuidado?
keh eh-dah-dehs teh-nee-ahn lohs nee-nyohs keh oo-stehd ah koo-ee-dah-doh

What were your duties?
¿Qué eran sus responsabilidades?
keh eh-rahn soos rrehs-pohn-sah-bee-lee-dah-dehs

Did you have any problems on your last job?
¿Tenía problemas en su último trabajo?
teh-nee-ah proh-bleh-mahs ehn soo ool-tee-moh trah-bah-hoh

If so, what were they?
¿Por ejemplo?
pohr eh-hehm-ploh

What do you feel is your most important responsibility on this job?
En su opinión, ¿cuál es la responsabilidad más importante de este trabajo?
ehn soo oh-pee-nee-ohn, koo-ahl ehs lah rrehs-pohn-sah-bee-lee-dahd mahs eem-pohr-tahn-teh deh ehs-teh trah-bah-hoh

Do you know how to cook?
¿Sabe cocinar?
sah-beh koh-see-nahr

Are you willing to cook?
¿Esta dispuesta a cocinar?
ehs-tah dees-poo-ehs-tah ah koh-see-nahr

Are you willing to do light housekeeping?
¿Está dispuesta a hacer una limpieza ligera?
ehs-tah dees-poo-ehs-tah ah ah-sehr oo-nah leem-pee-eh-sah lee-heh-rah

What activities do you like to do with children?
¿Qué actividades le gusta hacer con los niños?
keh ahk-tee-bee-dah-dehs leh goos-tah ah-sehr kohn lohs nee-nyohs

I (We) (do not) want you to discipline our son (daughter, children).
Yo (no) quiero (Nosotros [no] queremos) que usted castigue a nuestro hijo (nuestra hija, nuestros hijos).
yoh (noh) kee-eh-roh (noh-soh-trohs [noh] keh-reh-mohs) keh oo-stehd kahs-tee-geh ah noo-ehs-troh ee-hoh (noo-ehs-trah ee-hah, noo-ehs-trohs ee-hohs)

You may not hit our son (daughter, children).
Usted no puede golpear a nuestro hijo (nuestra hija, nuestros hijos)
oo-stehd noh poo-eh-deh gohl-peh-ahr ah noo-ehs-troh ee-hoh (noo-ehs-trah ee-hah, noo-ehs-trohs ee-hohs)

How long do you plan on staying?
¿Por cuánto tiempo piensa quedarse?
pohr koo-ahn-toh tee-ehm-poh pee-ehn-sah keh-dahr-seh

Do you have any problems living with our family?
¿Tiene problemas viviendo con nuestra familia?
tee-eh-neh proh-bleh-mahs bee-bee-ehn-doh kohn noo-ehs-trah fah-mee-lee-ah

Do you need your own bathroom (refrigerator)?
¿Necesita su propio baño (refrigerador)?
neh-seh-see-tah soo proh-pee-oh bah-nyoh (rreh-free-heh-rah-dohr)

Do you need your own entrance (private area)?
¿Necesita su propia entrada (área separada)?
neh-seh-see-tah soo proh-pee-ah ehn-trah-dah (ah-reh-ah seh-pah-rah-dah)

Do you stay up late? Do you go out late?
¿Se queda despierta tarde? ¿Sale usted tarde?
seh keh-dah dehs-pee-ehr-tah tahr-deh sah-leh oo-stehd tahr-deh

Do you have any pets?
¿Tiene usted mascotas?
tee-eh-neh oo-stehd mahs-koh-tahs

Will company be coming to visit you?
¿Tendrá usted visitas?
tehn-drah oo-stehd bee-see-tahs

Do you need a car during your time off?
¿Necesita un auto cuando tenga un día libre?
neh-seh-see-tah oon ah-oo-toh koo-ahn-doh tehn-gah oon dee-ah lee-breh

What do you do during your spare time?
¿Cómo pasa su tiempo libre?
koh-moh pah-sah soo tee-ehm-poh lee-breh

Are you willing to travel with us?
¿Está dispuesta a viajar con nosotros?
Ehs-tah dees-poo-ehs-tah ah bee-ah-hahr kohn noh-soh-trohs

Are you willing to adjust your schedule if I need (we need) to work
late or go out of town?
**¿Está dispuesta a cambiar su horario si necesito (necesitamos)
trabajar tarde o salir?**
*ehs-tah dees-poo-ehs-tah ah kahm-bee-ahr soo oh-rah-ree-oh see neh-seh-see-
toh (neh-seh-see-tah-mohs) trah-bah-hahr tahr-deh oh sah-leer*

Do you have recent CPR (first aid) certification?
¿Tiene un certificado reciente en CPR (primeros auxilios)?
*tee-eh-neh oon sehr-tee-fee-kah-doh rreh-see-ehn-teh ehn see-peh-erre
(pree-meh-rohs ah-ook-see-lee-ohs)*

Salary and Hours/Days of Employment

What day (days) do you want to work?
¿Qué día (días) quiere trabajar?
keh dee-ah (dee-ahs) kee-eh-reh trah-bah-hahr

How many days do you want to work?
¿Cuántos días quiere trabajar?
koo-ahn-tohs dee-ahs kee-eh-reh trah-bah-hahr

Is your schedule flexible?
¿Es flexible su horario?
ehs flehk-see-bleh soo oh-rah-ree-oh

Do you prefer to be a live-in or a daily worker?
¿Prefiere usted trabajar de interna o diariamente?
preh-fee-eh-reh oo-stehd trah-bah-hahr deh een-tehr-nah oh dee-ah-ree-ah-mehn-teh

How much do you charge per hour (day, week, month)?
¿Cuánto cobra por hora (al día, a la semana, al mes)?
koo-ahn-toh koh-brah pohr oh-rah (ahl dee-ah, ah lah seh-mah-nah, ahl mehs)

I am (We are) willing to pay _____ per hour (day, week, month).
Puedo (Podemos) pagar _____ por hora (al día, a la semana, al mes).
poo-eh-doh (poh-deh-mohs) pah-gahr _____ pohr oh-rah (ahl dee-ah, ah lah seh-mah-nah, ahl mehs)

If you work extra hours we will pay _____ dollars per hour (day) overtime.
Si usted trabaja horas extras, le pagaremos _____ dólares por hora (al día) por horas extras.
see oo-stehd trah-bah-hah oh-rahs ehks-trahs leh pah-gah-reh-mohs _____ doh-lah-rehs pohr oh-rah (ahl dee-ah) pohr oh-rahs ehks-trahs

Finishing the Interview

Is there anything in the job description that you are uncomfortable doing?
¿Hay algo en la descripción del trabajo que preferiría no hacer?
ah-ee ahl-goh ehn lah dehs-kreep-see-ohn dehl trah-bah-hoh keh preh-feh-ree-ree-ah noh ah-sehr

May I (we) have the names and addresses of your references?
¿Me (Nos) puede dar los nombres y las direcciones de sus referencias?
meh (nohs) poo-eh-deh dahr lohs nohm-brehs ee lahs dee-rehk-see-oh-nehs deh soos rreh-feh-rehn-see-ahs

Before you begin working for us we are going to check your references (do a background check).
Antes de empezar a trabajar para nosotros, vamos a revisar sus referencias (hacer una verificación de antecedentes penales).
ahn-tehs deh ehm-peh-sahr ah trah-bah-hahr pah-rah noh-soh-trohs bah-mohs ah rreh-bee-sahr soos rreh-feh-rehn-see-ahs (ah-sehr oo-nah beh-ree-fee-kah-see-ohn deh ahn-teh-seh-dehn-tehs peh-nah-lehs)

Let me discuss your application with my husband (wife).
Déjeme discutir su solicitud con mi esposo (esposa).
deh-heh-meh dees-koo-teer soo soh-lee-see-tood kohn mee ohs poh soh (ehs-poh-sah)

I will get back to you by _____.
Le contestaré en _____.
leh kohn-tehs-tah-reh ehn

What is the best way to contact you?
¿Cuál es la mejor manera de contactarla?
koo-ahl ehs lah meh-hohr mah-neh-rah deh kohn-tahk-tahr-lah

Goodbye.
Adiós.
ah dee ohs

Thank you for coming.
Gracias por venir.
grah-see-ahs pohr beh-neer

Have a nice day.
Qué tenga buen día.
keh tehn-gah boo-ehn dee-ah

Accepting or Rejecting the Applicant

Are you still interested in the job?
¿Todavía le interesa el trabajo?
toh-dah-bee-ah leh een-teh-reh-sah ehl trah-bah-hoh

I (We) would like you to work for us.
Me (Nos) gustaría que trabajara para nosotros.
meh (nohs) goos-tah-ree-ah keh trah-bah-hah-rah pah-rah noh-soh-trohs

When can you start?
¿Cuándo puede empezar?
koo-ahn-doh poo-eh-deh ehm-peh-sahr

Can you start on _____?
¿Puede empezar el _____?
poo-eh-deh ehm-peh-sahr ehl _____

See you in the morning at _____.
Nos veremos por la mañana a las _____.
nohs beh-reh-mohs pohr lah mah-nyah-nah ah lahs _____

You may move in on _____.
Usted puede mudarse el _____.
oo-stehd poo-eh-deh moo-dahr-seh ehl _____

I'm (very) sorry. I (We) have hired someone else for the job.
Lo siento (mucho). Ya he (hemos) escogido a otra persona para el trabajo.
loh see-ehn-toh moo-choh yah eh (eh-mohs) ehs-koh-hee-doh ah oh-trah pehr-soh-nah pah-rah ehl trah-bah-hoh

4

General Directions

Do's and Don'ts

Please _____ (_____).
Favor de _____.
fah-bohr deh _____

allow	**permitir**	*pehr-mee-teer*
answer	**contestar**	*kohn-tehs-tahr*
apply	**solicitar**	*soh-lee-see-tahr*
arrange	**arreglar**	*ah-rreh-glahr*
arrive	**llegar**	*yeh-gahr*
ask (a question)	**preguntar**	*preh-goon-tahr*
ask for	**pedir**	*peh-deer*
avoid	**evitar**	*eh-bee-tahr*
be careful	**tener cuidado**	*teh-nehr koo-ee-dah-doh*
begin	**empezar**	*ehm-peh-sahr*
bring	**traer**	*trah-ehr*
buy	**comprar**	*kohm-prahr*
call	**llamar**	*yah-mahr*
carry	**llevar**	*yeh-bahr*
change	**cambiar**	*kahm-bee-ahr*
check	**revisar**	*rreh-bee-sahr*
clean	**limpiar**	*leem-pee-ahr*
close	**cerrar**	*seh-rrahr*
come	**venir**	*beh-neer*
cook	**cocinar**	*koh-see-nahr*
cover	**cubrir**	*koo-breer*
cut	**cortar**	*kohr-tahr*

describe	**describir**	*dehs-kree-beer*
disinfect	**desinfectar**	*dehs-een-fehk-tahr*
divide	**dividir**	*dee-bee-deer*
do	**hacer**	*ah-sehr*
don't break	**no romper**	*noh rrohm-pehr*
don't touch	**no tocar**	*noh toh-kahr*
drink	**beber**	*beh-behr*
drive	**conducir**	*kohn-doo-seer*
dry	**secar**	*seh-kahr*
dust	**sacudir**	*sah-koo-deer*
eat	**comer**	*koh-mehr*
empty	**vaciar**	*bah-see-ahr*
enjoy (oneself)	**divertirse**	*dee-behr-teer-seh*
explain	**explicar**	*ehks-plee-kahr*
feed	**dar de comer**	*dahr deh koh-mehr*
fill	**llenar**	*yeh-nahr*
finish	**terminar**	*tehr-mee-nahr*
fluff	**mullir**	*moo-yeer*
fold	**doblar**	*doh-blahr*
follow	**seguir**	*seh-geer*
give	**dar**	*dahr*
go	**ir**	*eer*
hang	**colgar**	*kohl-gahr*
help	**ayudar**	*ah-yoo-dahr*
hurry	**apurarse**	*ah-poo-rahr-seh*
insert	**meter**	*meh-tehr*
keep	**guardar**	*goo-ahr-dahr*
leave (go out)	**salir**	*sah-leer*
leave (let remain)	**dejar**	*deh-hahr*
listen	**escuchar**	*ehs-koo-chahr*
load	**cargar**	*kahr-gahr*
lock	**cerrar (con llave)**	*seh-rrahr (kohn yah-beh)*
look/look at	**mirar**	*mee-rahr*
look for	**buscar**	*boos-kahr*
lower	**bajar**	*bah-hahr*
make	**hacer**	*ah-sehr*
mix	**mezclar**	*mehs-klahr*
mop	**trapear**	*trah-peh-ahr*
move	**mover**	*moh-behr*
notice	**notar**	*noh-tahr*

notify	notificar	noh-tee-fee-kahr
open	abrir	ah-breer
order	ordenar	ohr-deh-nahr
park	aparcar	ah-pahr-kahr
pay	pagar	pah-gahr
pick up	recoger	rreh-koh-hehr
plant	plantar	plahn-tahr
play	jugar	hoo-gahr
plug in	enchufar	ehn-choo-fahr
polish	lustrar	loos-trahr
prepare	preparar	preh-pah-rahr
pull	jalar	hah-lahr
push	empujar	ehm-poo-hahr
put/put in	meter	meh-tehr
put/put on	ponerse	poh-nehr-seh
put away	guardar	goo-ahr-dahr
raise	levantar	leh-bahn-tahr
rake	rastrillar	rrahs-tree-yahr
remember/ remember to	recordar	rreh-kohr-dahr
remove	quitar	kee-tahr
return (come back)	regresar	rreh-greh-sahr
return (something somewhere)	devolver	deh-bohl-behr
rinse	enjuagar	ehn-hoo-ah-gahr
scrub	fregar	freh-gahr
see	ver	behr
send	mandar	mahn-dahr
separate	separar	seh-pah-rahr
shake	agitar	ah-hee-tahr
shampoo	limpiar	leem-pee-ahr
show	mostrar	mohs-trahr
sign	firmar	feer-mahr
soak	remojar	rreh-moh-hahr
speak	hablar	ah-blahr
stack	amontonar	ah-mohn-toh-nahr
stay	quedar(se)	keh-dahr(seh)
stir	revolver	rreh-bohl-behr
stop	parar	pah-rahr
sweep	barrer	bah-rrehr

take	**tomar**	*toh-mahr*
take care of	**cuidar**	*koo-ee-dahr*
take out	**sacar**	*sah-kahr*
tell	**decir**	*deh-seer*
throw away	**botar**	*boh-tahr*
tie	**amarrar**	*ah-mah-rrahr*
touch	**tocar**	*toh-kahr*
trim	**recortar**	*rreh-kohr-tahr*
try to	**tratar de**	*trah-tahr deh*
turn	**doblar (voltear)**	*doh-blahr (bohl-teh-ahr)*
turn off	**apagar**	*ah-pah-gahr*
turn on	**prender**	*prehn-dehr*
unplug	**desenchufar**	*dehs-ehn-choo-fahr*
use	**usar**	*oo-sahr*
vacuum	**pasar la aspiradora**	*pah-sahr lah ah-spee-rah-doh-rah*
wait	**esperar**	*ehs-peh-rahr*
walk	**caminar**	*kah-mee-nahr*
wash	**lavar**	*lah-bahr*
water	**regar**	*rreh-gahr*
wax	**encerar**	*ehn-seh-rahr*
wear	**llevar**	*yeh-bahr*
work	**trabajar**	*trah-bah-hahr*
wrap	**envolver**	*ehn-bohl-behr*
write	**escribir**	*ehs-kree-beer*
the air-conditioner (the air-conditioners)	**el climatizador (los climatizadores)**	*ehl klee-mah-tee-sah-dohr (lohs klee-mah-tee-sah-doh-rehs)*
the answering machine (the answering machines)	**el contestador automático (los contestadores automáticos)**	*ehl kohn-tehs-tah-dohr ah-oo-toh-mah-tee-koh (lohs kohn-tehs-tah-doh-rehs ah-oo-toh-mah-tee-kohs)*
the banister (the banisters)	**el pasamanos (los pasamanos)**	*ehl pah-sah-mah-nohs (lohs pah-sah-mah-nohs)*
the baseboards	**los zócalos**	*lohs soh-kah-lohs*

the blinds	las persianas	lahs pehr-see-ah-nahs
the carpet	la moqueta	lah moh-keh-tah
(the carpets)	(las moquetas)	(lahs moh-keh-tahs)
the ceiling	el techo	ehl teh-choh
(the ceilings)	(los techos)	(lohs teh-chohs)
the chair	la silla	lah see-yah
(the chairs)	(las sillas)	(lahs see-yahs)
the closet	el armario	ehl ahr-mah-ree-oh
(the closets)	(los armarios)	(lohs ahr-mah-ree-ohs)
the curtains	las cortinas	lahs kohr-tee-nahs
the desk lamp	la lámpara	lah lahm-pah-rah
(the desk lamps)	(las lámparas) de escritorio	(lahs lahm-pah-rahs) deh ehs-kree-toh-ree-oh
the door	la puerta	lah poo-ehr-tah
(the doors)	(las puertas)	(lahs poo-ehr-tahs)
the doorknob	el pomo	ehl poh-moh
(the doorknobs)	(los pomos)	(lohs poh-mohs)
the draperies	las colgaduras	lahs kohl-gah-doo-rahs
the drawer	el cajón	ehl kah-hohn
(the drawers)	(los cajones)	(lohs kah-hoh-nehs)
the fan (the fans)	el ventilador	ehl behn-tee-lah-dohr
	(los ventiladores)	(lohs behn-tee-lah-doh-rehs)
the floor	el piso	ehl pee-soh
(the floors)	(los pisos)	(lohs pee-sohs)
the floor lamp	la lámpara	lah lahm-pah-rah
(the floor lamps)	(las lámparas)	(lahs lahm-pah-rahs)
the furniture	los muebles	lohs moo-eh-blehs
the lampshade	la pantalla	lah pahn-tah-yah
(the lampshades)	(las pantallas)	(lahs pahn-tah-yahs)
the light	la luz	lah loos
(the lights)	(las luces)	(lahs loo-sehs)
the light switch	el interruptor	ehl een-teh-rroop-tohr
(the light switches)	(los interruptores)	(lohs een-teh-rroop-toh-rehs)
the molding	la moldadura	lah mohl-dah-doo-rah
(the moldings)	(las moldaduras)	(lahs mohl-dah-doo-rahs)

the photograph	**la fotografía**	*lah foh-toh-grah-fee-ah*
(the photographs)	**(las fotografías)**	*(lahs foh-toh-grah-fee-ahs)*
the picture frame	**el marco**	*ehl mahr-koh*
(the picture frames)	**(los marcos)**	*(lohs mahr-kohs)*
the picture	**la pintura**	*lah peen-too-rah*
(the pictures)	**(las pinturas)**	*(lahs peen-too-rahs)*
the plant	**la planta**	*lah plahn-tah*
(the plants)	**(las plantas)**	*(lahs plahn-tahs)*
the rug (the rugs)	**la alfombra**	*lah ahl-fohm-brah*
	(las alfombras)	*(lahs ahl-fohm-brahs)*
the screen	**el biombo**	*ehl bee-ohm-boh*
(the screens)	**(los biombos)**	*(lohs bee-ohm-bohs)*
the sculpture	**la escultura**	*lah ehs-kool-too-rah*
(the sculptures)	**(las esculturas)**	*(lahs ehs-kool-too-rahs)*
the shades	**las persianas**	*lahs pehr-see-ah-nahs*
the shelf	**el estante**	*ehl ehs-tahn-teh*
(the shelves)	**(los estantes)**	*(lohs ehs-tahn-tehs)*
the shutter	**la contraventana**	*lah kohn-trah-behn-tah-nah (lahs kohn-trah-behn-tah-nahs)*
(the shutters)	**(las contraventanas)**	
the table	**la mesa**	*lah meh-sah*
(the tables)	**(las mesas)**	*(lahs meh-sahs)*
the telephone	**el teléfono**	*ehl teh-leh-foh-noh*
(the telephones)	**(los teléfonos)**	*(lohs teh-leh-foh-nohs)*
the wastepaper basket	**la papelera**	*lah pah-peh-leh-rah*
	(las papeleras)	*(lahs pah-peh-leh-rahs)*
the window	**la ventana**	*lah behn-tah-nah*
(the windows)	**(las ventanas)**	*(lahs behn-tah-nahs)*
the windowsill	**el aféizar**	*ehl ah-feh-ee-sahr*
(the windowsills)	**(los aféizares)**	*(lohs ah-feh-ee-sah-rehs)*

Note

To express that a person should not do something, simply put **no** in front of the verb:

Please don't answer the phone.
Favor de no contestar el teléfono.
fah-bohr deh noh kohn-tehs-tahr ehl teh-leh-foh-noh

Please answer the phone and take a message.
Favor de contestar el teléfono y tomar un mensaje.
fah-bohr deh kohn-tehs-tahr ehl teh-leh-foh-noh ee toh-mahr oon mehn-sah-heh

Please let the answering machine take the call.
Favor de permitir que la máquina de contestar tome un mensaje.
fah-bohr deh pehr-mee-teer keh lah mah-kee-nah deh kohn-tehs-tahr toh-meh oon mehn-sah-heh

Please arrange the closet.
Favor de arreglar el ropero
fah-bohr deh ah-rreh-glahr ehl rroh poh roh

Please arrive at work at _____.
Favor de llegar al trabajo a _____.
fah-bohr deh yeh-gahr ahl trah-bah hoh ah _____

Please buy whatever cleaning supplies (food) you need. I/We will reimburse you.
Favor de comprar lo que falte para limpiar (para comer). Los gastos le serán reembolsados.
fah-bohr deh kohm-prahr loh keh fahl-teh pah-rah leem-pee-ahr (pah-rah koh-mehr) lohs gahs-tohs leh seh-rahn rreh-ehm-bohl-sah-dohs

Please call me if you have any questions.
Favor de llamarme si usted tiene preguntas.
fah-bohr deh yah-mahr-meh see oo stehd too-eh-neh preh-guhn-tahs

Please change the batteries in the smoke (carbon monoxide) detector.
Favor de cambiar las baterías del detector de humo (monóxido de carbono).
fah-bohr deh kahm-bee-ahr lahs bah-teh-ree-ahs dehl deh-tehk-tohr deh oo-moh (moh-nohk-see-doh deh kahr-boh-noh).

Please change the light bulb.
Favor de cambiar la bombilla.
fah-bohr deh kahm-bee-ahr lah bohm-bee-yah

Please clean behind the furniture.
Favor de limpiar detrás de los muebles.
fah-bohr deh leem-pee-ahr deh-trahs deh lohs moo-eh-blehs

Please clean the shades (the shutters, the skylight).
Favor de limpiar las persianas (los postigos, la claraboya).
fah-bohr deh leem-pee-ahr lahs pehr-see-ah-nahs (lohs pohs-tee-gohs, lah klah-rah-boh-yah)

Please clean it again. It is still dirty.
Favor de limpiarlo (limpiarla) otra vez. Todavía está sucio (sucia).
fah-bohr deh leem-pee-ahr-loh (leem-pee-ahr-lah) oh-trah behs toh-dah-bee-ah ehs-tah soo-see-oh (soo-see-ah)

Please disinfect the phones.
Favor de desinfectar los teléfonos.
fah-bohr deh dehs-een-fehk-tahr lohs teh-leh-foh-nohs

Please do it this way (like this).
Favor de hacerlo de esta manera (así).
fah-bohr deh ah-sehr-loh deh ehs-tah mah-neh-rah (ah-see)

Please don't break anything.
Favor de no romper nada.
fah-bohr deh noh rrohm-pehr nah-dah

Please tell me if you break something.
Favor de avisarme si rompe algo.
fah-bohr deh ah-bee-sahr-meh see rrohm-peh ahl-goh

Please don't carry (lift) anything that is too heavy.
Favor de no llevar (levantar) nada que pese demasiado.
fah-bohr deh noh yeh-bahr (leh-bahn-tahr) nah-dah keh peh-seh deh-mah-see-ah-doh

Please don't change the temperature on the thermostat.
Favor de no cambiar la temperatura del termóstato.
fah-bohr deh noh kahm-bee-ahr lah tehm-peh-rah-too-rah dehl tehr-mohs-tah-toh

Please don't leave until all the chores are finished.
Favor de no salir hasta que todos los quehaceres estén terminados.
fah-bohr deh noh sah-leer ahs-tah keh toh-dohs lohs keh-ah-seh-rehs ehs-tehn tehr-mee-nah-dohs

Please don't mix _____.
Favor de no mezclar _____.
fah-bohr deh noh mehs-klahr _____

Please don't open any drawers in the _____.
Favor de no abrir los cajones en el (la) _____.
fah-bohr deh noh ah-breer lohs kah-hoh-nehs ehn ehl (lah) _____

Please don't permit strangers in the house.
Favor de no permitir que ningún extraño entre en la casa.
fah-bohr deh noh pehr-mee-teer keh neen-goon ehks-trah-nyoh ehn-treh ehn lah kah-sah

Please ask for identification.
Favor de pedir la identificación.
fah-bohr deh peh-deer lah ee-dehn-tee-fee-kah-see-ohn

Please don't touch anything.
Favor de no tocar nada.
fah-bohr deh noh toh-kahr nah-dah

Please dust the moldings (high hats, light fixtures, ceilings).
Favor de sacudir el polvo de las molduras (del cielo raso, de las luces, del techo).
fah-bohr deh sah-koo-deer ehl pol-boh deh lahs mohl-doo-rahs (dehl see-eh-loh rrah-soh, deh lahs loo-sehs, dehl teh-choh)

Please dust the pictures (television screen).
Favor de sacudir los cuadros (la pantalla del televisor).
fah-bohr deh sah-koo-deer lohs koo-ah-drohs (lah pahn-tah-yah dehl teh-leh-bee-sohr)

Please empty the garbage pails.
Favor de vaciar los basureros.
fah-bohr deh bah-see-ahr lohs bah-soo-reh-rohs

Please fluff the pillows.
Favor de mullir las almohadas.
fah-bohr deh moo-yeer lahs ahl-moh-hah-dahs

Please follow all directions carefully.
Favor de seguir todas las instrucciones con cuidado.
fah-bohr deh seh-geer toh-dahs lahs een-strook-see-oh-nehs kohn koo-ee-dah-doh

Here is the number to call if you have a problem.
Aquí está el número para llamar si usted tiene un problema.
ah-kee ehs-tah ehl noo-meh-roh pah-rah yah-mahr see oo-stehd tee-eh-neh oon proh-bleh-mah

Please ask for _____.
Favor de pedir a _____.
fah-bohr deh peh-deer ah _____.

I'm expecting a package (a letter). Please sign for it.
Espero un paquete (una carta). Favor de firmar.
ehs-peh-roh oon pah-keh-teh (oo-nah kahr-tah) fah-bohr deh feer-mahr

In case of an emergency, call 911.
En caso de emergencia, llame al nueve once.
ehn kah-soh deh eh-mehr-hehn-see-ah yah-meh ahl noo-eh-beh ohn-seh

Please leave on the lights.
Favor de dejar las luces encendidas.
fah-bohr deh deh-hahr lahs loo-sehs ehn-sehn-dee-dahs

Please leave on the stereo (the television).
Favor de dejar el estéreo (el televisor) encendido.
fah-bohr deh deh-hahr ehl ehs-teh-reh-oh (ehl teh-leh-bee-sohr) ehn-sehn-dee-doh

Please lock the door (the doors) (the window [the windows], the garage).
Favor de cerrar con llave la puerta (las puertas) (la ventana [las ventanas], el garaje).
fah-bohr deh seh-rrahr kohn yah-beh lah poo-ehr-tah (lahs poo-ehr-tahs) (lah behn-tah-nah [lahs behn-tah-nahs], ehl gah-rah-heh)

Please move the furniture.
Favor de mover los muebles.
fah-bohr deh moh-behr lohs moo-eh-blehs

Please open the window (the windows) (the door [the doors]).
Favor de abrir la ventana (las ventanas) (la puerta [las puertas]).
fah-bohr deh ah-breer lah behn-tah-nah (lahs behn-tah-nahs) (lah poo-ehr-tah [lahs poo-ehr-tahs])

Please pick up anything on the floor and put it away.
Favor de recoger cualquier cosa en el piso y guardarla.
fah-bohr deh rreh-koh-hehr koo-ahl-kee-ehr koh-sah ehn ehl pee-soh ee goo-ahr-dahr-lah

Please polish the furniture (the silver).
Favor de lustrar los muebles (la plata).
fah-bohr deh loos-trahr lohs moo-eh-blehs (lah plah-tah)

Please plug in the vacuum cleaner over there.
Favor de enchufar la aspiradora allá.
fah-bohr deh ehn-choo-fahr lah ah-spee-rah-doh-rah ah-yah

Please put away the toys.
Favor de guardar los juguetes.
fah-bohr deh goo-ahr-dahr lohs hoo-geh-tehs

Please put flowers in the _____.
Favor de poner flores en el _____.
fah-bohr deh poh-nehr floh-rehs ehn ehl _____

Please read the directions.
Favor de leer las instrucciones.
fah-bohr deh leh-ehr lahs eens-trook-see-oh-nehs

Please ask me if you don't understand anything.
Favor de preguntarme si usted no entiende algo.
fah-bohr deh preh-goon-tahr-meh see oo-stehd noh ehn-tee-ehn-deh ahl-goh

Please remember to _____.
Favor de recordar _____.
fah-bohr deh rreh-kohr-dahr _____

Please remove any fingerprints (marks, cobwebs) on the walls.
Favor de quitar las huellas digitales (manchas, telarañas) de las paredes.
fah-bohr deh kee-tahr lahs oo-eh-yahs dee-hee-tah-lehs (mahn-chahs, teh-lah-rah-nyahs) deh lahs pah-reh-dehs

Please send the draperies to the dry cleaner.
Favor de mandar las colgaduras a la tintorería.
fah-bohr deh mahn-dahr lahs kohl-gah-doo-rahs ah lah teen-toh-reh-ree-ah

Please shake out the rug (the rugs).
Favor de sacudir la alfombra (las alfombras).
fah-bohr deh sah-koo-deer lah ahl-fohm-brah (lahs ahl-fohm-brahs)

Please shampoo the rug.
Favor de limpiar la alfombra.
fah-bohr deh leem-pee-ahr lah ahl-fohm-brah

Please sweep the floor.
Favor de barrer el piso.
fah-bohr deh bah-rrehr ehl pee-soh

Please take out the garbage.
Favor de sacar la basura.
fah-bohr deh sah-kahr lah bah-soo-rah

Please throw away the old newspapers (the old magazines).
Favor de botar los periódicos viejos (las revistas viejas).
fah-bohr deh boh-tahr lohs peh-ree-oh-dee-kohs bee-eh-hohs (lahs rreh-bees-tahs bee-eh-hahs)

Please don't touch the fusebox (the hot water heater).
Favor de no tocar la caja de fusibles (el calentador de agua).
fah-bohr deh noh toh-kahr lah kah-hah deh foo-see-blehs (ehl kah-lehn-tah-dohr deh ah-goo-ah)

Please turn off the lights (the stereo, the television).
Favor de apagar las luces (el estéreo, el televisor).
fah-bohr deh ah-pah-gahr lahs loo-sehs (ehl ehs-teh-reh-oh, ehl teh-leh-bee-sohr)

Here is the light switch.
El interruptor está aquí.
ehl een-teh-rroop-tohr ehs-tah ah-kee

Please turn on the alarm (the air-conditioning).
Favor de prender la alarma (el aire acondicionado).
fah-bohr deh preh-dehr lah ah-lahr-mah (ehl ah-ee-reh ah-kohn-dee-see-oh-nah-doh)

Please unplug the iron.
Favor de desenchufar la plancha.
fah-bohr deh dehs-ehn-choo-fahr lah plahn-chah

Please vacuum the floors (the rugs, the furniture).
Favor de pasar la aspiradora en el piso (las alfombras, los muebles).
fah-bohr deh pah-sahr lah ahs-pee-rah-doh-rah ehn ehl pee-soh (lahs ahl-fohm-brahs, lohs moo-eh-blehs)

Please vacuum under (behind) the cushions (the furniture).
Favor de pasar la aspiradora debajo de (detrás de) los cojines (los muebles).
fah-bohr deh pah-sahr lah ahs-pee-rah-doh-rah deh-bah-hoh deh (deh-trahs deh) lohs koh-hee-nehs (lohs moo-eh-blehs)

Please vacuum the stairs (the steps).
Favor de pasar la aspiradora en las escaleras (los escalones).
fah-bohr deh pah-sahr lah ahs-pee-rah-doh-rah ehn lahs ehs-kah-leh-rahs (lohs ehs-kah-loh-nehs)

Please wash (mop, dust, sweep) the floors.
Favor de lavar (trapear, sacudir, barrer) el piso.
fah-bohr deh lah-bahr (trah-peh-ahr, sah-koo-deer, bah-rrehr) ehl pee-soh

Please wash _____ gently (by hand).
Favor de lavar _____ suavemente (a mano).
fah-bohr deh lah-bahr _____ soo-ah-beh-mehn-teh (ah mah-noh)

Please wash the curtains (the mirrors).
Favor de lavar las cortinas (los espejos).
fah-bohr deh lah-bahr lahs kohr-tee-nahs (lohs ehs-peh-hohs)

Please wash the windows inside and outside.
Favor de lavar las ventanas por dentro y por fuera.
fah-bohr deh lah-bahr lahs behn-tah-nahs pohr dehn-troh ee pohr foo-eh-rah

Please water the plants.
Favor de regar las plantas.
fah-bohr deh rreh-gahr lahs plahn-tahs

Please wax the furniture.
Favor de encerar los muebles.
fah-bohr deh ehn-seh-rahr lohs moo-eh-blehs

Please wear a uniform.
Favor de llevar uniforme.
fah-bohr deh yeh-bahr oo-nee-fohr-meh

Cleaning Agents

Please tell me which cleaning agents you prefer.
Favor de decirme cuáles productos de limpieza usted prefiere.
fah-bor deh deh-seer-meh koo-ah-lehs proh-dook-tohs deh leem-pee-eh-sah
oo-stehd preh-fee-eh-reh

I will buy (You may buy) them whenever you need them.
Yo los compraré (Usted puede comprarlos) cuando los necesite.
yoh lohs kohm-prah-reh (oo-stehd poo-eh-deh kohm-prahr-lohs) koo-ahn-doh
lohs neh-seh-see-teh

Please don't mix ammonia with bleach.
Favor de no mezclar el amoníaco con el blanqueador.
fah-bor deh noh mehs-klahr ehl ah-moh-nee-ah-koh kohn ehl
blahn-keh-ah-dohr

Please don't apply furniture polish.
Favor de no aplicar el lustrador de muebles.
fah-bor deh noh ah-plee-kahr ehl loos-trah-dohr deh moo-eh-blehs

Please don't use anything abrasive.
Favor de no usar nada abrasivo.
fah-bor deh noh oo-sahr nah-dah ah-brah-see-boh

Please be careful with chemicals.
Favor de tener cuidado con los químicos.
fah-bor deh teh-nehr koo-ee-dah-doh kohn lohs kee-mee-kohs

Please use a mask (rubber gloves) when necessary.
Favor de usar una máscara (guantes de goma) cuando sea
necesario.
fah-bor deh oo-sahr oo-nah mahs-kah-rah (goo-ahn-tehs deh goh-mah)
koo-ahn-doh seh-ah neh-seh-sah-ree-oh

This is the way I want it done.
Lo quiero hecho de esta manera.
loh kee-eh-roh eh-choh deh ehs-tah mah-neh-rah

Here are the products I use:

Aquí están los productos que uso:

ah-kee ehs-tahn lohs proh-dook-tohs keh oo-soh

all-purpose cleaner	**el limpiador de uso múltiple**	*ehl leem-pee-ah-dohr deh oo-soh mool-tee-pleh*
ammonia	**el amoníaco**	*ehl ah-moh-nee-ah-koh*
baking soda	**el bicarbonato de soda**	*ehl bee-kahr-boh-nah-toh deh soh-dah*
bleach	**el blanqueador**	*ehl blahn-keh-ah-dohr*
carpet cleaner	**el limpiador de alfombras**	*ehl leem-pee-ah-dohr deh ahl-fohm-brahs*
cleanser (liquid, cream, powder, spray)	**el limpiador (líquido, en crema, en polvo, en aerosol)**	*ehl leem-pee-ah-dohr (lee-kee-doh, ehn kreh-mah, ehn pohl-boh, ehn ah-eh-roh-sohl)*
cream	**la crema**	*lah kreh-mah*
detergent (laundry, dishwasher)	**el detergente (para ropa, para lavaplatos)**	*ehl deh-tehr-hehn-teh (pah-rah rroh-pah, pah-rah lah-bah-plah-tohs)*
disinfectant	**el desinfectante**	*ehl dehs-een-fehk-tahn-teh*
fabric protector	**el protector de telas**	*ehl proh-tehk-tohr deh teh-lahs*
fabric softener	**el suavizador**	*ehl soo-ah-bee-sah-dohr*
floor cleaner	**el limpiador de pisos**	*ehl leem-pee-ah-dohr deh pee-sohs*
furniture oil	**el aceite para muebles**	*ehl ah-seh-ee-teh pah-rah moo-eh-blehs*
glass cleaner	**el limpiador para cristal**	*ehl leem-pee-ah-dohr pah-rah krees-tahl*
grout cleaner	**el limpiador para lechada**	*ehl leem-pee-ah-dohr pah-rah leh-chah-dah*

liquid cleaner for stainless-steel (dishes)	**el líquido para acero (platos)**	*ehl lee-kee-doh pah-rah ah-seh-roh (plah-tohs)*
liquid for delicate washes	**el líquido para ropa delicada**	*ehl lee-kee-doh pah-rah rroh-pah deh-lee-kah-dah*
nonabrasive cleaner	**el limpiador no-abrasivo**	*ehl leem-pee-ah-dohr noh-ah-brah-see-boh*
oven cleaner	**el limpiador de hornos**	*ehl leem-pee-ah-dohr deh ohr-nohs*
polish (silver, brass, copper, chrome)	**el lustrador para (plata, latón, cobre, cromo)**	*ehl loos-trah-dohr pah-rah (plah-tah, lah-tohn, koh-breh, kroh-moh)*
polish (furniture)	**el lustrador de muebles**	*ehl loos-trah-dohr deh moo-eh-blehs*
room deodorizer	**el desodorante para cuartos**	*ehl deh-soh-doh-rahn-teh pah-rah koo-ahr-tohs*
shampoo	**el champú**	*ehl chahm-poo*
soap (antibacterial)	**el jabón con protección antibacterial**	*ehl hah-bohn kohn proh-tehk-see-ohn ahn-tee-bahk-teh-ree-ahl*
spot remover	**el quitamanchas**	*ehl kee-tah-mahn-chahs*
spray starch	**el almidón en aerosol**	*ehl ahl-mee-dohn ehn ah-eh-roh-sohl*
vinegar	**el vinagre**	*ehl bee-nah-greh*
water	**el agua**	*ehl ah-goo-ah*
wax	**la cera**	*lah seh-rah*
wipes (antibacterial, countertop)	**las toallitas (con protección antibacterial, para las encimeras)**	*lahs toh-ah-yee-tahs (kohn proh-tehk-see-ohn ahn-tee-bahk-teh-ree-ahl, pah-rah lahs ehn-see-meh-rahs)*

Note

You may refer to a particular brand by using **el** (the) followed by the name of the product: *El Shine-Brite*.

The brand I prefer is _____.
La marca que yo prefiero es _____.
lah mahr-kah keh yoh preh-fee-eh-roh ehs _____

Cleaning Supplies

Please apply (use) the product with _____.
Favor de aplicar (usar) el producto con _____.
fah-bohr deh ah-plee-kahr (oo-sahr) ehl proh-dook-toh kohn _____

a brush (scrub)	**un cepillo (limpiasuelos)**	*oon seh-pee-yoh (leem-pee-ah-soo-eh-lohs)*
a mop	**un trapeador**	*oon trah-peh-ah-dohr*
a paper towel	**una toalla de papel**	*oo-nah toh-ah-yah deh pah-pehl*
a rag	**un trapo**	*oon-trah-poh*
a scouring pad	**un estropajo**	*oon ehs-troh-pah-hoh*
a sponge	**una esponja**	*oo-nah ehs-pohn-hah*
a toothbrush	**un cepillo de dientes**	*oon seh-pee-yoh deh dee-ehn-tehs*
a towel	**una toalla**	*oo-nah toh-ah-yah*

Use as many as you need to do the job correctly.
Favor de usar cuantos sean necesarios para hacer el trabajo correcto.
fah-bohr deh oo-sahr koo-ahn-tohs seh-ahn neh-seh-sah-ree-ohs pah-rah ah-sehr ehl trah-bah-hoh koh rrehk-toh

Make sure what you use is _____.
Favor de estar segura de lo que usa sea _____.
fah-bohr deh ehs-tahr seh-goo-rah deh loh keh oo-sah seh-ah _____

clean	**limpio**	*leem-pee-oh*
cold	**frio**	*free-oh*
cool	**fresco**	*frehs-koh*
dry	**seco**	*seh-koh*
hot	**caliente**	*kah-lee-ehn-teh*
moist	**húmedo**	*oo-meh-doh*
nonabrasive	**no-abrasivo**	*noh-ah-brah-see-boh*
soft	**suave**	*soo-ah-beh*
warm	**tibio**	*tee-bee-oh*
wet	**mojado**	*moh-hah-doh*

Other supplies you may need are _____.
Otros productos que puede necesitar son _____.
oh-trohs proh-dook-tohs keh poo-eh-deh neh-seh-see-tahr sohn _____

a broom	**una escoba**	*oo-nah ehs-koh-bah*
a bucket	**un balde**	*oon bahl-deh*
a dustpan	**una pala de recoger basura**	*oo-nah pah-lah deh rreh-koh-hehr bah-soo-rah*
a feather duster	**un plumero**	*oon ploo-meh-roh*
garbage bags	**bolsas para basura**	*bohl-sahs pah-rah bah-soo-rah*
an iron	**una plancha**	*oo-nah plahn-chah*
an ironing board	**una tabla de planchar**	*oo-nah tah-blah deh plahn-chahr*
a ladder	**una escalera**	*oo-nah ehs-kah-leh-rah*
a laundry basket	**una canasta para la ropa**	*oo-nah kah-nahs-tah pah-rah lah rroh-pah*
a mask	**una máscara**	*oo-nah mahs-kah-rah*
a pail	**un cubo**	*oon koo-boh*
rubber gloves	**guantes de goma**	*goo-ahn-tehs deh goh-mah*
scissors	**tijeras**	*tee-heh-rahs*
a scraper	**un raspador**	*oon rrahs-pah-dohr*
a squeegee	**un utensilio para limpiar cristales**	*oon oo-tehn-see-lee-oh pah-rah leem-pee-ahr krees-tah-lehs*
a stepladder	**una escalera de mano**	*oo-nah ehs-kah-leh-rah deh mah-noh*
a trash bag	**una bolsa para basura**	*oo-nah bohl-sah pah-rah bah-soo-rah*
a trash can	**un cesto para basura**	*oon sehs-toh pah-rah bah-soo-rah*
a vacuum cleaner	**una aspiradora**	*oo-nah ahs-pee-rah-doh-rah*
a vacuum cleaner bag	**una bolsa para aspiradora**	*oo-nah bohl-sah pah-rah ahs-pee-rah-doh-rah*
a wastepaper basket	**un papelero**	*oon pah-peh-leh-roh*

Praise

You did a great (good) job.
Hizo un (buen) trabajo formidable.
ee-soh oon (boo-ehn) trah-bah-hoh fohr-mee-dah-bleh

Thank you very much.
Muchas gracias.
moo-chahs grah-see-ahs

I'm very grateful.
Estoy muy agradecido (agradecida).
ehs-toh-ee moo-ee ah-grah-deh-see-doh (ah-grah-deh-see-dah)

It's perfect.
Es perfecto.
ehs pehr-fehk-toh

Especially for Renters

The doorman is holding (has received) a package for me (us).
Please go downstairs to pick it up.
**El portero tiene (ha recibido) un paquete para mí (nosotros).
Favor de bajar para recogerlo.**
*ehl pohr-teh-roh tee-eh-neh (ah rreh-see-bee-doh) oon pah-keh-teh pah-rah
mee (noh-soh-trohs) fah-bohr deh bah-hahr pah-rah rreh-koh-hehr-loh*

There is a problem in the bathroom (the kitchen). Please call the
superintendent.
**Hay un problema en el baño (la cocina). Favor de llamar al
superintendente.**
*ah-ee oon proh-bleh-mah ehn ehl bah-nyoh (lah koh-see-nah) fah-bohr deh
yah-mahr ahl soo-peh-reen-tehn-dehn-teh*

You are (not) allowed to use the building's parking lot.
**Usted (no) tiene permiso de usar el estacionamiento del
edificio.**
*oo-stehd (noh) tee-eh-neh pehr-mee-soh deh oo-sahr ehl ehs-tah-see-oh-nah-
mee-ehn-toh dehl eh-dee-fee-see-oh*

If you ever forget your key, the superintendent (the concierge) has a spare.
Si usted se olvida de la llave, el superintendente (el conserje) tiene otra.
see oo-stehd seh ohl-bee-dah deh lah yah-beh ehl soo-peh-reen-tehn-dehn-teh (ehl kohn-sehr-heh) tee-eh-neh oh-trah

The elevators are (not) working today.
Los ascensores (no) están funcionando hoy.
lohs ah-sehn-soh-rehs (noh) ehs-tahn foon-see-oh-nahn-doh oh-ee

Please go downstairs to the mailbox and pick up the mail.
Favor de bajar al buzón y recoger el correo.
fah-bohr deh bah-hahr ahl boo-sohn ee rreh-koh-hehr ehl koh-rreh-oh

You don't have to carry packages upstairs. The porter/doorman (the concierge) will help you.
Usted no tiene que cargar los paquetes arriba. El portero (El conserje) le ayudará.
oo-stehd noh tee-eh-neh keh kahr-gahr lohs pah-keh-tehs ah-ree-bah ehl pohr-teh-roh (ehl kohn-sehr-heh) leh ah-yoo-dah-rah

Please give him/her this tip.
Favor de darle esta propina.
fah-bohr deh dahr-leh ehs-tah proh-pee-nah

5

Cleaning in
the Kitchen

General Directions

Please _____.
Favor de _____.
fah-bohr deh _____

arrange	**arreglar**	*ah-rreh-glahr*
change	**cambiar**	*kahm-bee-ahr*
clean	**limpiar**	*leem-pee-ahr*
defrost	**descongelar**	*dehs-kohn-heh-lahr*
disinfect	**desinfectar**	*dehs-een-fehk-tahr*
dry	**secar**	*seh-kahar*
empty	**vaciar**	*bah-see-ahr*
keep	**guardar**	*goo-ahr-dahr*
label	**etiquetar**	*eh-tee-keh-tahr*
leave	**salir (dejar)**	*sah-leer (deh-hahr)*
mop	**tropear**	*troh-peh-ahr*
press	**exprimir**	*ehks-pree-meer*
pull	**jalar**	*hah-lahr*
push	**empujar**	*ehm-poo-hahr*
put	**poner**	*poh-nehr*
remove	**quitar**	*kee-tahr*
rinse	**enjuagar**	*ehn-hoo-ah-gahr*
rotate	**voltear**	*bohl-teh-ahr*
scrub	**fregar**	*freh-gahr*
set (the table)	**poner (la mesa)**	*poh-nehr (lah meh-sah)*

spray	**rociar**	*rroh-see-ahr*
stack	**amontonar**	*ah-mohn-toh-nahr*
store	**guardar**	*goo-ahr-dahr*
sweep	**barrer**	*bah-rrehr*
take out	**sacar**	*sah-kahr*
tell	**decir**	*deh-seer*
use	**usar**	*oo-sahr*
vacuum	**pasar la**	*pah-sahr lah*
	aspiradora	*ahs-pee-rah-doh-rah*
wash	**lavar**	*lah-bahr*
wear	**llevar (usar)**	*yeh-bahr (oo-sahr)*
wipe	**pasarle**	*pah-sahr-leh*
	un trapo a...	*oon trah-poh ah*

Please arrange the cans in the pantry.
Favor de arreglar las latas en la despensa.
fah-bohr deh ah-rreh-glahr lahs lah-tahs ehn lah dehs-pehn-sah

Please change the tablecloth.
Favor de cambiar el mantel.
fah-bohr deh kahm-bee-ahr ehl mahn-tehl

Please clean the cabinets (the island).
Favor de limpiar los gabinetes (la isla).
fah-bohr deh leem-pee-ahr lohs gah-bee-neh-tehs (lah ees-lah)

Please clean the light fixture (floor lamp) with a feather duster.
Favor de limpiar la luz (lámpara) con un plumero.
fah-bohr deh leem-pee-ahr lah loos (lahm-pah-rah) kohn oon ploo-meh-roh

Please clean the sponges in the dishwasher (microwave).
Favor de limpiar las esponjas en el lavaplatos (microoondas).
fah-bohr deh leem-pee-ahr lahs ehs-pohn-hahs ehn ehl lah-bah-plah-tohs
(mee-kroh-ohn-dahs)

Please defrost the freezer once a month.
Favor de descongelar el congelador una vez al mes.
fah-bohr deh dehs-koh-heh-lahr ehl kohn-heh-lah-dohr oo-nah behs ahl mehs.

Please disinfect the countertops.
Favor de desinfectar los mostradores.
fah-bohr deh dehs-een-fehk-tahr lohs moh-strah-doh-rehs

Please dry the dishes in the sink.
Favor de secar los platos en el lavabo.
fah-bohr deh seh-kahr lohs plah-tohs ehn ehl lah-bah-boh

Please empty the garbage pail every evening.
Favor de vaciar el basurero cada noche.
fah-bohr deh bah-see-ahr ehl bah-soo-reh-roh kah-dah noh-cheh

Please keep the kitchen clean at all times.
Favor de mantener la cocina limpia siempre.
fah-bohr deh mahn-teh-nehr lah koh-see-nah leem-pee-ah see-ehm-preh

Please label the containers.
Favor de etiquetar los envases.
fah-bohr deh eh-tee-keh-tahr lohs ehn-bah-sehs

Please leave the sponge in the holder on the sink.
Favor de dejar la esponja en el platillo sobre el lavabo.
fah-bohr deh deh-hahr lah ehs-pohn-hah ehn ehl plah-tee-yoh soh-breh ehl lah-bah-boh

Please mop the floor with warm (hot) water.
Favor de tropear el piso con agua tibia (caliente).
fah-bohr deh troh-peh-ahr ehl pee-soh kohn ah-goo-ah tee-bee-ah (kah-lee-ehn-teh)

Please press (pull, push) this button to turn on the dishwasher.
Favor de oprimir (jalar, empujar) este botón para prender el lavaplatos.
fah-bohr deh oh-pree-meer (hah-lahr, ehm-poo-hahr) ehs-teh boh-tohn pah-rah prehn-dehr ehl lah-bah-plah-tohs

Please put these utensils in this (that) drawer.
Favor de poner estos utensilios en este (ese) cajón.
fah-bohr deh poh-nehr ehs-tohs oo-tehn-see-lee-ohs ehn ehs-teh (eh-seh) kah-hohn

Please put all plastics and metal cans in the garbage pail (garbage bag).
Favor de poner todos los plásticos y latas en el basurero (la bolsa de basura).
fah-bohr deh poh-nehr toh-dohs lohs plahs-tee-kohs ee lah-tahs ehn ehl bah-soo-reh-roh (lah bohl-sah deh bah-soo-rah)

Please put knives point down in the dishwasher.
Favor de poner los cuchillos en el lavaplatos con la punta hacia abajo.
fah-bohr deh poh-nehr lohs koo-chee-yohs ehn ehl lah-bah-plah-tohs kohn lah poon-tah ah-see-ah ah-bah-hoh

Please (don't) put these (those) knives in the dishwasher.
Favor de (no) poner estos (esos) cuchillos en el lavaplatos.
fah-bohr deh (noh) poh-nehr ehs-tohs (eh-sohs) koo-chee-yohs ehn ehl lah-bah-plah-tohs

Please remove the soap scum from the sink.
Favor de quitar el desecho de jabón del lavabo.
fah-bohr deh kee-tahr ehl deh-seh-choh deh hah-bohn dehl lah-bah-boh

Please rinse the dishes before loading them in the dishwasher.
Favor de enjuagar los platos antes de ponerlos en el lavaplatos.
fah-bohr deh ehn-hoo-ah-gahr lohs plah-tohs ahn-tehs deh poh-nehr-lohs ehn ehl lah-bah-plah-tohs

Please rotate the canned goods in the pantry.
Favor de voltear las latas en la despensa.
fah-bohr deh bohl-teh-ahr lahs lah-tahs ehn lah dehs-pehn-sah

Please scrub the floor.
Favor de fregar el piso.
fah-bohr deh freh-gahr ehl pee-soh

Please separate the garbage.
Favor de separar la basura.
fah-bohr deh seh-pah-rahr lah bah-soo-rah

Please set the dishwasher for the gentle (energy-saving, normal, scrub) cycle.
Favor de poner el lavaplatos al ciclo de delicado (para conservar energía, normal, fregar).
fah-bohr deh poh-nehr ehl lah-bah-plah-tohs ahl see-kloh deh deh-lee-kah-doh (pah-rah kohn-sehr-bahr eh-nehr-hee-ah, nohr-mahl, freh-gahr)

Please spray the countertops with this.
Favor de rociar los mostradores con ésto.
fah-bohr deh rroh-see-ahr lohs mohs-trah-doh-rehs kohn ehs-toh

Please stack the dishes in this (that) cabinet.
Favor de amontonar los platos en este (ese) gabinete.
fah-bohr deh ah-mohn-toh-nahr lohs plah-tohs ehn ehs-teh (eh-seh) gah-bee-neh-teh

Please store all paper goods in the pantry.
Favor de guardar todas las cosas de papel en la despensa.
fah-bohr deh goo-ahr-dahr toh-dahs lahs koh-sahs deh pah-pehl ehn lah dehs-pehn-sah

Please sweep the floor.
Favor de barrer el piso.
fah-bohr deh bah-rrehr ehl pee-soh

Please take out the garbage.
Favor de sacar la basura.
fah-bohr deh sah-kahr lah bah-soo-rah

Please tell me if there are any cleaning products that you need.
Favor de decirme qué productos para limpiar necesita.
fah-bohr deh deh-seer-meh keh proh-dook-tohs pah-rah leem-pee-ahr neh-seh-see-tah

Please use this product.
Favor de usar este producto.
fah-bohr deh oo-sahr ehs-teh proh-dook-toh

Please vacuum the refrigerator coils.
Favor de pasar la aspiradora por las bobinas del refrigerador.
fah-bohr deh pah-sahr lah ahs-pee-rah-doh-rah pohr lahs boh-bee-nahs dehl rreh-free-heh-rah-dohr

Please wax the kitchen floor.
Favor de encerar el piso de la cocina.
fah-bohr deh ehn-seh-rahr ehl pee-soh deh lah koh-see-nah

Please wash the dishes immediately.
Favor de fregar los platos en seguida.
fah-bohr deh freh-gahr lohs plah-tohs ehn seh-gee-dah

Please wear rubber gloves when you clean.
Favor de usar guantes de goma cuando usted limpie.
fah-bohr deh oo-sahr goo-ahn-tehs deh goh-mah koo-ahn-doh oo-stehd leem-pee-eh

Please wipe the countertops thoroughly.
Favor de limpiar completamente los mostradores con un trapo húmedo.
fah-bohr deh leem-pee-ahr kohm-pleh-tah-mehn-teh lohs mohs-trah-doh-rehs kohn oon trah-poh oo-meh-doh

The cork floor is (the countertops are) very porous. Please be careful not to spill anything on it (them).
El piso de corcho es (Los mostradores son) muy poroso (porosos). Favor de tener cuidado de no derramar nada sobre él (ellos).
ehl pee-soh deh kohr-choh ehs (lohs mohs-trah-doh-rehs sohn)
moo-ee poh-roh-soh (poh-roh-sohs) fah-bohr deh teh-nehr koo-ee-dah-doh deh noh deh-rrah-mahr nah-dah soh-breh ehl (eh-yohs)

The tile floor shows crumbs. Please sweep them immediately.
El suelo de baldosas muestra migas. Favor de barrerlas en seguida.
ehl soo-eh-loh deh bahl-doh-sahs moo-ehs-trah mee-gahs fah-bohr deh bah-rrehr-lahs ehn seh-gee-dah

The lineoleum (cork, tile, vinyl) floor needs to be cleaned every evening.
El piso de linóleo (corcho, loceta, vinilo) hay que limpiarlo cada noche.
ehl pee-soh deh lee-noh-leh-oh (kohr-choh, loh-seh-tah, bee-nee-loh) ah-ee keh leem-pee-ahr-loh kah-dah noh-cheh

The _____ needs to be cleaned once (twice) a day (a week, a month, a year).
Hay que limpiar el (la) _____ una vez (dos veces) al día (a la semana, al mes, al año).
ah-ee keh leem-pee-ahr ehl (lah) _____ oo-nah behs (dohs beh-sehs) ahl dee-ah (ah lah seh-mah-nah, ahl mehs, ahl ah-nyoh)

We recycle.
Nosotros reciclamos.
noh-soh-trohs rreh-see-klah-mohs

Please tie up paper, old newspapers, old magazines, and cardboard.
Favor de atar papeles, periódicos viejos, revistas viejas y cartón.
fah-bohr deh ah-tahr pah-peh-lehs, peh-ree-oh-dee-kohs bee-eh-hohs, rreh-bees-tahs bee-eh-hahs ee kahr-tohn

Pantry, Drawers, and Cabinets

Pantry

We keep only nonperishable foods in the pantry.
Guardamos sólo comestibles no perecederos en la despensa.
goo-ahr-dah-mohs soh-loh koh-mehs-tee-blehs noh peh-reh-seh-deh-rohs ehn lah dehs-pehn-sah

Please arrange the cans (the bottles, the boxes, the packages) by their expiration dates.
Favor de arreglar las latas (las botellas, las cajas, los paquetes) según las fechas de expiración.
fah-bohr deh ah-rreh-glahr lahs lah-tahs (lahs boh-teh-yahs, lahs kah-hahs, lohs pah-keh-tehs) seh-goon lahs feh-chahs deh ehks-pee-rah-see-ohn

Please put the most recently dated product in the front.
Favor de poner enfrente el producto con la fecha más reciente.
fah-bohr deh poh-nehr ehn-frehn-teh ehl proh-dook-toh kohn lah feh-chah mahs rreh-see-ehn-teh

Please rotate the items.
Favor de voltear las cosas.
fah-bohr deh bohl-teh-ahr lahs koh-sahs

Please clean the pantry once a week (a month).
Favor de limpiar la despensa una vez a la semana (al mes).
fah-bohr deh leem-pee-ahr lah dehs-pehn-sah oo-nah behs ah lah seh-mah-nah (ahl mehs)

Please tell me when we run out of something.
Favor de avisarme cuando nos falte algo.
fah-bohr deh ah-bee-sahr-meh koo-ahn-doh nohs fahl-teh ahl-goh

Drawers and Cabinets

I keep (We keep) the _____ in this (that) drawer (cabinet).
Yo guardo (Nosotros guardamos) el (la) _____ en este (ese) cajón (gabinete).
yoh goo-ahr-doh (noh-soh-trohs goo-ahr-dah-mohs) ehl (lah) _____ ehn ehs-teh (eh-seh) kah-hohn (gah-bee-neh-teh)

_____ is (are) in the pantry.
. _____ **está (están) en la despensa.**
_____ *ehs-tah (ehs-tahn) ehn lah dehs-pehn-sah*

The aluminum foil	**El papel de aluminio**	*ehl pah-pehl deh ah-loo-mee-nee-oh*
The apron (The aprons)	**El delantal (Los delantales)**	*ehl deh-lahn-tahl (lohs deh-lahn-tah-lehs)*
The ashtray (The ashtrays)	**El cenicero (Los ceniceros)**	*ehl seh-nee-seh-roh (lohs seh-nee-seh-rohs)*
The bag (The bags) (paper, plastic)	**La bolsa (Las bolsas) (de papel, de plástico)**	*lah bohl-sah (lahs bohl-sahs) (deh pah-pehl, deh plahs-tee-koh)*
The bakeware	**Las fuentes para el horno**	*lahs foo-ehn-tehs pah-rah*
The baking dish (The baking dishes)	**El molde (Los moldes) de hornear**	*ehl mohl-deh (lohs mohl-dehs) deh ohr-neh ahr*
The bottle opener (The bottle openers)	**El abre-botellas (Los abre-botellas)**	*ehl ah-breh boh-teh-yahs (lohs ah-breh-boh-teh-yahs)*
The bowl (The bowls) (mixing)	**El tazón (Los tazones) (para mezclar)**	*ehl tah-sohn (lohs tah-soh-nehs) (pah-rah mehs-klahr)*
The bread basket (The bread baskets)	**La canasta (Las canastas)**	*lah kah-nahs-tah (lahs kah-nahs-tahs)*
The bundt pan (The bundt pans)	**La caserola de bundt (Las caserolas de bundt)**	*lah kah-seh-roh-lah deh buhnt (lahs kah-seh-roh-lahs deh buhnt)*
The butter dish (The butter dishes)	**La mantequillera (Las mantequilleras)**	*lah mahn-teh-kee-yeh-rah (lahs mahn-teh-kee-yeh-rahs)*
The cake pan (The cake pans)	**El molde para torta (Los moldes para tortas)**	*ehl mohl-deh pah-rah tohr-tah (lohs mohl-dehs pah-rah tohr-tahs)*

The can opener (The can openers)	**El abrelatas** (**Los abrelatas**)	*ehl ah-breh lah-tahs* (*lohs ah-breh-lah-tahs*)
The carafe (The carafes)	**La garrafa** (**Las garrafas**)	*lah gah-rrah-fah* (*lahs gah-rrah-fahs*)
The casserole (The casseroles)	**La caserola** (**Las caserolas**)	*lah kah-seh-roh-lah* (*lahs kah-seh-roh-lahs*)
The cleanser (The cleansers)	**El limpiador** (**Los limpiadores**)	*ehl leem-pee-ah-dohr* (*lohs leem-pee-ah-doh-rehs*)
The coffee filter (The coffee filters)	**El filtro de café** (**Los filtros de café**)	*ehl feel-troh deh kah-feh* (*lohs fool trohs deh kah-feh*)
The colander (The colanders)	**El escurridor** (**Los escurridores**)	*ehl ehs-koo-rree-dohr* (*lohs ehs-koo-rree-doh-rehs*)
The cookie sheet (The cookie sheets)	**La hoja metálica para el horno** (**Las hojas metálicas para el horno**)	*lah oh-hah meh-tah-lee-kah pah-rah ehl ohr-noh* (*lahs oh-hahs meh-tah-lee-kahs pah-rah ehl ohr-noh*)
The cork (The corks)	**El corcho** (**Los corchos**)	*ehl kohr-choh* (*lohs kohr-chohs*)
The corkscrew (The corkscrews)	**El sacacorchos** (**Los sacacorchos**)	*ehl sah-kah-kohr-chohs* (*lohs sah-kah-kohr-chohs*)
The cover (The covers) (for pots or pans)	**La tapa** (**Las tapas**)	*lah tapa (lahs tah-pahs*)
The creamer	**La cremera**	*lah kreh-meh-rah*
The cup (The cups) (paper, plastic)	**La taza** (**Las tazas**) (**de papel, plásticas**)	*lah tah sah (lahs tah-sahs*) (*deh pah-pehl, plahs-tee-kahs*)
The cutting board (The cutting boards)	**La tabla para cortar** (**Las tablas para cortar**)	*lah tah-blah pah-rah kohr-tahr (lahs tah-blahs pah-rah kohr-tahr*)
The dish rack (The dish racks)	**El escurreplatos** (**Los escurreplatos**)	*ehl ehs-koo-rreh-plah-tohs* (*lohs ehs-koo-rreh-plah-tohs*)
The dishwashing detergent	**El detergente del lavaplatos**	*ehl deh-tehr-hehn-teh dehl lah-bah-plah-tohs*

The double boiler (The double boilers)	**La olla de baño maría (Las ollas de baño maría)**	*lah oh-yah deh bah-nyoh mah-ree-ah (lahs oh-yahs deh bah-nyoh mah-ree-ah)*
The drain board (The drainboards)	**El escurridero (Los escurrideros)**	*ehl ehs-koo-rree-deh-roh (lohs ehs-koo-rree-deh-rohs)*
The Dutch oven (The Dutch ovens)	**El horno holandés (Los hornos holandeses)**	*ehl ohr-noh oh-lahn-dehs (lohs ohr-nohs oh-lahn-deh-sehs)*
The fork (The forks) (plastic, silver, stainless steel)	**El tenedor (Los tenedores) (plásticos, de plata, de acero inoxidable)**	*ehl teh-neh-dohr (lohs teh-neh-doh-rehs) (plahs-tee-kohs, deh plah-tah, deh ah-seh-roh een-ohk-see-dah-bleh)*
The frying pan (The frying pans)	**La sartén (Las sartenes)**	*lah sahr-tehn (lahs sahr-teh-nehs)*
The funnel (The funnels)	**El embudo (Los embudos)**	*ehl ehm-boo-doh (lohs ehm-boo-dohs)*
The garlic press	**La prensa de ajo**	*lah prehn-sah deh ah-hoh*
The glass (The glasses)	**El vaso (Los vasos)**	*ehl bah-soh (lohs bah-sohs)*
The glove (The gloves) (rubber)	**El guante (Los guantes) (de goma)**	*ehl goo-ahn-teh (lohs goo-ahn-tehs) (deh goh-mah)*
The grater (The graters)	**El rallador (Los ralladores)**	*ehl rrah-yah-dohr (lohs rrah-yah-doh-rehs)*
The ice bucket (The ice buckets)	**La hielera (Las hieleras)**	*lah ee-eh-leh-rah (lahs ee-eh-leh-rahs)*
The ice cream scoop (The ice cream scoops)	**La heladera (Las heladeras)**	*lah eh-lah-deh-rah (lahs eh-lah-deh-rahs)*
The knife (The knives) (electric, plastic, silver, stainless steel)	**El cuchillo (Los cuchillos) (eléctricos, plásticos, de plata, de acero inoxidable)**	*ehl koo-chee-yoh (lohs koo-chee-yohs) (eh-lehk-tree-kohs, plahs-tee-kohs, deh plah-tah, deh ah-seh-roh een-ohk-see-dah-bleh)*

The ladle (The ladles)	**El cucharón (Los cucharones)**	*ehl koo-chah-rohn (lohs koo-chah-roh-nehs)*
The lid (The lids)	**La tapa (Las tapas)**	*lah tah-pah (lahs tah-pahs)*
The loaf pan (The loaf pans)	**El molde para pan (Los moldes para pan)**	*ehl mohl-deh pah-rah pahn (lohs mohl-dehs pah-rah pahn)*
The match (The matches)	**El fósforo (Los fósforos)**	*ehl fohs-foh-roh (lohs fohs-foh-rohs)*
The measuring cup (The measuring cups)	**La taza de medir (Las tazas de medir)**	*lah tah-sah deh meh-deer (lahs tah-sahs deh meh-deer)*
The measuring spoon (The measuring spoons)	**La cuchara para medir (Las cucharas para medir)**	*lah koo-chah-rah pah-rah meh-deer (lahs koo-chah-rahs pah-rah meh-deer)*
The microplane (The microplanes)	**El microplano (Los microplanos)**	*ehl mee-kroh-plah-noh (lohs mee-kroh-plah-nohs)*
The muffin tin (The muffin tins)	**El molde metálico para molletes (Los moldes metálicos para molletes)**	*ehl mohl-deh meh-tah-lee-koh pah-rah moh-yeh-tehs (lohs mohl-dehs meh-tah-lee-kohs pah-rah moh-yeh-tehs)*
The napkin (The napkins)	**La servilleta (Las servilletas)**	*lah sehr-bee-yeh-tah (lahs sehr-bee-yeh-tahs)*
The napkin holder (The napkin holders)	**El servilletero (Los servilleteros)**	*ehl sehr-bee-yeh-teh-roh (lohs sehr-bee-yeh-teh-rohs)*
The oven mitt (The oven mitts)	**El guante del horno (Los guantes del horno)**	*ehl goo-ahn-teh dehl ohr-noh (lohs goo-ahn-tehs dehl ohr-noh)*
The pan (The pans)	**La sartén (Las sartenes)**	*lah sahr-tehn (lahs sahr-teh-nehs)*
The paper goods	**Los productos de papel**	*lohs proh-dook-tohs deh pah-pehl*
The parchment paper	**El papel de pergamino**	*ehl pah-pehl deh pehr-gah-mee-noh*

The pastry brush (The pastry brushes)	El cepillo para pasteles (Los cepillos para pasteles)	*ehl seh-pee-yoh pah-rah pahs-teh-lehs (lohs seh-pee-yohs pah-rah pahs-teh-lehs)*
The pepper shaker (The pepper shakers)	El pimentero (Los pimenteros)	*ehl pee-mehn-teh-roh (lohs pee-mehn-teh-rohs)*
The pitcher (The pitchers)	La jarra (Las jarras)	*lah hah-rrah (lahs hah-rrahs)*
The placemat (The placemats)	El mantel individual (Los manteles individuales)	*ehl mahn-tehl een-dee-bee-doo-ahl (lohs mahn-teh-lehs een-dee-bee-doo-ah-lehs)*
The plastic container (The plastic containers)	El envase plástico (Los envases plásticos)	*ehl ehn-bah-seh plahs-tee-koh (lohs ehn-bah-sehs plahs-tee-kohs)*
The plastic silverware	Los cubiertos de plástico	*lohs koo-bee-ehr-tohs deh plahs-tee-koh*
The plastic wrap	El papel de plástico	*ehl pah-pehl deh plahs-tee-koh*
The plate (The plates) (dinner, paper, plastic)	El plato (Los platos) (de cena, de papel, de plástico)	*ehl plah-toh (lohs plah-tohs) (deh seh-nah, deh pah-pehl, deh plahs-tee-koh)*
The potholder (The potholders)	El portaolla (Los portaollas)	*ehl pohr-tah-oh-yah (lohs pohr-tah-oh-yahs)*
The pot (The pots)	La olla (Las ollas)	*lah oh-yah (lahs oh-yahs)*
The pressure cooker (The pressure cookers)	La olla de presión (Las ollas de presión)	*lah oh-yah deh preh-see-ohn (lahs oh-yahs deh preh-see-ohn)*
The roasting pan (The roasting pans)	El asador (Los asadores)	*ehl ah-sah-dohr (lohs ah-sah-doh-rehs)*
The rolling pin (The rolling pins)	El rodillo (Los rodillos)	*ehl rroh-dee-yoh (lohs rroh-dee-yohs)*

The salad bowl (The salad bowls)	La ensaladera (Las ensaladeras)	*lah ehn-sah-lah-deh-rah (lahs ehn-sah-lah-deh-rahs)*
The salt shaker (The salt shakers)	El salero (Los saleros)	*ehl sah-leh-roh (lohs sah-leh-rohs)*
The saucepan (The saucepans)	La cacerola (Las cacerolas)	*lah kah-seh-roh-lah (lahs kah-seh-roh-lahs)*
The saucer (The saucers)	El platillo (Los platillos)	*ehl plah-tee-yoh (lohs plah-tee-yohs)*
The scissors	Las tijeras	*lahs tee-heh-rahs*
The serving dish (The serving dishes)	El plato de servir (Los platos de servir)	*ehl plah-toh deh sehr-beer (lohs plah-tohs deh sehr-beer)*
The serving pieces	Los utensilios para servir	*lohs oo-tehn-see-lee-ohs pah-rah sehr-beer*
The silverware	Los cubiertos	*lohs koo-bee-ehr-tohs*
The skewer (The skewers)	El pincho (Los pinchos)	*ehl peen-choh (lohs peen-chohs)*
The skillet (The skillets)	La sartén (Las sartenes)	*lah sahr-tehn (lahs sahr-teh-nehs)*
The slow cooker (The slow cookers)	La vasija de barro (Las vasijas de barro)	*lah bah-see-hah deh bah-rroh (lahs bah-see-hahs deh bah-rroh)*
The spatula (The spatulas)	La espátula (Las espátulas)	*lah ehs-pah-too-lah (lahs ehs-pah-too-lahs)*
The spoon (The spoons) (plastic, silver, stainless steel, wooden)	La cuchara (Las cucharas) (de plástico, de plata, de acero inoxidable, de madera)	*lah koo-chah-rah (lahs koo-chah-rahs) (deh plahs-tee-koh, deh plah-tah, deh ah-seh-roh een-ohk-see-dah-bleh, deh mah-deh-rah)*
The springform pan (The springform pans) (9-inch)	La caserola de springform (Las caserolas de springform) (de nueve pulgadas)	*lah kah-seh-roh-lah deh spreeng-fohrm (lahs kah-seh-roh-lahs deh spreeng-fohrm) (deh noo-eh-beh pool-gah-dahs)*

The strainer	El colador	*ehl koh-lah-dohr*
(The strainers)	(Los coladores)	*(lohs koh-lah-doh-rehs)*
The sugar bowl	La azucarera	*lah ah-soo-kah-reh-rah*
(The sugar bowls)	(Las azucareras)	*(lahs ah-soo-kah-reh-rahs)*
The tablecloth	El mantel	*ehl mahn-tehl*
(The tablecloths)	(Los manteles)	*(lohs mahn-teh-lehs)*
(linen, paper, plastic)	(de lino, de papel, de plástico)	*(deh lee-noh, deh pah-pehl, deh plahs-tee-koh)*
The teapot	La tetera	*lah teh-teh-rah*
(The teapots)	(Las teteras)	*(lahs teh-teh-rahs)*
The thermometer (The thermometers)	El termómetro (Los termómetros)	*ehl tehr-moh-meh-troh (lohs tehr-moh-meh-trohs)*
(instant read, oven)	(de lectura instantánea, de horno)	*(deh lehk-too-rah een-stahn-tah-neh-ah, deh ohr-noh)*
The Thermos	El termo	*ehl tehr-moh*
(The Thermoses)	(Los termos)	*(lohs tehr-mohs)*
The timer (The timers)	El reloj de cocina (Los relojes de cocina)	*ehl rreh-loh deh koh-see-nah (lohs rreh-loh-hehs deh koh-see-nah)*
The tin (The tins)	La lata (Las latas)	*lah lah-tah (lahs lah-tahs)*
The tongs	Las tenazas	*lahs teh-nah-sahs*
The toothpicks	El palillo de dientes (Los palillos de dientes)	*ehl pah-lee-yoh deh dee-ehn-tehs (lohs pah-lee-yohs deh dee-ehn-tehs)*
The towel (The towels) (kitchen)	La toalla (Las toallas) (de cocina)	*lah toh-ah-yah (lahs toh-ah-yahs) (deh koh-see-nah)*
The tray (The trays)	La bandeja (Las bandejas)	*lah bahn-deh-hah (lahs bahn-deh-hahs)*
The tube pan (The tube pans)	La caserola de tubo (las caserolas de tubo)	*lah kah-seh-roh-lah deh too-boh (lahs kah-seh-roh-lahs deh too-boh)*
The utensils	Los utensilios	*lohs oo-tehn-see-lee-ohs*

The vegetable peeler (The vegetable peelers)	**El pelador (Los peladores)**	*ehl peh-lah-dohr (lohs peh-lah-doh-rehs)*
The wax paper	**El papel encerado**	*ehl pah-pehl ehn-seh-rah-doh*
The whisk (The whisks)	**El batidor (Los batidores)**	*ehl bah-tee-dohr (lohs bah-tee-doh-rehs)*
The wok (The woks)	**El wok (Los woks)**	*ehl wohk (lohs wohks)*

Please bring me _____.
Favor de traerme _____.
fah-bohr deh trah-ehr-meh _____

Please take out _____.
Favor de sacar _____.
fah-bohr deh sah-kahr _____

You will need _____.
Usted va a necesitar _____.
oo-stehd bah ah neh-seh-see-tahr _____

I (We) will reimburse you. Please buy _____.
Yo (Nosotros) le reembolsaré (reembolsaremos). Favor de comprar _____.
yoh (noh-soh-trohs) leh rreh-ehm-bohl-sah-reh (rreh-ehm-bohl-sah-reh-mohs) fah-bohr deh kohm-prahr

Please clean the interior and exterior of all cabinets and drawers.
Favor de limpiar dentro y fuera de los gabinetes y los cajones.
fah-bohr deh leem-pee-ahr dehn-troh ee foo-eh-rah deh lohs gah-bee-neh-tehs ee lohs kah-hoh-nehs

Please dry everything immediately and put it away.
Favor de secar todo en seguida y guardarlo.
fah-bohr deh seh-kahr toh-doh ehn seh-gee-dah ee goo-ahr-dahr-loh

Please keep the cabinets (drawers) neat at all times.
Favor de mantener los gabinetes (los cajones) siempre arreglados.
fah-bohr deh mahn-teh-nehr lohs gah-bee-neh-tehs (lohs kah-hoh-nehs) see-ehm-preh ah-rreh-glah-dohs

Please don't leave dirty dishes in the sink.
Favor de no dejar platos sucios en el fregadero.
fah-bohr deh noh deh-hahr plah-tohs soo-see-ohs ehn ehl freh-gah-deh-roh

Please (don't) put _____ in the dishwasher.
Favor de (no) poner _____ en el lavaplatos.
fah-bohr deh (noh) poh-nehr _____ ehn ehl lah-bah-plah-tohs

Please remove everything from the kitchen cabinets (the drawers) before cleaning.
Favor de sacar todo de los gabinetes (los cajones) de la cocina antes de limpiarlos.
fah-bohr deh sah-kahr toh-doh deh lohs gah-bee-neh-tehs (lohs kah-hoh-nehs) deh lah koh-see-nah ahn-tehs deh leem-pee-ahr-lohs

Please (don't) reorganize the cabinets (the drawers, the pantry).
Favor de (no) reorganizar los gabinetes (los cajones, la despensa).
fah-bohr deh (noh) rreh-ohr-gah-nee-sahr lohs gah-bee-neh-tehs (lohs kah-hoh-nehs, lah dehs-pehn-sah)

Please set the timer for _____ minutes.
Favor de poner el reloj de cocina por _____ minutos.
fah-bohr deh poh-nehr ehl rreh-loh deh koh-see-nah pohr _____ mee-noo-tohs

You will need a ladder (a stepstool) to clean on top of the cabinets.
Usted va a necesitar una escalera (una taburete escalera) para limpiar encima de los gabinetes.
oo-stehd bah ah neh-seh-see-tahr oo-nah ehs-kah-leh-rah (oo-nah tah-boo-reh-teh ehs-kah-leh-rah) pah-rah leem-pee-ahr ehn-see-mah deh lohs gah-bee-neh-tehs

Appliances and Electrics

Please clean _____.
Favor de limpiar _____.
fah-bohr deh leem-pee-ahr _____

the blender	**la licuadora**	*lah lee-koo-ah-doh-rah*
the can opener (electric)	**el abrelatas (eléctrico)**	*ehl ah-breh-lah-tahs (eh-lehk-tree-koh)*
the coffeemaker	**la cafetera**	*lah kah-feh-teh-rah*
the dishwasher	**el lavaplatos**	*ehl lah-bah-plah-tohs*

the electric fry pan	la sartén eléctrica	lah sahr-tehn eh-lehk-tree-kah
the electric knife	el cuchillo eléctrico	ehl koo-chee-yoh eh-lehk-tree-koh
the food processor	el procesador de comida	ehl proh-seh-sah-dohr deh koh-mee-dah
the freezer	el congelador	ehl kohn-heh-lah-dohr
the garbage disposal	el desechador	ehl deh-seh-chah-dohr
the griddle	el comal	ehl koh-mahl
the grill	la parrilla	lah pah-rree-yah
the grinder	el molino	ehl moh-lee-noh
the ice maker	la hielera	lah ee-eh-leh-rah
the immersion blender	la licuadora de immersión	lah lee-koo-ah-doh-rah deh ee-mehr-see-ohn
the knife sharpener	la afiladora de cuchillos	lah ah-fee-lah-doh-rah deh koo-chee-yohs
the microwave oven	el microondas	ehl mee-kroh ohn dahs
the mixer	la batidora	lah bah-tee-doh-rah
the oven	el horno	ehl ohr-noh
the range	el fogón	ehl foh-gohn
the range hood	la cubierta del fogón	lah koo-bee-ehr-tah dehl foh-gohn
the refrigerator	el refrigerador	ehl rreh-free-heh-rah-dohr
the steamer	la olla de vapor	lah oh-yah deh bah-pohr
the stove	la estufa	lah ehs-too-fah
the toaster	el tostador	ehl tohs-tah-dohr
the trash compactor	el comprimidor de basura	ehl kohm-pree-mee-dohr deh bah-soo-rah
the waffle iron	la plancha para gofres	lah plahn-chah pah-rah goh-frehs

The _____ needs to be washed.
Hay que (Hace falta) lavar _____.
ah-ee keh (ah-seh fahl-tah) lah-bahr _____

Please clean the _____.
Favor de limpiar _____.
fah-bohr deh leem-pee-ahr _____

It is dirty (sticky, grimy, greasy).
Está sucio/sucia (pegajoso/pegajosa, mugriento/mugrienta, grasoso/grasosa).
ehs-tah soo-see-oh/soo-see-ah (peh-gah-hoh-soh/peh-gah-hoh-sah, moo-gree-ehn-toh/moo-gree-ehn-tah, grah-soh-soh/grah-soh-sah)

There are crumbs (spots/stains). Please remove them.
Hay migas (manchas). Favor de quitarlas.
ah-ee mee-gahs (mahn-chahs) fah-bohr deh kee-tahr-lahs

The blades (The grates, The burners, The racks) are dirty.
Las hojas de cuchillo (Las rejillas, Los quemadores, Los estantes del horno) están sucias/sucios.
lahs oh-hahs deh koo-chee-yoh (lahs rreh-hee-yahs, lohs keh-mah-doh-rehs, lohs ehs-tahn-tehs dehl ohr-noh) ehs-tahn soo-see-ahs/soo-see-ohs

Please vacuum the refrigerator (freezer) coils.
Favor de pasar la aspiradora por las bobinas del refrigerador (congelador).
fah-bohr deh pah-sahr lah ah-spee-rah-doh-rah pohr lahs boh-bee-nahs dehl rreh-free-heh-rah-dohr (kohn-heh-lah-dohr)

Before you vacuum them you must turn off the circuit breaker to the kitchen.
Antes de limpiarlas con la aspiradora, usted debe apagar el cortacircuitos en la cocina.
ahn-tehs deh leem-pee-ahr-lahs kohn lah ahs-pee-rah-doh-rah oo-stehd deh-beh ah-pah-gahr ehl kohr-tah-seer-koo-ee-tohs ehn lah koh-see-nah

Please let me show you where it is.
Favor de permitirme mostrarle donde está.
fah-bohr deh pehr-mee-teer-meh mohs-trahr-leh dohn-deh ehs-tah

Then you have to remove the piece at the bottom.
Después usted tiene que quitar la pieza del fondo.
dehs-poo-ehs oo-stehd tee-eh-neh keh kee-tahr lah pee-eh-sah dehl fohn-doh

Please clean the filters for the range hood.
Favor de limpiar los filtros de la tapa del fogón.
fah-bohr deh leem-pee-ahr lohs feel-trohs deh lah tah-pah dehl foh-gohn

Please change the filter to the water purifier.
Favor de cambiar el filtro del depurador de agua.
fah-bohr deh kahm-bee-ahr ehl feel-troh dehl deh-poo-rah-dohr deh ah-goo-ah

This is how it's done.
Se hace así.
seh ah-see ah-see

Please do not put your fingers in the _____.
Favor de no meter los dedos en _____.
fah-bohr deh noh meh-tehr lohs deh-dohs ehn _____

Please empty the _____.
Favor de vaciar el (la) _____.
fah-bohr deh bah-see-ahr ehl (lah) _____

Please defrost the freezer.
Favor de descongelar el congelador.
fah-bohr deh dehs-kohn-heh-lahr ehl kohn-heh-lah-dohr

The _____ needs to be emptied.
Hay que vaciar el (lah) _____.
ah-ee keh bah-see-ahr ehl (lah) _____

Please load (empty) the dishwasher.
Favor de meter (sacar) los platos al (del) lavaplatos.
fah-bohr deh meh-tehr (sah-kahr) lohs plah-tohs al (dehl) lah-bah-plah-tohs

You may use the stepstool (ladder).
Usted puede usar el taburete (escalera).
oo-stehd poo-eh-deh oo-sahr ehl tah-boo-reh-teh (ehs-kah-leh-rah)

Please remove any outdated foods.
Favor de sacar los comestibles expirados.
fah-bohr deh sah-kahr lohs koh-mehs-tee-blehs ehks-pee-rah-dohs

Please (do not) use dry (damp, wet) paper towels.
Favor de (no) usar toallas de papel secas (húmedas, mojadas).
fah-bohr deh (noh) oo-sahr toh-ah-yahs deh pah-pehl seh-kahs (oo-meh-dahs, moh-hah-dahs)

Please (do not) use a dry (damp, wet) sponge.
Favor de (no) usar una esponja seca (húmeda, mojada).
fah-bohr deh (noh) oo-sahr oo-nah ehs-pohn-hah seh-kah (oo-meh-dah, moh-hah-dah)

Please (do not) use a dry (damp, wet) rag.
Favor de (no) usar un trapo seco (húmedo, mojado).
fah-bohr deh (noh) oo-sahr oon trah-poh seh-koh (oo-meh-doh, moh-hah-doh)

Please (do not) use an abrasive cleaner.
Favor de (no) usar un limpiador abrasivo.
fah-bohr deh (noh) oo-sahr oon leem-pee-ah-dohr ah-brah-see-boh

Here is the product I use (we use).
Aquí está el producto que yo uso (nosotros usamos).
ah-kee ehs-tah ehl proh-dook-toh keh yoh oo-soh (noh-soh-trohs oo-sah-mohs)

Please wear rubber gloves.
Favor de usar guantes de goma.
fah-bohr deh oo-sahr goo-ahn-tehs deh goh-mah

Please (do not) scrub.
Favor de (no) fregar.
fah-bohr deh (noh) freh-gahr

We have a/an electric (gas) stove.
Tenemos una estufa eléctrica (de gas).
teh-neh-mohs oo-nah ehs-too-fah eh-lehk-tree-kah (deh gahs)

We have a/an electric (gas) oven.
Tenemos un horno eléctrico (de gas).
teh-neh-mohs oon ohr-noh eh-lehk-tree-koh (deh gahs)

Here's how it works.
Así es como funciona.
ah-see ehs koh-moh foon-see-oh-nah

The oven is self-cleaning.
El horno se limpia solo.
ehl ohr-noh seh leem-pee-ah soh-loh

Please press (push, pull) the on (off, pause) button/switch.
Favor de oprimir (empujar, jalar) el botón/interruptor de encender (apagar, pausar).
fah-bohr deh oh-pree-meer (ehm-poo-hahr, hah-lahr) ehl boh-tohn/een-teh-rroop-tohr deh ehn-sehn-dehr (ah-pah-gahr, pah-oo-sahr)

Please do this to cancel the setting.
Favor de hacer esto para cancelar la posición.
fah-bohr deh ah-sehr ehs-toh pah-rah kahn-seh-lahr lah poh-see-see-ohn

Please turn the knob (dial).
Favor de dar vueltas al pomo (dial).
fah-bohr deh dahr boo-ehl-tahs ahl poh-moh (dee-ahl)

Please set the clock (timer, thermostat).
Favor de poner el reloj (reloj de cocina, termóstato).
fah-bohr deh poh-nehr ehl rreh-loh (rreh-loh deh koh-see-nah, tehr-mohs-tah-toh)

Please put all poisonous (dangerous) substances out of the reach of the children.
Favor de poner todas las cosas tóxicas (peligrosas) donde los niños no puedan tocarlas.
fah-bohr deh poh-nehr toh-dahs lahs koh-sahs tohk-see-kahs (peh-lee-groh-sahs) dohn-deh lohs nee-nyohs noh poo-eh-dahn toh-kahr-lahs

We keep a kosher home.
Mantenemos una casa kosher.
mahn-teh-neh-mohs oo-nah kah-sah koh-shehr

Please put dishes used for dairy products in this dishwasher.
Favor de poner los platos usados para productos lácteos en este lavaplatos.
fah-bohr deh poh-nehr lohs plah-tohs oo-sah-dohs pah-rah proh-dook-tohs lahk-teh-ohs ehn ehs-teh lah-bah-plah-tohs

Please put dishes used for meat products in this dishwasher.
Favor de poner los platos usados para los productos de carne en este lavaplatos.
fah-bohr deh poh-nehr lohs plah-tohs oo-sah-dohs pah-rah lohs proh-dook-tohs deh kahr-neh ehn ehs-teh lah-bah-plah-tohs

If you have a question, please ask me (us).
Si tiene una pregunta, favor de preguntarme (preguntarnos).
see tee-eh-neh oo-nah preh-goon-tah fah-bohr deh preh-goon-tahr-meh (preh-goon-tahr-nohs)

Please don't put bones in the garbage disposal.
Favor de no poner huesos en el desechador.
fah-bohr deh noh poh-nehr oo-eh-sohs ehn ehl dehs-eh-chah-dohr

Please do not let silverware fall into the garbage disposal.
Favor de no dejar caer los cubiertos en el desechador.
fah-bohr deh noh deh-hahr kah-ehr lohs koo-bee-ehr-tohs ehn ehl dehs-eh-chah-dohr

Please use the stepstool (ladder) when you want to clean hard-to-reach areas.
Favor de usar el taburete (escalera) cuando usted quiera limpiar lugares difíciles de alcanzar.
fah-bohr deh oo-sahr ehl tah-boo-reh-teh (ehs-kah-leh-rah) koo-ahn-doh oo-stehd kee-eh-rah leem-pee-ahr loo-gah-rehs dee-fee-see-lehs deh ahl-kahn-sahr

Working with Food in the Kitchen

Foods

Meats and Poultry

I (We) like my/our meat rare (medium, medium-rare, well done).
Me (Nos) gusta la carne poca hecha (término medio, mediano crudo, bien hecha).
meh (nohs) goos-tah lah kahr-neh poh-kah eh-chah (tehr-mee-noh meh-dee-oh, meh-dee-ah-noh kroo-doh, bee-ehn eh-chah)

I (We) (don't) like sauces/gravies.
(No) Me (Nos) gustan las salsas/guisos.
(noh) meh (nohs) goos-tahn lahs sahl-sahs/gee-sohs

When you shop, only buy lean meat.
Cuando usted vaya de compras, compre sólo carne magra.
koo-ahn-doh oo-stehd bah-yah deh kohm-prahs, kohm-preh soh-loh kahr-neh mah-grah

Please prepare _____.
Favor de preparar _____.
fah-bohr deh preh-pah-rahr _____

the bacon	**el tocino**	*ehl toh-see-noh*
the beef	**la carne de vaca**	*lah kahr-neh deh bah-kah*
the chicken	**el pollo**	*ehl poh-yoh*
the duck	**el pato**	*ehl pah-toh*

the ham	el jamón	ehl hah-mohn
the hamburger	la hamburguesa	lah ahm-boor-geh-sah
the hen	la gallina	lah gah-yee-nah
the hot dog	el perro caliente	ehl peh-rroh kah-lee-ehn-teh
the lamb	el cordero	ehl kohr-deh-roh
the liver	el hígado	ehl ee-gah-doh
the meat	la carne	lah kahr-neh
the meatballs	las albóndigas	lahs ahl-bohn-dee-gahs
the pork	el cerdo	ehl sehr-doh
the porkchop	la chuleta de cerdo	lah choo-leh-tah deh sehr-doh
the roast beef	el rosbif	ehl rrohs-beef
the sausages	las salchichas	lahs sahl-chee-chahs
the steak	el bistec	ehl bees-tehk
the stew	el cocido	ehl koh-see-doh
the turkey	el pavo	ehl pah-boh
the veal roast	la ternera asada	lah tehr-neh-rah ah-sah-dah

Fish and Shellfish

Please don't overcook the fish.
Favor de no cocinar demasiado el pescado.
fah-bohr deh noh koh-see-nahr deh-mah-see-ah-doh ehl pehs-kah-doh

It should be opaque in the middle.
Debe ser opaco en el medio.
deh-beh sehr oh-pah-koh ehn ehl meh-dee-oh

I (We) like my/our fish well done.
Me (Nos) gusta el pescado bien hecho.
meh (nohs) goos-tah ehl pehs-kah-doh bee-ehn eh-choh

Please bake (broil, fry) the _____.
Favor de hornear (asar a la parrilla, freir) el (la) _____.
fah-bohr deh ohr-neh-ahr (ah-sahr ah lah pah-rree-yah, freh-eer) ehl (lah) _____

Please clean (use, wash) _____.
Favor de limpiar (usar, lavar) _____.
fah-bohr deh leem-pee-ahr (oo-sahr, lah-bahr) _____

the anchovies	las anchoas	*lahs ahn-choh-ahs*
the bass	la lubina	*lah loo-bee-nah*
the clams	las almejas	*lahs ahl-meh-hahs*
the cod	el bacalao	*ehl bah-kah-lah-oh*
the crabmeat	la carne de cangrejo	*lah kahr-neh deh kahn-greh-hoh*
the crabs	los cangrejos	*lohs kahn-greh-hohs*
the flounder	el lenguado	*ehl lehn-goo-ah-doh*
the grouper	el mero	*ehl meh-roh*
the herring	el arenque	*ehl ah-rehn-keh*
the lobster	la langosta	*lah lahn-gohs-tah*
the mackerel	la caballa	*lah kah-bah-yah*
the monkfish	el rape	*ehl rruh-peh*
the mussels	los mejillones	*lohs meh-hee-yoh-nehs*
the oysters	las ostras	*lahs ohs-trahs*
the red snapper	el pargo del golfo	*ehl pahr-goh dehl gohl-foh*
the salmon	el salmón	*ehl sahl-mohn*
the sardines	las sardinas	*lahs sahr-dee-nahs*
the scallops	las vieiras	*lahs bee-eh-ee-rahs*
the shrimp	el camarón	*chl kah-mah-rohn*
the snails	los caracoles	*lohs kah-rah-koh-lehs*
the sole	el lenguado	*ehl lehn-goo-ah-doh*
the squid	el calamar	*ehl kah-lah-mahr*
the swordfish	el pez espada	*ehl pehs ehs-pah-dah*
the trout	la trucha	*lah troo-chah*
the tuna	el atún	*ehl ah-toon*

Vegetables

Please steam (boil, roast) the vegetables.

Favor de cocer al vapor (hervir, asar) los vegetales.

fah-bohr deh koh-sehr ahl bah-pohr (ehr-beer, ah-sahr) lohs beh-heh-tah-lehs

When you shop, make sure the vegetables are fresh.

Cuando usted vaya de compras, asegúrese de que los vegetales sean frescos.

koo-ahn-doh oo-stehd bah-yah deh kohm-prahs, ah-seh-goo-reh-seh deh keh lohs beh-heh-tah-lehs seh-ahn frehs-kohs

Please buy _____ in the supermarket (the grocery store, the market).

Favor de comprar _____ en el supermercado (la bodega, el mercado).

fah-bohr deh kohm-prahr _____ ehn ehl soo-pehr-mehr-kah-doh (lah boh-deh-gah, ehl mehr-kah-doh)

the artichokes	**las alcachofas**	*lahs ahl-kah-choh-fahs*
the asparagus	**los espárragos**	*lohs ehs-pah-rrah-gohs*
the beans	**los frijoles**	*lohs free-hoh-lehs*
the beets	**las remolachas**	*lahs rreh-moh-lah-chahs*
the broccoli	**el bróculi**	*ehl broh-koo-lee*
the Brussels sprouts	**los repollitos de Bruselas**	*lohs rreh-poh-yee-tohs deh broo-seh-lahs*
the cabbage	**la col**	*lah kohl*
the carrots	**las zanahorias**	*lahs sah-nah-oh-ree-ahs*
the cauliflower	**la coliflor**	*lah koh-lee-flohr*
the celery	**el apio**	*ehl ah-pee-oh*
the chickpeas	**los garbanzos**	*lohs gahr-bahn-sohs*
the corn	**el maíz**	*ehl mah-ees*
the cucumbers	**los pepinos**	*lohs peh-pee-nohs*
the eggplant	**la berenjena**	*lah beh-rehn-heh-nah*
the endives	**las endivias**	*lahs ehn-dee-bee-ahs*
the leeks	**los puerros**	*lohs poo-eh-rrohs*
the lentils	**las lentejas**	*lahs lehn-teh-hahs*
the lettuce	**la lechuga**	*lah leh-choo-gah*
the lima beans	**los frijoles de lima**	*lohs free-hoh-lehs deh lee-mah*
the mushrooms	**los champiñones**	*lohs cham-pee-nyoh-nehs*
the onions	**las cebollas**	*lahs seh-boh-yahs*
the peas	**los guisantes**	*lohs gee-sahn-tehs*
the peppers (green, red, orange, yellow)	**los pimientos (verdes, rojos, anaranjados, amarillos)**	*lohs pee-mee-ehn-tohs (behr-dehs, rroh-hohs, ah-nah-rahn-hah-dohs, ah-mah-ree-yohs)*
the potatoes	**las papas**	*lahs pah-pahs*
the pumpkin	**la calabaza**	*lah kah-lah-bah-sah*
the radishes	**los rábanos**	*lohs rrah-bah-nohs*
the rice	**el arroz**	*ehl ah-rrohs*
the spinach	**la espinaca**	*lah ehs-pee-nah-kah*
the squash	**la calabaza**	*lah kah-lah-bah-sah*

the tomatoes	**los tomates**	*lohs toh-mah-tehs*
the turnips	**los nabos**	*lohs nah-bohs*
the yams	**las batatas**	*lahs bah-tah-tahs*
the zucchini	**el calabacín**	*ehl kah-lah-bah-seen*

Fruits and Nuts

Squeeze (Smell) the _____ to make sure it's ripe.
Favor de apretar (oler) el (la) _____ para verificar que esté maduro (madura).
fah-bohr deh ah-preh-tahr (oh-lehr) ehl (lah) _____ pah-rah beh-ree-fee-kahr keh ehs-teh mah-doo-roh ('mah-doo-rah)

Please don't buy any fruits with bruises.
Favor de no comprar frutas machacadas.
fah-bohr deh noh kohm-prahr froo-tahs mah-chah-kah-dahs

Please buy these fruits (nuts).
Favor de comprar estas frutas (nueces).
fah-bohr deh kohm-prahr ehs-tahs froo-tahs (noo-eh-sehs)

Please buy _____.
Favor de comprar _____.
fah-bohr deh kohm-prahr _____

the almond	**la almendra**	*lah ahl-mehn-drah*
(the almonds)	**(las almendras)**	*(lahs ahl-mehn-drahs)*
the apple	**la manzana**	*lah mahn-sah-nah*
(the apples)	**(las manzanas)**	*(lahs mahn-sah-nahs)*
the apricot	**el durazno**	*ehl doo-rahs-noh*
(the apricots)	**(los duraznos)**	*(lohs doo-rahs-nohs)*
the avocado	**el aguacate**	*ehl ah-goo-ah-kah-teh*
(the avocados)	**(los aguacates)**	*(lohs ah-goo-ah-kah-tehs)*
the banana	**la banana**	*lah bah-nah-nah*
(the bananas)	**(las bananas)**	*(lahs bah-nah-nahs)*
the blackberry (the blackberries)	**la mora** **(las moras)**	*lah moh-rah* *(lahs moh-rahs)*
the blueberry (the blueberries)	**el arándano** **(los arándanos)**	*ehl ah-rahn-dah-noh* *(lohs ah-rahn-dah-nohs)*

the cherry	la cereza	*lah seh-reh-sah*
(the cherries)	(las cerezas)	*(lahs seh-reh-sahs)*
the chestnut	la castaña	*lah kahs-tah-nyah*
(the chestnuts)	(las castañas)	*(lahs kahs-tah-nyahs)*
the coconut	el coco	*ehl koh-koh*
(the coconuts)	(los cocos)	*(lohs koh-kohs)*
the cranberry	el arándano	*ehl ah-rahn-dah-noh*
(the	agrio (los	*ah-gree-oh (lohs*
cranberries)	arándanos	*ah-rahn-dah-nohs*
	agrios)	*ah-gree-ohs)*
the date	el dátil	*ehl dah-teel*
(the dates)	(los dátiles)	*(lohs dah-tee-lehs)*
the fig (the figs)	el higo (los higos)	*ehl ee-goh (lohs ee-gohs)*
the grapefruit	la toronja	*lah toh-rohn-hah*
(the grapefruits)	(las toronjas)	*(lahs toh-rohn-hahs)*
the grape	la uva (las uvas)	*lah oo-bah (lahs oo-bahs)*
(the grapes)		
the hazelnut	la avellana	*lah ah-beh-yah-nah*
(the hazelnuts)	(las avellanas)	*(lahs ah-beh-yah-nahs)*
the kiwi	el kiwi (los kiwis)	*ehl kee-wee (lohs kee-wees)*
(the kiwis)		
the lemon	el limón	*ehl lee-mohn*
(the lemons)	(los limones)	*(lohs lee-moh-nehs)*
the lime	la lima	*lah lee-mah*
(the limes)	(las limas)	*(lahs lee-mahs)*
the mango	el mango	*ehl mahn-goh*
(the mangoes)	(los mangos)	*(lohs mahn-gohs)*
the melon	el melón	*ehl meh-lohn*
(the melons)	(los melones)	*(lohs meh-loh-nehs)*
the nectarine	la nectarina	*lah nehk-tah-ree-nah*
(the nectarines)	(las nectarinas)	*(lahs nehk-tah-ree-nahs)*
the olive	la aceituna	*lah ah-seh-ee-too-nah*
(the olives)	(las aceitunas)	*(lahs ah-seh-ee-too-nahs)*
the orange	la naranja	*lah nah-rahn-hah*
(the oranges)	(las naranjas)	*(lahs nah-rahn-hahs)*
the peach	el melocotón (los	*ehl meh-loh-koh-tohn (lohs*
(the peaches)	melocotones)	*meh-loh-koh-toh-nehs)*
the peanut	el cacahuete	*ehl kah-kah-oo-eh-teh*
(the peanuts)	(los cacahuetes)	*(lohs kah-kah-oo-eh-tehs)*
the pear	la pera (las peras)	*lah peh-rah (lahs peh-rahs)*
(the pears)		

the pineapple (the pineapples)	la piña (las piñas)	*lah pee-nyah (lahs pee-nyahs)*
the plum (the plums)	la ciruela (las ciruelas)	*lah see-roo-eh-lah (lahs see-roo-eh-lahs)*
the pomegranate (the pomegranates)	la granada (las granadas)	*lah grah-nah-dah (lahs grah-nah-dahs)*
the prune (the prunes)	la ciruela pasa (las ciruelas pasas)	*lah see-roo-eh-lah pah-sah (lahs see-roo-eh-lahs pah-sahs)*
the raisin (the raisins)	la pasa (las pasas)	*lah pah-sah (lahs pah-sahs)*
the raspberry (the raspberries)	la frambuesa (las frambuesas)	*lah frahm-boo-eh-sah (lahs frahm-boo-eh-sahs)*
the rhubarb (the rhubarbs)	el ruibarbo (los ruibarbos)	*ehl rroo-ee-bahr-boh (lohs rroo-ee-bahr-bohs)*
the strawberry (the strawberries)	la fresa (las fresas)	*lah freh-sah (lahs freh-sahs)*
the tangerine (the tangerines)	la mandarina (las mandarinas)	*lah mahn-dah-ree-nah (lahs mahn-dah-ree-nahs)*
the walnut (the walnuts)	la nuez (las nueces)	*lah noo-ehs (lahs noo-eh-sehs)*
the watermelon (the watermelons)	la sandía (las sandías)	*lah sahn-dee-ah (lahs sahn-dee-ahs)*

Dairy Products

Do we need _____?
¿Necesitamos _____?
neh-seh-see-tah-mohs _____

Please pass _____.
Favor de pasar _____.
fah-bohr deh pah-sahr _____.

the butter	la mantequilla	*lah mahn-teh-kee-yah*
the buttermilk	el suero de leche	*ehl soo-eh-roh deh leh-cheh*
the cheese	el queso	*ehl keh-soh*
the condensed milk	la leche condensada	*lah leh-cheh kohn-dehn-sah-dah*

the cottage cheese	**el queso cottage**	*ehl keh-soh koh-tahg*
the cream	**la crema**	*lah kreh-mah*
the cream cheese	**el queso crema**	*ehl keh-soh kreh-mah*
the egg substitute	**el substituto de huevo**	*ehl soob-stee-too-toh deh oo-eh-boh*
the eggs	**los huevos**	*lohs oo-eh-bohs*
the evaporated milk	**la leche evaporada**	*lah leh-cheh eh-bah-poh-rah-dah*
the ice cream (low-fat)	**el helado (bajo en grasa)**	*ehl eh-lah-doh (bah-hoh ehn grah-sah)*
the margarine	**la margarina**	*lah mahr-gah-ree-nah*
the milk (skim, 1 percent, 2 percent, whole)	**la leche (desnatada, 1 por ciento, 2 por ciento entera)**	*lah leh-cheh (dehs-nah-tah-dah, deh oon pohr-see-ehn-toh, deh dohs pohr-see-ehn-toh ehn-teh-rah)*
the Parmesan cheese	**el queso parmesano**	*ehl keh-soh pahr-meh-sah-noh*
the sour cream	**la crema agria**	*lah kreh-mah ah-gree-ah*
the yogurt	**el yogur**	*ehl yoh-goor*

Herbs, Spices, and Condiments

The recipe calls for _____.
La receta indica _____.
lah rreh-seh-tah een-dee-kah _____

I (We) (don't) like our food (too) spicy.
(No) Me (Nos) gusta la comida (muy) picante.
(noh) meh (nohs) goos-tah lah koh-mee-dah (moo-ee) pee-kahn-teh

Please use spices (herbs) sparingly.
Favor de usar pocas especias (hierbas).
fah-bohr deh oo-sahr poh-kahs ehs-peh-see-ahs (ee-ehr-bahs)

Please use _____ in this (that) recipe.
Favor de usar _____ en esta (esa) receta.
fah-bohr deh oo-sahr _____ ehn ehs-tah (eh-sah) rreh-seh-tah

| basil | **la albahaca** | *lah ahl-bah-ah-kah* |
| baking powder | **el polvo de hornear** | *ehl pohl-boh deh ohr-neh-ahr* |

baking soda	el bicarbonato de soda	ehl bee-kahr-boh-nah-toh deh soh-dah
barbecue sauce	la salsa de barbacoa	lah sahl-sah deh bahr-bah-koh-ah
bay leaf	la hoja de laurel	lah oh-hah deh lah-oo-rehl
breadcrumbs	el pan rallado	ehl pahn rrah-yah-doh
capers	las alcaparras	lahs ahl-kah-pah-rrahs
chives	el cebollín	ehl seh-boh-yeen
cinnamon	la canela	lah kah-neh-lah
cloves	los clavos	lohs klah-bohs
dill	el eneldo	ehl eh-nehl-doh
flour	la harina	lah ah-ree-nah
garlic	el ajo	ehl ah-hoh
ginger	el gengibre	ehl hehn-hee-breh
gravy	la salsa	lah sahl-sah
honey	la miel	lah mee-ehl
horseradish	el rábano picante	ehl rrah-bah-noh pee-kahn-teh
jam/jelly	la mermelada	lah mehr-meh-lah-dah
ketchup	la salsa de tomate	lah sahl-sah deh toh-mah-teh
maple syrup	el jarabe de arce	ehl hah-rah-beh deh ahr-seh
mayonnaise	la mayonesa	lah mah-yoh-neh-sah
mint	la menta	lah mehn-tah
mustard	la mostaza	lah mohs-tah-sah
nutmeg	la nuez moscada	lah noo-ehs mohs-kah-dah
oil (olive, virgin olive, vegetable, canola, corn)	el aceite (de oliva, de oliva virgen, vegetal, de canola, de maíz)	ehl ah-seh-ee-teh (deh oh-lee-bah, deh oh-lee-bah beer-hehn, beh-heh-tahl, deh kah-noh-lah, deh mah-ees)
oregano	el orégano	ehl oh-reh-gah-noh
paprika	el pimentón dulce	ehl pee-mehn-tohn dool-seh
parsley	el perejil	ehl peh-reh-heel
pepper	la pimienta	lah pee-mee-ehn-tah
rosemary	el romero	ehl rroh-meh-roh
saffron	el azafrán	ehl ah-sah-frahn
sage	la salvia	lah sahl-bee-ah
salad dressing	la salsa para la ensalada	lah sahl-sah pah-rah lah ehn-sah-lah-dah
salt	la sal	lah sahl

soy sauce	**la salsa de soja**	*lah sahl-sah deh soh-hah*
sugar	**el azúcar**	*ehl ah-soo-kahr*
sweetener (artificial)	**el dulcificante (artificial)**	*ehl dool-see-fee-kahn-teh (ahr-tee-fee-see-ahl)*
teriyaki sauce	**la salsa japonesa**	*lah sahl-sah hah-poh-neh-sah*
thyme	**el tomillo**	*ehl toh-mee-yoh*
vanilla	**la vainilla**	*lah bah-ee-nee-yah*
vinegar (balsamic)	**el vinagre (balsámico)**	*ehl bee-nah-greh (bahl-sah-mee-koh)*
Worchestershire sauce	**la salsa inglesa**	*lah sahl-sah een-gleh-sah*

Breads and Desserts

Please serve _____.
Favor de servir _____.
fah-bohr deh sehr-beer _____.

the bread (white, rye, whole wheat)	**el pan (blanco, de centeno, integral)**	*ehl pahn (blahn-koh, deh sehn-teh-noh, een-teh-grahl)*
the cake (the cakes)	**la torta (las tortas)**	*lah tohr-tah (lahs tohr-tahs)*
the caramel custard	**el flan**	*ehl flahn*
the cookie (the cookies)	**la galletita (las galletitas)**	*lah gah-yeh-tee-tah (lahs gah-yeh-tee-tahs)*
the cracker (the crackers)	**la galleta (las galletas)**	*lah gah-yeh-tah (lahs gah-yeh-tahs)*
the fruit salad	**la ensalada de fruta**	*lah ehn-sah-lah-dah de froo-tah*
the pie (the pies)	**la tarta (las tartas)**	*lah tahr-tah (lahs tahr-tahs)*
the pudding	**el pudín**	*ehl poo-deen*
the rice pudding	**el pudín de arroz**	*ehl poo-deen deh ah-rrohs*
the roll (the rolls)	**el panecillo (los panecillos)**	*ehl pah-neh-see-yoh (lohs pah-neh-see-yohs)*
the sponge cake (the sponge cakes)	**el pastel esponjoso (los pasteles esponjosos)**	*ehl pahs-tehl ehs-pohn-hoh-soh (lohs pahs-teh-lehs ehs-pohn-hoh-sohs)*

| the tart | **la tarta** | *lah tahr-tah* |
| (the tarts) | **(las tartas)** | *(lahs tahr-tahs)* |

Drinks

Please put the _____ on the table.
Favor de poner el (la) _____ sobre la mesa.
fah-bohr deh poh-nehr ehl (lah) _____ soh-breh lah meh-sah

I (We) would like to drink a/an/some _____.
Me (Nos) gustaría beber _____.
meh (nohs) goos-tah-ree-ah beh-behr _____

cappucino	**el capuchino**	*ehl kah-poo-chee-noh*
cider	**la cidra**	*lah see-drah*
cocoa	**el cacao**	*ehl kah-kah-oh*
coffee	**el café**	*ehl kah-feh*
(decaffeinated,	**(descafeinado,**	*(dehs-kah-feh-ee-nah-doh,*
hot, iced)	**caliente,**	*kah-lee-ehn-teh,*
	helado)	*eh-lah-doh)*
espresso	**el espreso**	*ehl ehs-preh-soh*
hot chocolate	**el chocolate**	*ehl choh-koh-lah-teh*
	caliente	*kah-lee-ehn-teh*
juice (apple,	**el jugo (de**	*ehl hoo-goh (deh*
orange,	**manzana, de**	*mahn-sah-nah, deh*
pineapple,	**naranja, de**	*nah-rahn-hah, deh*
grapefruit,	**piña, de**	*pee nyah, doh*
grape, lemon,	**toronja, de uva,**	*toh-rohn-hah, deh oo-bah,*
lime, cranberry)	**de limón,**	*deh lee-mohn,*
	de lima, de	*deh lee-mah, deh*
	arándano	*ah-rahn-dah-noh*
	agrio)	*ah-gree-oh)*
lemonade	**la limonada**	*lah lee-moh-nah-dah*
milk	**la leche**	*lah leh-cheh*
milkshake	**el batido**	*ehl bah-tee-doh*
mineral water	**el agua mineral**	*ehl ah-goo-ah mee-neh-rahl*
(carbonated,	**(gaseosa,**	*(gah-seh-oh-sah,*
noncarbonated)	**sin gas)**	*seen gahs)*
punch	**el ponche**	*ehl pohn-cheh*
soda (diet,	**la gaseosa**	*lah gah-seh-oh-sah*
decaffeinated)	**(de dieta,**	*(deh dee-eh-tah,*
	descafeinada)	*dehs-kah-feh-ee-nah-dah)*

| tea (herbal, decaffeinated, iced, hot) | el té (de hierbas, descafeinado, helado, caliente) | ehl teh (deh ee-ehr-bahs, dehs-kah-feh-ee-nah-doh, eh-lah-doh, kah-lee-ehn-teh) |
| water | el agua | ehl ah-goo-ah |

Miscellaneous

Where is (are) _____?
¿Dónde está (están) _____?
dohn-deh ehs-tah (ehs-tahn) _____

the appetizers	los aperitivos	lohs ah-peh-ree-tee-bohs
the broth	el caldo	ehl kahl-doh
the candy	el dulce	ehl dool-seh
the cereal	el cereal	ehl seh-reh-ahl
the chocolate (dark, milk, semisweet, white)	el chocolate (oscuro, de leche, semi-dulce, blanco)	ehl choh-koh-lah-teh (ohs-koo-roh, deh leh-cheh, seh-mee-dool-seh, blahn-koh)
the flour	la harina	lah ah-ree-nah
the French toast	la tostada francesa	lah tohs-tah-dah frahn-seh-sah
the gum	el chicle	ehl chee-kleh
the ice cubes	los cubitos de hielo	lohs koo-bee-tohs deh ee-eh-loh
the gelatin	la gelatina	lah heh-lah-tee-nah
the macaroni	los macarrones	lohs mah-kah-rroh-nehs
the noodles	los fideos	lohs fee-deh-ohs
the oatmeal	la avena	lah ah-beh-nah
the omelet	la tortilla	lah tohr-tee-yah
the pancakes	los panqueques	lohs pahn-keh-kehs
the pasta	la pasta	lah pahs-tah
the peanut butter	la crema de maní	lah kreh-mah deh mah-nee
the pickles	los encurtidos	lohs ehn-koor-tee-dohs
the pizza	la pizza	lah pee-sah
the sauce	la salsa	lah sahl-sah
the soup	la sopa	lah soh-pah
the spaghetti	el espagueti	ehl ehs-pah-geh-tee
the waffles	los gofres	lohs goh-frehs

Quantities

Please use a _____ of _____ in this (that) recipe.
Favor de usar _____ de _____ en esta (esa) receta.
fah-bohr deh oo-sahr _____ deh _____ ehn ehs-tah (eh-sah) rreh-seh-tah

Please buy a _____ of _____ in the supermarket.
Favor de comprar _____ de _____ en el supermercado.
fah-bohr deh kohm-prahr _____ deh _____ ehn ehl soo-pehr-mehr-kah-doh

I need (We need) _____ of _____.
Yo necesito (Nosotros necesitamos) _____ de _____.
yoh neh-seh-see-toh (nohs-oh-trohs neh-seh-see-tah-mohs) _____ deh _____

a bag	**una bolsa**	*oo-nah bohl-sah*
a bar	**una barra**	*oo-nah bah-rrah*
a bottle	**una botella**	*oo-nah boh-teh-yah*
a box	**una caja**	*oo-nah kah-hah*
a bunch	**un atado**	*oon ah-tah-doh*
a can	**una lata**	*oo-nah lah-tah*
a cup	**una taza**	*oo-nah tah-sah*
a dozen	**una docena**	*oo-nah doh-seh-nah*
a gallon	**un galón**	*oon gah-lohn*
a gram	**un gramo**	*oon grah-moh*
a half-pound	**media libra**	*meh-dee-ah lee-brah*
a jar	**un frasco**	*oon frahs-koh*
a kilogram	**un kilo**	*oon kee-loh*
a liter	**un litro**	*oon lee-troh*
an ounce	**una onza**	*oo-nah ohn-sah*
a package	**un paquete**	*oon pah-keh-teh*
a piece	**un pedazo**	*oon peh-dah-soh*
a pinch	**una pizca**	*oo-nah pees-kah*
a pint	**una pinta**	*oo-nah peen-tah*
a pound	**una libra**	*oo-nah lee-brah*
a quart	**un cuartillo**	*oon koo-ahr-tee-yoh*
a slice	**una tajada**	*oo-nah tah-hah-dah*
a tablespoon	**una cuchara**	*oo-nah koo-chah-rah*
a teaspoon	**una cucharadita**	*oo-nah koo-chah-rah-dee-tah*

Food Preparation

To prepare this recipe, please (don't) _____ the food (the vegetables, the meat, the eggs).

Para preparar esta receta, favor de (no) _____ la comida (los vegetales, la carne, los huevos).

pah-rah preh-pah-rahr ehs-tah rreh-seh-tah fah-bohr deh (noh) _____ lah koh-mee-dah (lohs beh-heh-tah-lehs, lah kahr-neh, lohs oo-eh-bohs)

add	**añadir**	*ah-nyah-deer*
bake	**hornear**	*ohr-neh-ahr*
barbecue	**asar a la parrilla**	*ah-sahr ah lah pah-ree-yah*
beat	**batir**	*bah-teer*
blanch	**blanquear**	*blahn-keh-ahr*
blend	**mezclar**	*mehs-klahr*
boil (liquid)	**hervir**	*ehr-beer*
bread	**empanizar**	*ehm-pah-nee-sahr*
broil	**asar**	*ah-sahr*
brown	**dorar**	*doh-rahr*
burn	**quemar**	*keh-mahr*
chill	**enfriar**	*ehn-free-ahr*
chop	**cortar en pedacitos**	*kohr-tahr ehn peh-dah-see-tohs*
clean	**limpiar**	*leem-pee-ahr*
combine	**combinar**	*kohm-bee-nahr*
cook	**cocinar**	*koh-see-nahr*
cover	**tapar**	*tah-pahr*
cut	**cortar**	*kohr-tahr*
defrost	**descongelar**	*dehs-kohn-heh-lahr*
dice	**cortar en cubitos**	*kohr-tahr ehn koo-bee-tohs*
dissolve	**disolver**	*dee-sohl-behr*
dry	**secar**	*seh-kahr*
flip	**voltear**	*bohl-teh-ahr*
flour	**enharinar**	*ehn-ah-ree-nahr*
fold	**doblar**	*doh-blahr*
freeze	**congelar**	*kohn-heh-lahr*
fry	**freir**	*freh-eer*
grate	**rallar**	*rrah-yahr*
grease	**engrasar**	*ehn-grah-sahr*
grill	**asar a la parrilla**	*ah-sahr ah lah pah-rree-yah*
grind	**moler**	*moh-lehr*
heat	**calentar**	*kah-lehn-tahr*

insert	**meter**	*meh-tehr*
liquefy	**licuar**	*lee-koo-ahr*
make	**hacer**	*ah-sehr*
mash	**machacar**	*mah-chah-kahr*
measure	**medir**	*meh-deer*
melt	**derretirse**	*deh-rreh-teer-seh*
mix	**mezclar**	*mehs-klahr*
peel	**pelar**	*peh-lahr*
plug in	**enchufar**	*ehn-choo-fahr*
pour	**verter**	*behr-tehr*
preheat	**precalentar**	*preh-kah-lehn-tahr*
prepare	**preparar**	*preh-pah-rahr*
put (on the burner)	**prender**	*prehn-dehr*
reduce	**reducir**	*rreh-doo-seer*
reheat	**recalentar**	*rreh-kah-lehn-tahr*
remove	**quitar**	*kee-tahr*
rinse	**enjuagar**	*ehn-hoo-ah-gahr*
roast	**asar**	*ah-sahr*
sauté	**sofreír**	*soh-freh-eer*
scrape	**rallar**	*rrah-yahr*
season	**sazonar**	*sah-soh-nahr*
serve	**servir**	*sehr-beer*
shred	**cortar en tiras**	*kohr-tahr ehn tee-rahs*
sift	**tamizar**	*tah-mee-sahr*
simmer	**hervir a fuego lento**	*ehr-beer ah foo-eh-goh lehn-toh*
skim	**espumar**	*ehs-poo-mahr*
slice	**cortar en tajadas**	*kohr-tahr ehn tah-hah-dahs*
soak	**remojar**	*rreh-moh-hahr*
spill	**derramar**	*deh-rrah-mahr*
sprinkle	**rociar**	*rroh-see-ahr*
start	**empezar**	*ehm-peh-sahr*
stir	**revolver**	*rreh-bohl-behr*
stop	**parar**	*pah-rahr*
strain	**colar**	*koh-lahr*
stuff	**rellenar**	*rreh-yeh-nahr*
thicken	**espesar**	*ehs-peh-sahr*
toast	**tostar**	*tohs-tahr*
toast	**brindar por**	*breen-dahr pohr*

turn	**dar vueltas a**	*dahr boo-ehl-tahs ah*
turn off	**apagar**	*ah-pah-gahr*
turn on	**prender**	*prehn-dehr*
uncover	**destapar**	*dehs-tah-pahr*
unmold	**desmoldear**	*dehs-mohl-deh-ahr*
warm	**calentar**	*kah-lehn-tahr*
wash	**lavar**	*lah-bahr*
whip	**batir**	*bah-teer*

Meals

It is time to eat breakfast (lunch, a snack, dinner).
Es hora de comer el desayuno (el almuerzo, una merienda, la cena).
ehs oh-rah deh koh-mehr ehl deh-sah-yoo-noh (ehl ahl-moo-ehr-soh, oo-nah meh-ree-ehn-dah, lah seh-nah)

We generally eat our meals in the breakfast area.
Generalmente, comemos las comidas donde nos desayunamos.
heh-neh-rahl-mehn-teh koh-meh-mohs lahs koh-mee-dahs dohn-deh nohs deh-sah-yoo-nah-mohs

Please set four places at the table.
Favor de poner la mesa para cuatro.
fah-bohr deh poh-nehr lah meh-sah pah-rah koo-ah-troh

For breakfast (lunch, a snack, dinner) I (my husband, my wife, my son, my daughter) generally eat (eats) _____.
Para el desayuno (el almuerzo, la merienda, la cena) yo (mi esposo, mi esposa, mi hijo, mi hija) generalmente como (come) _____.
pah-rah ehl deh-sah-yoo-noh (ehl ahl-moo-ehr-soh, lah meh-ree-ehn-dah, lah seh-nah) yoh (mee ehs-poh-soh, mee ehs-poh-sah, mee ee-hoh, mee ee-hah) heh-neh-rahl-mehn-teh koh-moh (koh-meh) _____

I (We) like my/our eggs scrambled (soft-boiled, hard-boiled, fried, poached).
Me (Nos) gusta comer los huevos revueltos (pasados por agua, duros, fritos, escalfados).
meh (nohs) goos-tah koh-mehr lohs oo-eh-bohs rreh-boo-ehl-tohs (pah-sah-dohs pohr ah-goo-ah, doo-rohs, free-tohs, ehs-kahl-fah-dohs)

Please prepare the meal now.
Favor de preparar la comida ahora.
fah-bohr deh preh-pah-rahr lah koh-mee-dah ah-oh-rah

Here is how the gas oven (stove) works.
El horno (La estufa) de gas funciona asi.
ehl ohr-noh (lah ehs-too-fah) deh gahs foon-see-oh-nah ah-see

Here is how the electric oven (the electric stove) works.
El horno eléctrico (La estufa eléctrica) funciona así.
ehl ohr-noh eh-lehk-tree-koh (lah ehs-too-fah eh-lehk-tree-kah) foon-see-oh-nah ah-see

Please have _____ ready by _____ o'clock.
Favor de tener el (la) _____ listo (lista) para las _____.
fah-bohr deh teh-nehr ehl (lah) _____ lees-toh (lees-tah) pah-rah lahs _____

Never put metal or aluminum foil in the microwave.
Favor de nunca poner metal o papel de aluminio en el horno de microondas.
fah-bohr deh noon-kah poh-nehr meh-tahl oh pah-pehl deh ah-loo-mee-nee-oh ehn ehl ohr-noh deh mee-kroh-dahs

You may use plastic in the microwave.
Usted puede usar plástico en el horno de microondas.
oo-stehd poo-eh-deh oo-sahr plahs-tee-koh ehn ehl ohr-noh deh mee kroh ohn dahs

Only put microwave-safe dishes (containers) in the microwave.
Favor de sólo usar los platos (envases) hechos especialmente para el horno de microondas.
fah-bohr deh soh-loh oo-sahr lohs plah-tohs (ehn-bah-sehs) eh-chohs ehs-peh see-ahl-mehn-teh pah-rah ehl ohr-noh deh mee-kroh-ohn-dahs

Never put plastic containers in the oven.
Nunca ha de poner envases de plástico en el horno.
noon-kah ah deh poh-nehr ehn-bah-sehs deh plahs-tee-koh ehn ehl ohr-noh

I am (We are) on a diet.
Yo estoy (Nosotros estamos) a dieta.
yoh ehs-toh-ee (noh-soh-trohs ehs-tah-mohs) ah dee-eh-tah

I am a vegetarian.
Soy vegetariano (vegetariana).
soh-ee beh-heh-tah-ree-ah-noh (beh-heh-tah-ree-ah-nah)

We are vegetarians.
Somos vegetarianos.
soh-mohs beh-heh-tah-ree-ah-nohs

I eat (We eat) only kosher (organic) food.
Sólo como (comemos) comida kosher (orgánica).
soh-loh koh-moh (koh-meh-mohs) koh-mee-dah koh-shehr (ohr-gah-nee-kah)

I (We) can't eat anything made with _____.
No puedo (podemos) comer nada (algo) hecha con _____.
noh poo-eh-doh (poh-deh-mohs) koh-mehr nah-dah (ahl-goh) eh-chah kohn
_____

I am (My husband is, My wife is, My son is, My daughter is) allergic to _____.
Soy (Mi esposo es, Mi esposa es, Mi hijo es, Mi hija es) alérgico (alérgica) a _____.
soh-ee (mee ehs-poh-soh ehs, mee ehs-poh-sah ehs, mee ee-hoh ehs, mee ee-hah ehs) ah-lehr-hee-goh (ah-lehr-hee-gah) ah _____

I can't (My husband can't, My wife can't, My son can't, My daughter can't) have any dairy products (alcohol, shellfish, saturated fats).
Yo no puedo (Mi esposo no puede, Mi esposa no puede, Mi hijo no puede, Mi hija no puede) tener productos lácteos (alcohol, mariscos, grasas saturadas).
yoh noh poo-deh-doh (mee ehs-poh-soh noh poo-eh-deh, mee ehs-poh-sah noh poo-eh-deh, mee ee-hoh noh poo-eh-deh, mee ee-hah noh poo-eh-deh) teh-nehr proh-dook-tohs lahk-teh-ohs (ahl-koh-ohl, mah-rees-kohs, grah-sahs sah-too-rah-dahs)

Please cook meals high in fiber (low in cholesterol, low in fat, low in sodium).
Favor de cocinar las comidas altas en fibra (bajas en colesterol, bajas en grasa, bajas en sal).
fah-bohr deh koh-see-nahr lahs koh-mee-dahs ahl-tahs ehn fee-brah (bah-hahs ehn koh-lehs-teh-rohl, bah-hahs ehn grah-sah, bah-hahs ehn sahl)

I (We) like our food bland (salt-free, spicy, sugar-free, well seasoned, without artificial preservatives).

Me (Nos) gusta la comida sosa (sin sal, picante, sin azúcar, bien sazonada, sin preservativos artificiales).
meh (nohs) goos-tah lah koh-mee-dah soh-sah (seen sahl, pee-kahn-teh, seen ah-soo-kahr, bee-ehn sah-soh-nah-dah, seen preh-sehr-bah-tee-bohs ahr-tee-fee-see-ah-lehs)

The _____ is _____.
El (La) _____ está _____.
ehl (lah) _____ ehs-tah _____

bitter	**amargo (amarga)**	*ah-mahr-goh (ah-mahr-gah)*
burned	**quemado (quemada)**	*keh-mah-doh (keh-mah-dah)*
cold	**frío (fría)**	*free-oh (free-ah)*
delicious	**delicioso (deliciosa)**	*deh-lee-see-oh-soh (deh-lee-see-oh-sah)*
dry	**seco (seca)**	*seh-koh (seh-kah)*
fresh	**fresco (fresca)**	*frehs-koh (frehs-kah)*
frozen	**congelado (congelada)**	*kohn-heh-lah-doh (kohn-heh-lah-dah)*
hard	**duro (dura)**	*doo-roh (doo-rah)*
lukewarm	**tibio (tibia)**	*tee-bee-oh (tee-bee-ah)*
moist	**húmedo (humeda)**	*oo-meh-doh (oo-meh-dah)*
rare	**poco hecho (hecha)**	*poh-koh eh-choh (eh-chah)*
raw	**crudo (cruda)**	*kroo-doh (kroo-dah)*
sour	**agrio (agria)**	*ah-gree-oh (ah-gree-ah)*
tasty	**sabroso (sabrosa)**	*sah-broh-soh (sah-broh-sah)*
tender	**tierno (tierna)**	*tee-ehr-noh (tee-ehr-nah)*
too salty	**demasiado salado (demasiada salada)**	*deh-mah-see-ah-doh sah-lah-doh (deh-mah-see-ah-dah sah-lah-dah)*
too spicy	**demasiado picante**	*deh-mah-see-ah-doh pee-kahn-teh*
too sweet	**demasiado dulce**	*deh-mah-see-ah-doh dool-seh*
tough	**duro (dura)**	*doo-roh (doo-rah)*
undercooked	**poco cocinado (poca cocinada)**	*poh-koh koh-see-nah-doh (poh-kah koh-see-nah-dah)*

Please eat with us.
Favor de comer con nosotros.
fah-bohr deh koh-mehr kohn noh-soh-trohs

You may have what ever you like.
Coma lo que quiera.
koh-mah loh keh kee-eh-rah

Please help yourself to anything in the refrigerator or freezer.
Favor de escoger cualquier cosa en el refrigerador o en el congelador.
fah-bohr deh ehs-koh-hehr koo-ahl-kee-ehr koh-sah ehn ehl rreh-free-heh-rah-dohr oh ehn ehl kohn-heh-lah-dohr

What foods do you (not) like?
¿Qué comidas (no) le gustan?
keh koh-mee-dahs (noh) leh goos-tahn

We are ordering takeout food.
Ordenamos comida preparada para comprar.
ohr-deh-nah-mohs koh-mee-dah preh-pah-rah-dah pah-rah kohm-prahr

Do you like Italian (Chinese, Mexican) food?
¿Le gusta la comida italiana (china, mexicana)?
leh goos-tah lah koh-mee-dah ee-tah-lee-ah-nah (chee-nah, meh-hee-kah-nah)

Shopping

You may buy whatever you like in the supermarket.
Compre lo que quiera en el supermercado.
kohm-preh loh keh kee-eh-rah ehn ehl soo-pehr-mehr-kah-doh

Please go grocery shopping on _____.
Favor de ir de compras el _____.
fah-bohr deh eer deh kohm-prahs ehl _____

Please buy _____ at _____.
Favor de comprar _____ en _____.
fah-bohr deh kohm-prahr _____ ehn _____

the bakery	**la panadería**	*lah pah-nah-deh-ree-ah*
the butcher shop	**la carnicería**	*lah kahr-nee-seh-ree-ah*
the candy store	**la confitería**	*lah kohn-fee-teh-ree-ah*

the delicatessen	la tienda especializada en comida exótica	*lah tee-ehn-dah ehs-peh-see-ah-lee-sah-dah ehn koh-mee-dah ehk-soh-tee-kah*
the fish store	la pescadería	*lah pehs-kah-deh-ree-ah*
the fruit and vegetable market	la verdulería	*lah behr-doo-leh-ree-ah*
the grocery store	la bodega	*lah boh-deh-gah*
the liquor store	la tienda de licores	*lah tee-ehn-dah deh lee-koh-rehs*
the supermarket	el supermercado	*ehl soo-pehr-mehr-kah-doh*

7

In the Dining Room or Breakfast Area

Furniture and Accessories

Please clean (wash) _____.
Favor de limpiar (lavar) _____.
fah-bohr de leem-pee-ahr (lah-bahr) _____

the blinds	**las persianas**	*lahs pehr-see-ah-nahs*
the buffet server	**el aparador**	*ehl ah-pah-rah-dohr*
the candlesticks	**los candeleros**	*lohs kahn-deh-leh-rohs*
the carpet (wall to wall)	**la alfombra (de pared a pared)**	*lah ahl-fohm-brah (deh pah-rehd ah pah-rehd)*
the carving knife (fork)	**el cuchillo (el tenedor) de cortar**	*ehl koo-chee-yoh (ehl teh-neh-dohr) deh kohr-tahr*
the ceiling	**el techo**	*ehl teh-choh*
the chairs	**las sillas**	*lahs see-yahs*
the china	**la porcelana**	*lah pohr-seh-lah-nah*
the crystal	**el cristal**	*ehl krees-tahl*
the curtains	**las cortinas**	*lahs kohr-tee-nahs*
the dishes	**los platos**	*lohs plah-tohs*
the drapes	**las cortinas**	*lahs kohr-tee-nahs*
the floor (wood, tile)	**el piso (de madera, de baldosas)**	*ehl pee-soh (deh mah-deh-rah, deh bahl-doh-sahs)*
the floral arrangement	**el arreglo floral**	*ehl ah-rreh-gloh floh-rahl*

the flowers	**las flores**	*lahs floh-rehs*
the folding chairs	**las sillas plegables**	*lahs see-yahs pleh-gah-blehs*
the French doors	**las puertas francesas**	*lahs poo-ehr-tahs frahn-seh-sahs*
the glass door(s)	**la (las) puerta (puertas) de cristal**	*lah (lahs) poo-ehr-tah (poo-her-tahs) deh krees-tahl*
the pictures/ paintings	**los cuadros**	*lohs koo-ah-drohs*
the rugs	**las alfombras**	*lahs ahl-fohm-brahs*
the serving pieces	**las cosas de servir**	*lahs koh-sahs deh sehr-beer*
the shades	**las sombras**	*lahs sohm-brahs*
the silverware	**los cubiertos**	*lohs koo-bee-ehr-tohs*
the slipcovers	**las fundas removibles**	*lahs foon-dahs rreh-moh-bee-blehs*
the table	**la mesa**	*lah meh-sah*
the table leaves	**las extensiones de mesa**	*lahs ehks-tehn-see-oh-nehs deh meh-sah*
the table pads	**las almohadillas de mesa**	*lahs ahl-moh-ah-dee-yahs deh meh-sah*
the table runner	**el salvamanteles**	*ehl sahl-bah-mahn-teh-lehs*
the tea cart	**el carrito de té**	*ehl kah-rree-toh deh teh*
the tea service (silver)	**el servicio de té (de plata)**	*ehl sehr-bee-see-oh deh teh (deh plah-tah)*
the vase	**el florero**	*ehl floh-reh-roh*
the windows	**las ventanas**	*lahs behn-tah-nahs*

Please dust the blinds.
Favor de quitar el polvo de las persianas.
fah-bohr deh kee-tahr ehl pohl-boh deh lahs pehr-see-ah-nahs

Please organize the serving pieces in the buffet server.
Favor de organizar las cosas de servir en el aparador.
fah-bohr deh ohr-gah-nee-sahr lahs koh-sahs deh sehr-beer ehn ehl ah-pah-rah-dohr

Please clean the wax off the candlestick holders.
Favor de limpiar la cera de los candeleros.
fah-bohr deh leem-pee-ahr lah seh-rah deh lohs kahn-deh-leh-rohs

Please sharpen the carving knife.
Favor de afilar el cuchillo de cortar.
fah-bohr deh ah-fee-lahr ehl koo-chee-yoh deh kohr-tahr

Please rearrange the chairs.
Favor de arreglar las sillas.
fah-bohr deh ah-rreh-glahr lahs see-yahs

Please do not put the fine china (crystal) in the dishwasher.
Favor de no poner la porcelana fina (el cristal) en el lavaplatos.
fah-bohr deh noh poh-nehr lah pohr-seh-lah-nah fee-nah (ehl krees-tahl) ehn ehl lah-bah-plah-tohs

Please sweep the floor.
Favor de barrer el piso.
fah-bohr deh bah-rrehr ehl pee-soh

Please wash the floor with a damp mop (rag).
Favor de lavar el piso con un trapeador (trapo) húmedo.
fah-bohr deh lah-bahr ehl pee-soh kohn oon trah-peh-ah-dohr (trah-poh) oo-meh-doh

Please put the flowers in a vase.
Favor de poner las flores en un florero.
fah-bohr deh poh-nehr lahs floh-rehs ehn oon floh-reh-roh

Please put the floral arrangement on the table.
Favor de poner el arreglo floral sobre la mesa.
fah-bohr deh poh-nehr ehl ah-rreh-gloh floh-rahl soh-breh lah meh-sah

Please change the water often.
Favor de cambiar el agua a menudo.
fah-bohr deh kahm-bee-ahr ehl ah-goo-ah ah meh-noo-doh

Please open the folding chairs and place them around the table.
Favor de abrir las sillas plegables y ponerlas alrededor de la mesa.
fah-bohr deh ah-breer lahs see-yahs pleh-gah-blehs ee poh-nehr-lahs ahl-reh-deh-dohr deh lah meh-sah

Please clean the glass in the French doors.
Favor de limpiar el cristal de las puertas francesas.
fah-bohr deh leem-pee-ahr ehl krees-tahl deh lahs poo-ehr-tahs frahn-seh-sahs

Please dust the pictures/paintings.
Favor de quitar el polvo de los cuadros.
fah-bohr deh kee-tahr ehl pohl-boh deh lohs koo-ah-drohs

Please vacuum the rug/carpet.
Favor de pasar la aspiradora en la alfombra.
fah-bohr deh pah-sahr lah ahs-pee-rah-doh-rah ehn lah ahl-fohm-brah

Please polish the silver.
Favor de pulir la plata.
fah-bohr deh poo-leer lah plah-tah

Please insert the table leaves from underneath the table.
Favor de meter las extensiones de mesa por debajo de la mesa.
fah-bohr deh meh-tehr lahs ehks-tehn-see-oh-nehs deh meh-sah pohr deh-bah-hoh deh lah meh-sah

Please put the table pads on top of the table and then put on the tablecloth.
Favor de poner las almohadillas sobre la mesa y después poner el mantel.
fah-bohr deh poh-nehr lahs ahl-moh-ah-dee-yahs soh-breh lah meh-sah ee dehs-poo-ehs poh-nehr ehl mahn-tehl

Please remove the table runner before putting on the tablecloth (setting the table).
Favor de quitar el salvamanteles antes de poner el mantel (poner la mesa).
fah-bohr deh kee-tahr ehl sahl-bah-mahn-teh-lehs ahn-tehs deh poh-nehr ehl mahn-tehl (poh-nehr lah meh-sah)

Please only use a soft (damp) cloth.
Favor de usar solo una toallita suave (húmeda).
fah-bohr deh oo-sahr soh-loh oo-nah toh-ah-yee-tah soo-ah-beh (oo-meh-dah)

Please use clear (cool, warm) water.
Favor de usar agua clara (fresca, tibia).
fah-bohr deh oo-sahr ah-goo-ah klah-rah (frehs-kah, tee-bee-ah)

Please do not use any spray.
Favor de no usar aerosol.
fah-bohr deh noh oo-sahr ah-eh-roh-sohl

Lighting

Please dim the lights.
Favor de bajar las luces.
fah-bohr deh bah-hahr lahs loo-sehs

Please replace any broken light bulbs.
Favor de cambiar las bombillas rotas.
fah-bohr deh kahm-bee-ahr lahs bohm-bee-yahs rroh-tahs

Please dust (clean, wash) the light fixture.
Favor de quitar el polvo de (limpiar, lavar) la luz.
fah-bohr deh kee-tahr ehl pohl-boh deh (leem-pee-ahr, lah-bahr) lah loos

The chandelier is dirty (dusty).
El candelabro está sucio (cubierto de polvo).
ehl kahn-deh-lah-broh ehs-tah soo-see-oh (koo-bee-ehr-toh deh pohl-boh)

Please use the feather duster to remove any dust.
Favor de usar el plumero para quitar el polvo.
fah-bohr deh oo-sahr ehl ploo-meh-roh pah-rah kee-tahr ehl pohl-boh

Each crystal of the chandelier must be cleaned (washed) individually.
Cada cristal del candelabro debe limpiarse (lavarse) individualmente.
kah-dah krees-tahl dehl kahn-deh-lah-broh deh-beh leem-pee-ahr-seh (lah-bahr-seh) een-dee-bee-doo-ahl-mehn-teh

Please handle the crystals gently. They are very fragile.
Favor de tratar los cristales con cuidado. Son muy delicados.
fah-bohr deh trah-tahr lohs krees-tah-lehs kohn koo-ee-dah-doh sohn moo-ee deh-lee-kah-dohs

Be careful. Take your time.
Tenga cuidado. Tómese su tiempo.
tehn-gah koo-ee-dah-doh toh-meh-seh soo tee-ehm-poh

I will help you.
Yo le ayudaré.
yoh leh ah-yoo-dah-reh

Please call me if you need my help.
Favor de llamarme si me necesita.
fah-bohr deh yah-mahr-meh see meh neh-seh-see-tah

Please stand on a ladder (stepstool).
Favor de pararse en una escalera (un taburete).
fah-bohr deh pah-rahr-seh ehn oo-nah ehs-kah-leh-rah (oon tah-boo-reh-teh)

Please be careful not to fall.
Favor de tener cuidado de no caerse.
fah-bohr deh teh-nehr koo-ee-dah-doh deh noh kah-ehr-seh

Entertaining

The dining room is for formal occasions.
El comedor es para ocasiones formales.
ehl koh-meh-dohr ehs pah-rah oh-kah-see-oh-nehs fohr-mah-lehs

There are stains on the tablecloth (the napkins).
Hay manchas en el mantel (las servilletas).
ah-ee mahn-chahs ehn ehl mahn-tehl (lahs sehr-bee-yeh-tahs)

Please wash the tablecloth (the napkins).
Favor de lavar el mantel (las servilletas).
fah-bohr deh lah-bahr ehl mahn-tehl (lahs sehr-bee-yeh-tahs)

Please take them to the dry cleaner.
Favor de llevarlos a la tintorería.
fah-bohr deh yeh-bahr-lohs ah lah teen-toh-reh-ree-ah

I am (We are) having a party.
Tengo (Tenemos) una fiesta.
tehn-goh (teh-neh-mohs) oo-nah fee-ehs-tah

I am (We are) having a cocktail party.
Tengo (Tenemos) un cóctel.
tehn-goh (teh-neh-mohs) oon kohk-tehl

I am (We are) having a brunch (a lunch, a dinner).
Tengo (Tenemos) un brunch (un almuerzo, una cena).
tehn-goh (teh-neh-mohs) oon bruhnch (oon ahl-moo-ehr-soh, oo-nah seh-nah)

I am (We are) having guests.
Tengo (Tenemos) invitados.
tehn-goh (teh-neh-mohs) een-bee-tah-dohs

I (We) have invited _____ people.
He (Hemos) invitado a _____ personas.
eh (eh-mohs) een-bee-tah-doh ah _____ pehr-soh-nahs

It is a surprise.
Es una sorpresa.
ehs oo-nah sohr-preh-sah

It is a formal party.
Es una fiesta formal.
ehs oo-nah fee-ehs-tah fohr-mahl

It is an informal gathering.
Es una reunión informal.
ehs oo-nah rreh-oo-nee-ohn een-fohr-mahl

It will be a sit-down (buffet) meal.
Será una comida a la mesa (bufet).
seh-rah oo-nah koh-mee-dah ah lah meh-sah (boo-feh)

Do you know how to cook (bake)?
¿Sabe usted cocinar (hornear)?
sah-beh oo-stehd koh-see-nahr (ohr-neh-ahr)

Will you be available to help (cook, serve, prepare) on _____
at _____?
¿Estará usted disponible para ayudar (cocinar, servir, preparar) el _____ a la (las) _____?
ehs-tah-rah oo-stehd dees-poh-nee-bleh pah-rah ah-yoo-dahr (koh-see-nahr, sehr-beer, preh-pah-rahr) ehl _____ ah lah (lahs) _____

Do you have any friends (family members) who can help?
¿Tiene amigos (familiares) que puedan ayudar?
tee-eh-neh ah-mee-gohs (fah-mee-lee-ah-rehs) keh poo-eh-dahn ah-yoo-dahr

I need (We need) two or three more people.
Necesito (Necesitamos) dos o tres personas más.
neh-seh-see-toh (neh-seh-see-tah-mohs) dohs oh trehs pehr-soh-nahs mahs

Before the party, please set the table for _____ people.
Antes de la fiesta, favor de poner la mesa para _____ personas.
ahn-tehs deh lah fee-ehs-tah fah-bohr deh poh-nehr lah meh-sah pah-rah _____ pehr-soh-nahs

Before the party, please use the fine china (the crystal).
Antes de la fiesta, favor de usar la porcelana fina (el cristal).
ahn-tehs deh lah fee-ehs-tah fah-bohr deh oo-sahr lah pohr-seh-lah-nah fee-nah (ehl krees-tahl)

Before the party, please use the good silverware.
Antes de la fiesta, favor de usar los cubiertos buenos.
ahn-tehs deh lah fee-ehs-tah fah-bohr deh oo-sahr lohs koo-bee-ehr-tohs boo-eh-nohs

Before the party, please take _____ out from the cabinet (buffet server).
Antes de la fiesta, favor de sacar _____ del gabinete (aparador).
ahn-tehs deh lah fee-ehs-tah fah-bohr deh sah-kahr _____ dehl gah-bee-neh-teh (ah-pah-rah-dohr)

Before the party, please make sure it is all clean.
Antes de la fiesta, favor de asegurar que todo esté limpio.
ahn-tehs deh lah fee-ehs-tah fah-bohr deh ah-seh-goo-rahr keh toh-doh ehs-teh leem-pee-oh

Before the party, please polish the silverware (silver tea service) before you put it on the table.
Antes de la fiesta, favor de pulir los cubiertos (el servicio de té de plata) antes de ponerlos (ponerlo) en la mesa.
ahn-tehs deh lah fee-ehs-tah fah-bohr deh poo-leer lohs koo-bee-ehr-tohs (ehl sehr-bee-see-oh deh teh deh plah-tah) ahn-tehs deh poh-nehr-lohs (poh-nehr-loh) ehn lah meh-sah

Before the party, please go to the store and buy ice.
Antes de la fiesta, favor de ir a la tienda y comprar hielo.
ahn-tehs deh lah fee-ehs-tah fah-bohr deh eer ah lah tee-ehn-dah ee kohm-prahr ee-eh-loh

Before the party, please light the candles.
Antes de la fiesta, favor de encender las velas.
ahn-tehs deh lah fee-ehs-tah fah-bohr deh ehn-sehn-dehr lahs beh-lahs

Before the party, please write the place cards.
Antes de la fiesta, favor de escribir las tarjetas de identifi-cación que indican el asiento en la mesa.
ahn-tehs deh lah fee-ehs-tah fah-bohr deh ehs-kree-beer lahs tahr-heh-tahs deh ee-dehn-tee-fee-kah-see-ohn keh een-dee-kahn ehl ah-see-ehn-toh ehn lah meh-sah

Before the party, please put the slipcovers on the dining-room chairs.
Antes de la fiesta, favor de poner las fundas removibles en las sillas del comedor.
ahn-tehs deh lah fee-ehs-tah fah bohr deh poh nehr lahs foon-dahs rreh-moh-bee-blehs ehn lahs see-yahs dehl koh-meh-dohr

Before the party, please take out the folding chairs.
Antes de la fiesta, favor de sacar las sillas plegables.
ahn-tehs deh lah fee-ehs-tah fah-bohr deh sah-kahr lahs see-yahs pleh gah blehs

During the party, please pass the appetizers.
Durante la fiesta, favor de pasar los aperitivos.
doo-rahn-teh lah fee-ehs-tah fah-bohr deh pah-sahr lohs ah-peh-ree-tee-bohs

During the party, please replenish the trays of food.
Durante la fiesta, favor de mantener llenas las bandejas de comida.
doo-rahn-teh lah fee-ehs-tah fah-bohr deh mahn-teh-nehr yeh-nahs lahs bahn-deh-hahs deh koh-mee-dah

During the party, please get another bottle (tray).
Durante la fiesta, favor de traer otra botella (bandeja).
doo-rahn-teh lah fee ehs tah fah-bohr deh trah-ehr oh-trah boh-teh-yah (bahn-deh-hah)

During the party, please serve the drinks.
Durante la fiesta, favor de servir las bebidas.
doo-rahn-teh lah fee-ehs-tah fah-bohr deh sehr-beer lahs beh-bee-dahs

During the party, please empty the ashtrays often.
Durante la fiesta, favor de vaciar los ceniceros a menudo.
doo-rahn-teh lah fee-ehs-tah fah-bohr deh bah-see-ahr lohs seh-nee-seh-rohs ah meh-noo-doh

During the party, please heat the food and then serve it.
Durante la fiesta, favor de calentar la comida y después servirla.
doo-rahn-teh lah fee-ehs-tah fah-bohr deh kah-lehn-tahr lah koh-mee-dah ee dehs-poo-ehs sehr-beer-lah

During the party, please make the coffee.
Durante la fiesta, favor de preparar el café.
doo-rahn-teh lah fee-ehs-tah fah-bohr deh preh-pah-rahr ehl kah-feh

During the party, please serve the tea.
Durante la fiesta, favor de servir el té.
doo-rahn-teh lah fee-ehs-tah fah-bohr deh sehr-beer ehl teh

During the party, please run the dishwasher as often as possible.
Durante la fiesta, favor de usar el lavaplatos con frecuencia.
doo-rahn-teh lah fee-ehs-tah fah-bohr deh oo-sahr ehl lah-bah-plah-tohs kohn freh-koo-ehn-see-ah

After the party, please clear the dirty dishes (the dirty glasses, the dirty cups) immediately.
Después de la fiesta, favor de quitar los platos sucios (los vasos sucios, las tazas sucias) inmediatamente.
dehs-poo-ehs deh lah fee-ehs-tah fah-bohr deh kee-tahr lohs plah-tohs soo-see-ohs (lohs bah-sohs soo-see-ohs, lahs tah-sahs soo-see-ahs) een-meh-dee-ah-tah-mehn-teh

After the party, please throw away the empty bottles (cups).
Después de la fiesta, favor de botar las botellas (tazas) vacías.
dehs-poo-ehs deh lah fee-ehs-tah fah-bohr deh boh-tahr lahs boh-teh-yahs (tah-sahs) bah-see-ahs

After the party, please throw away the empty plates (glasses).
Después de la fiesta, favor de botar los platos (vasos) vacíos.
dehs-poo-ehs deh lah fee-ehs-tah fah-bohr deh boh-tahr lohs plah-tohs (bah-sohs) bah-see-ohs

After the party, please remove the pads (leaves) from the table.
Después de la fiesta, favor de quitar las almohadillas (extensiones) de la mesa.
dehs-poo-ehs deh lah fee-ehs-tah fah-bohr deh kee-tahr lahs ahl-moh-ah-dee-yahs (ehks-tehn-see-oh-nehs) deh lah meh-sah

After the party, please put the pads (leaves) away.
Después de la fiesta, favor de poner las almohadillas (extensiones) en su lugar.
dehs-poo-ehs deh lah fee-ehs-tah fah-bohr deh poh-nehr lahs ahl-moh-ah-dee-yahs (ehks-tehn-see-oh-nehs) ehn soo loo-gahr

After the party, please put everything back in its proper place.
Después de la fiesta, favor de poner todo en su lugar apropiado.
dehs-poo-ehs deh lah fee-ehs-tah fah-bohr deh poh-nehr toh-doh ehn soo loo-gahr ah-proh-pee-ah-doh

The Bar

Please take out the _____.
Favor de sacar _____.
fah-bohr deh sah-kahr _____

Please put _____ on the table (the counter).
Favor de poner _____ sobre la mesa (el mostrador).
fah-bohr deh poh-nehr _____ soh-breh lah meh-sah (ehl mohs-trah-dohr)

the bottles	**las botellas**	*lahs boh-teh-yahs*
the cocktail napkins	**las servilletas de cóctel**	*lahs sehr-bee-yeh-tahs deh kohk-tehl*
the corkscrew	**el sacacorchos**	*ehl sah-kah-kohr-chohs*
the crushed ice	**el hielo molido**	*ehl ee-eh-loh moh-lee-doh*
the flutes	**las copas**	*lahs koh-pahs*
the fruit slices	**las rodajas de frutas**	*lahs rroh-dah-hahs deh froo-tahs*
the (liquor, wine) glasses	**los vasos (de licor, de vino)**	*lohs bah-sohs (deh lee-kohr, deh bee-noh)*
the ice (cubes)	**el hielo (en cubitos)**	*ehl ee-eh-loh (ehn koo-bee-tohs)*
the ice bucket	**la cubitera**	*lah koo-bee-teh-rah*
the juices	**los jugos**	*lohs hoo-gohs*
the mixer	**la batidora**	*lah bah-tee-doh-rah*
the pitcher	**el cántaro**	*ehl kahn-tah-roh*
the shaker	**la coctelera**	*lah kohk-teh-leh-rah*
the shot glass	**el vasito de tragos**	*ehl bah-see-toh deh trah-gohs*
the stirrers	**los agitadores**	*lohs ah-hee-tah-doh-rehs*
the tongs	**las pinzas**	*lahs peen-sahs*
the tonic	**el tónico**	*ehl toh-nee-koh*
the toothpicks	**los palillos**	*lohs pah-lee-yohs*
the wine decanter	**la licorera de vino**	*lah lee-koh-reh-rah deh bee-noh*

Do you know how to mix drinks?
¿Sabe usted mezclar bebidas?
sah-beh oo-stehd mehs-klahr beh-bee-dahs

Do you know a bartender?
¿Conoce a un barman?
koh-noh-seh ah oon bahr-mahn

He (She, You) must know how to blend (mix, prepare, serve, shake, stir) drinks.

Él (Ella, Usted) debe saber combinar (mezclar, preparar, servir, agitar, revolver) las bebidas.

ehl (eh-yah, oo-stehd) deh-beh sah-behr kohm-bee-nahr (mehs-klahr, preh-pah-rahr, sehr-beer, ah-hee-tahr, rreh-bohl-behr) lahs beh-bee-dahs

We need a bowl of cherries (olives, onions).

Necesitamos un tazón de cerezas (aceitunas, cebollas).

neh-seh-see-tah-mohs oon tah-sohn deh seh-reh-sahs (ah-seh-ee-too-nahs, seh-boh-yahs)

Please slice the celery (the lemon, the lime, the orange, the pineapple).

Favor de cortar el apio (el limón, la lima, la naranja, la piña).

fah-bohr deh kohr-tahr ehl ah-pee-oh (ehl lee-mohn, lah lee-mah, lah nah-rahn-hah, lah pee-nyah)

We need a pitcher of cranberry (grapefruit, lemon, lime, orange, pineapple, tomato) juice.

Necesitamos un cántaro de jugo de arándano (toronja, limón, lima, naranja, piña, tomate).

neh-seh-see-tah-mohs oon kahn-tah-roh deh hoo-goh deh ah-rahn-dah-noh (toh-rohn-hah, lee-mohn, lee-mah, nah-rahn-hah, pee-nyah, toh-mah-teh)

Please make sure there is water on the table.

Favor de asegurarse que haya agua en la mesa.

fah-bohr deh ah-seh-goo-rahr-seh keh ah-yah ah-goo-ah ehn lah meh-sah

Here is a tray for the drinks.

Aquí está una bandeja para las bebidas.

ah-kee ehs-tah oo-nah bahn-deh-hah pah-rah lahs beh-bee-dahs

Please put a bottle (the bottles) of _____ on the bar (table, counter).

Favor de poner una botella (las botellas) de _____ en el bar (la mesa, el mostrador).

fah-bohr deh poh-nehr oo-nah boh-teh-yah (lahs boh-teh-yahs) deh _____ ehn ehl bahr (lah meh-sah, ehl mohs-trah-dohr)

| beer (light, domestic, imported)) | **cerveza (ligera, doméstica, importada)** | *sehr-beh-sah (lee-heh-rah, doh-mehs-tee-kah, eem-pohr-tah-dah)* |
| bourbon | **whisky americano** | *oo-ees-kee ah-meh-ree-kah-noh* |

brandy	**coñac**	*koh-nyahk*
champagne	**champaña**	*chahm-pah-nyah*
gin	**ginebra**	*hee-neh-brah*
liqueur	**licor**	*lee-kohr*
port	**oporto**	*oh-pohr-toh*
rum	**ron**	*rrohn*
rye	**whisky de centeno**	*oo-ees-kee deh sehn-teh-noh*
scotch	**escocés**	*ehs-koh-sehs*
sherry	**jerez**	*heh-rehs*
vermouth	**vermut**	*behr-moot*
vodka	**vodca**	*bohd-kah*
whisky	**whisky**	*oo-ees-kee*
wine (red, white, rosé, sparkling)	**vino (tinto blanco, rosado, espumante)**	*bee-noh (teen-toh blahn-koh, rroh-sah-doh, ehs-poo-mahn-teh)*

Note

Some alcoholic drinks are also known in Spanish by their English names (for example, el scotch).

8

In the Bathroom

Bathroom Fixtures

Please clean (organize) _____.

Favor de limpiar (organizar) _____.

fah-bohr deh leem-pee-ahr (ohr-gah-nee-sahr) _____

the bathmat	**la alfombrilla**	*lah ahl-fohm-hree-yah*
the bathtub	**la bañera**	*lah bah-nyeh-rah*
the bench	**el banco**	*ehl bahn-koh*
the bidet	**el bidé**	*ehl bee-deh*
the cabinet	**el gabinete**	*ehl gah-bee-neh-teh*
the chair	**la silla**	*lah see-yah*
the closet	**el armario**	*ehl ahr-mah-ree-oh*
the countertop	**la encimera**	*lah ehn-see-meh-rah*
the cup	**la taza**	*lah tah-sah*
the drain	**el desagüe**	*ehl dehs-ah-goo-eh*
the drawer	**el cajón**	*ehl kah-hohn*
(the drawers)	**(los cajones)**	*(lohs kah-hoh-nehs)*
the dressing area	**el vestidor**	*ehl behs-tee-dohr*
the electrical outlet	**el enchufe**	*ehl ehn-choo-feh*
the fan (the fans)	**el ventilador**	*ehl behn-tee-lah-dohr*
(ceiling)	**(los ventiladores)**	*(lohs behn-tee-lah-doh-*
	(de techo)	*rehs) (deh teh-choh)*
the faucet	**el grifo**	*ehl gree-foh*
(cold water,	**(agua fría,**	*(ah-goo-ah free-ah,*
hot water)	**agua caliente)**	*(ah-goo-ah kah-lee-*
		ehn-teh)

the floor tiles	**las baldosas**	*lahs bahl-doh-sahs*
the hot-tub	**la bañera de hidromasaje**	*lah bah-nyeh-rah deh ee-droh-mah-sah-heh*
the Jacuzzi	**el jacuzzi**	*ehl hah-koo-see*
the light (the lights)	**la luz (las luces)**	*lah loos (lahs loo-sehs)*
the light switch (the light switches)	**el interruptor (los interruptores)**	*ehl een-teh-rroop-tohr (lohs een-teh-rroop-toh-rehs)*
the magazine rack	**el revistero**	*ehl rreh-bees-teh-roh*
the medicine cabinet (the medicine cabinets)	**el botiquín (los botiquines)**	*ehl boh-tee-keen (lohs boh-tee-kee-nehs)*
the mirror	**el espejo**	*ehl ehs-peh-hoh*
the scale	**la pesa**	*lah peh-sah*
the shelf	**el estante**	*ehl ehs-tahn-teh*
the shower	**la ducha**	*lah doo-chah*
the shower curtain	**la cortina de ducha**	*lah kohr-tee-nah deh doo-chah*
the shower door	**la puerta de ducha**	*lah poo-ehr-tah deh doo-chah*
the shower tiles	**los azulejos**	*lohs ah-soo-leh-hohs*
the sink	**el lavabo**	*ehl lah-bah-boh*
the soap dish	**la jabonera**	*lah hah-boh-neh-rah*
the toilet	**el inodoro**	*ehl ee-noh-doh-roh*
the toilet-paper holder	**el dispensador de papel higiénico**	*ehl dees-pehn-sah-dohr deh pah-pehl ee-hee-eh-nee-koh*
the toothbrush holder	**el estuche del cepillo de dientes**	*ehl ehs-too-cheh dehl seh-pee-yoh deh dee-ehn-tehs*
the towel rack	**el toallero**	*ehl toh-ah-yeh-roh*
the vanity (the vanities)	**el tocador (los tocadores)**	*ehl.toh-kah-dohr (lohs toh-kah-doh-rehs)*
the wastebasket	**la papelera**	*lah pah-peh-leh-rah*
the window treatment	**la decoración de la ventana**	*lah deh-koh-rah-see-ohn deh lah behn-tah-nah*

Please scrub the bathtub after each use.
Favor de limpiar la bañera después de cada uso.
fah-bohr deh leem-pee-ahr lah bah-nyeh-rah dehs-poo-ehs deh kah-dah oo-soh

Please clean the bidet the same way you clean the toilet.
Favor de limpiar el bidé como usted limpia el inodoro.
*fah-bohr deh leem-pee-ahr ehl bee-deh koh-moh oo-stehd leem-pee-ah ehl
ee-noh-doh-roh*

Please vacuum any hairs on the floor.
Favor de pasar la aspiradora para recoger los pelos del piso.
*fah-bohr deh pah-sahr lah ahs-pee-rah-doh-rah pah-rah rreh-koh-hehr lohs
peh-lohs dehl pee-soh*

Please wash the countertops (the floor tiles) with water (this
product).
**Favor de lavar las encimeras (las baldosas) con agua (este
producto).**
*fah-bohr deh lah-bahr lahs ehn-see-meh-rahs (lahs bahl-doh-sahs) kohn ah-
goo-ah (ehs-teh proh-dook toh)*

Please remove any hair from the drains.
Favor de remover los pelos de los desagües.
fah-bohr deh rreh-moh-behr lohs peh-lohs deh lohs dehs-ah-goo-ehs

Please do not let hair or any foreign object go down the drain.
Favor de no dejar caer pelo o ningún objeto en el desagüe.
*fah-bohr deh noh deh-hahr kah-ehr peh-loh oh neen-goon ohh-heh-toh ehn ehl
dehs-ah-goo-eh*

Please keep the dressing area neat.
Favor de mantener el vestidor en orden.
fah-bohr deh mahn-teh-nehr ehl behs-tee-dohr ehn ohr-dehn

Please run the fan when the bathroom is in use.
Favor de prender el ventilador cuando se use el baño.
*fah-bohr deh prehn-dehr ehl behn-tee-lah-dohr koo-ahn-doh seh oo-seh ehl
bah-nyoh*

Please do not put any oils (lotions) in the Jacuzzi.
Favor de no poner aceites (lociones) en el jacuzzi.
fah-bohr deh noh poh-nehr ah-seh-ee-tehs (loh-see-oh-nehs) ehn ehl hah-koo-see

Please tidy the magazines in the magazine rack.
Favor de arreglar las revistas en el revistero.
fah-bohr deh ah-rreh-glahr lahs rreh-bees-tahs ehn ehl rreh-bees-teh-roh

Please remove expired medicines from the medicine cabinet.
Favor de sacar las medicinas expiradas del botiquín.
fah-bohr deh sah-kahr lahs meh-dee-see-nahs ehks-pee-rah-dahs dehl boh-tee-keen

Please remove all spots from the mirror (from the mirrors).
Favor de quitar todas las manchas del espejo (de los espejos).
fah-bohr deh kee-tahr toh-dahs lahs mahn-chahs dehl ehs-peh-hoh (deh lohs ehs-peh-hohs)

Please dry (squeegee) the shower walls (door, floor, tiles) after each use.
Favor de secar las paredes de la ducha (de la puerta, del suelo, de las baldosas) después de cada uso.
fah-bohr deh seh-kahr lahs pah-reh-dehs deh lah doo-chah (deh lah poo-ehr-tah, dehl soo-eh-loh, deh lahs bahl-doh-sahs) dehs-poo-ehs deh kah-dah oo-soh

Please scrub the shower tiles.
Favor de limpiar los azulejos.
fah-bohr deh leem-pee-ahr lohs ah-soo-leh-hohs

Please remove any mold (mildew, soap scum) with this spray (this foam).
Favor de quitar el moho (mildiu, desecho) con este aerosol (esta espuma).
fah-bohr deh kee-tahr ehl moh-oh (meel-dee-oo, deh-seh-choh) kohn ehs-teh ah-eh-roh-sohl (ehs-tah ehs-poo-mah)

Please empty the wastebasket every day.
Favor de vaciar la papelera cada día.
fah-bohr deh bah-see-ahr lah pah-peh-leh-rah kah-dah dee-ah

The electrical outlets (light switches) are over here (there).
Los enchufes (interruptores) están aquí (allí).
lohs ehn-choo-fehs (een-teh-rroop-toh-rehs) ehs-tahn ah-kee (ah-yee)

Cleaning Tools

Please use _____ to clean.
Favor de usar _____ para limpiar.
fah bohr deh oo sahr _____ pah-rah leem-pee-ahr

an antibacterial soap	**un jabón antibacterial**	*oon hah-bohn ahn-tee-bahk-teh-ree-ahl*
a brush (scrub)	**un cepillo (de fregar)**	*oon seh-pee-yoh (deh freh-gahr)*
a bucket	**el cubo**	*ehl koo-boh*
deodorizer	**un desodorante**	*oon deh-soh-doh-rahn-teh*
detergent	**un detergente**	*oon deh-tehr-hehn-teh*
disinfectant	**un desinfectante**	*oon dehs-een-fehk-tahn-teh*
foam	**espuma**	*ehs-poo-mah*
a mop	**un trapeador**	*oon trah-peh-ah-dohr*
a pail	**un cubo**	*oon koo-boh*
a rag	**un trapo**	*oon trah-poh*
a sponge	**una esponja**	*oo-nah ehs-pohn-hah*
spray	**una rociada**	*oo-nah rroh-see-ah-dah*
a vacuum	**la aspiradora**	*lah ahs-pee-rah-doh-rah*
wipes (throwaway)	**toallitas desechables**	*toh-ah-yee-tahs dehs-eh-chah-blehs*

It is in the closet (drawer, vanity).
Está en el armario (cajón, tocador).
ehs-tah ehn ehl ahr-mah-ree-oh (kah-hohn, toh-kah-dohr)

It is in the storage room (the basement, the garage, the kitchen, the laundry room).
Está en el depósito (el sótano, el garaje, la cocina, la lavandería).
ehs-tah ehn ehl deh-poh-see-toh (ehl soh-tah-noh, ehl gah-rah-heh, lah koh-see-nah, lah lah-bahn-deh-ree-ah)

Use an old towel (undershirt) as a rag.
Favor de usar de trapo una toalla (camiseta) vieja.
fah-bohr deh oo-sahr deh trah-poh oo-nah toh-ah-yah (kah-mee-seh-tah) bee-eh-hah

Bathroom Items

In the medicine cabinet (drawers, closet) you will find _____.
En el botiquín (los cajones, el armario) usted encontrará

_____**.**

ehn ehl boh-tee-keen (lohs kah-hoh-nehs, ehl ahr-mah-ree-oh) oo-stehd ehn-kohn-trah-rah _____

aftershave lotion	**la loción para después del afeitado**	*lah loh-see-ohn pah-rah dehs-poo-ehs dehl ah-feh-ee-tah-doh*
air freshener	**el ambientador**	*ehl ahm-bee-ehn-tah-dohr*
alcohol	**el alcohol**	*ehl ahl-koh-ohl*
aloe	**el aloe**	*ehl ah-loh-eh*
an antacid	**un antiácido**	*oon ahn-tee-ah-see-doh*
an antihistamine	**un antihistamínico**	*oon ahn-tee-ees-tah-mee-nee-koh*
an antiseptic	**un antiséptico**	*oon ahn-tee-sehp-tee-koh*
aspirin	**las aspirinas**	*lahs ahs-pee-ree-nahs*
bandages	**vendas**	*behn-dahs*
Band-Aids	**curitas**	*koo-ree-tahs*
bath oil	**el aceite para el baño**	*ehl ah-seh-ee-teh pah-rah ehl bah-nyoh*
a bathtub mat	**una alfombrilla del baño**	*oo-nah ahl-fohm-bree-yah dehl bah-nyoh*
a brush	**un cepillo**	*oon seh-pee-yoh*
cologne	**la colonia**	*lah koh-loh-nee-ah*
a comb	**un peine**	*oon peh-ee-neh*
conditioner	**el suavizador para el pelo**	*ehl soo-ah-bee-sah-dohr pah-rah ehl peh-loh*
cotton	**el algodón**	*ehl ahl-goh-dohn*
cotton balls	**bolitas de algodón**	*boh-lee-tahs deh ahl-goh-dohn*
cotton swabs	**hisopos**	*ees-oh-pohs*
cough drops	**pastillas para la tos**	*pahs-tee-yahs pah-rah lah tohs*
cough syrup	**el jarabe para la tos**	*ehl hah-rah-beh pah-rah lah tohs*
dental floss	**el hilo dental**	*ehl ee-loh dehn-tahl*
deodorant	**el desodorante**	*ehl dehs-oh-doh-rahn-teh*
deodorizer (room)	**el desodorante para el cuarto**	*ehl dehs-oh-doh-rahn-teh pah-rah ehl koo-ahr-toh*

a diffuser	**una difusora**	*oo-nah dee-foo-soh-rah*
an electric razor	**una rasuradora eléctrica**	*oo-nah rrah-soo-rah-doh-rah eh-lehk-tree-kah*
eyedrops	**el colirio**	*ehl koh-lee-ree-oh*
a first-aid kit	**un botiquín de primeros auxilios**	*oon boh-tee-keen deh pree-meh-rohs ah-oo-see-lee-ohs*
gauze	**la gasa**	*lah gah-sah*
a hairdryer	**un secador de pelo**	*oon seh-kah-dohr deh peh-loh*
hair gel	**la gomina**	*lah goh-mee-nah*
hairpins	**las horquillas**	*lahs ohr-kee-yahs*
hairspray	**la laca**	*lah lah-kah*
hamper	**la canasta**	*lah kah-nahs-tah*
hand lotion	**la crema para las manos**	*lah kreh-mah pah-rah lahs mah-nohs*
a heating pad	**una placa de calentamiento**	*oo-nah plah-kah deh kah-lehn-tah-mee-ehn-toh*
a hot-water bag	**una bolsa de agua caliente**	*oo-nah bohl-sah deh ah-goo ah kah-lee-ehn-teh*
an ice pack	**una bolsa de hielo**	*oo-nah bohl-sah deh ee-eh-loh*
insect repellent	**el repelente contra insectos**	*ehl rreh-peh-lehn-teh kohn-trah een-sehk-tohs*
laxatives	**los laxantes**	*lohs lahk-sahn-tehs*
a manicure set	**un estuche de manicura**	*oon ehs-too-cheh deh mah-nee-koo-rah*
makeup	**el maquillaje**	*ehl mah-kee-yah-heh*
moisturizer	**la crema hidratante**	*lah kreh-mah ee-drah-tahn-teh*
mouthwash	**el enjuague bucal**	*ehl ehn-hoo-ah-geh boo-kahl*
nail clippers	**el cortaúñas**	*ehl kohr-tah-oo-nyahs*
a nail file	**una lima de uñas**	*oo-nah lee-mah deh oo-nyahs*
nail polish	**el esmalte de uñas**	*ehl ehs-mahl-teh deh oo-nyahs*
nail polish remover	**el quitaesmalte**	*ehl kee-tah-ehs-mahl-teh*
nose drops	**las gotas para la nariz**	*lahs goh-tahs pah-rah lah nah-rees*

perfume	**el perfume**	*ehl pehr-foo-meh*
petroleum jelly	**la vaselina**	*lah bah-seh-lee-nah*
potpourri	**el popurrí**	*ehl poh-poo-rree*
prescription medicine	**el medicamento recetado**	*ehl meh-dee-kah-mehn-toh rreh-seh-tah-doh*
a razor	**la rasuradora**	*lah rrah-soo-rah-doh-rah*
razor blades	**las hojas de afeitar**	*lahs oh-hahs deh ah-feh-ee-tahr*
safety pins	**los imperdibles**	*lohs eem-pehr-dee-blehs*
sanitary napkins	**las toallas sanitarias**	*lahs toh-ah-yahs sah-nee-tah-ree-ahs*
scissors	**las tijeras**	*lahs tee-heh-rahs*
shampoo (dandruff)	**el champú (para la caspa)**	*ehl chahm-poo (pah-rah lah kahs-pah)*
shaving cream (lotion)	**la crema de afeitar**	*lah kreh-mah deh ah-feh-ee-tahr*
soap	**el jabón**	*ehl hah-bohn*
suntan lotion (with sun block)	**la crema protectora**	*lah kreh-mah proh-tehk-toh-rah*
talcum powder	**el talco**	*ehl tahl-koh*
tampons	**tampones**	*tahm-poh-nehs*
a thermometer	**un termómetro**	*oon tehr-moh-meh-troh*
tissues	**pañuelos de papel**	*pah-nyoo-eh-lohs deh pah-pehl*
toilet paper	**el papel higiénico**	*ehl pah-pehl ee-hee-eh-nee-koh*
a toothbrush	**un cepillo de dientes**	*oon seh-pee-yoh deh dee-ehn-tehs*
toothpaste	**la pasta de dientes**	*lah pahs-tah deh dee-ehn-tehs*
tweezers	**las pinzas**	*lahs peen-sahs*
vitamins	**las vitaminas**	*lahs bee-tah-mee-nahs*

Note

To express "the," replace *un* with *el* and *una* with *la*. Use *los* for nouns that end in –os and *las* for nouns that end in –as.

I need (We need) _____.
Necesito (Necesitamos) _____.
neh-seh-see-toh (neh-seh-see-tah-mohs) _____

Please buy _____ at the drugstore.
Favor de comprar _____ en la farmacia.
fah-bohr deh kohm-prahr _____ ehn lah fahr-mah-see-ah

Have you seen the _____?
¿Ha visto el (la) _____?
ah bees-toh ehl (lah) _____

Where is (are) the _____?
¿Dónde está (están) el/la (los/las) _____?
dohn-deh ehs-tah (ehs-tahn) ehl/lah (lohs/lahs) _____

Please go to the drugstore and have this prescription filled.
Favor de ir a la farmacia y llenar esta receta.
fah-bohr deh eer ah lah fahr-mah-see-ah ee yeh-nahr ehs-tah rreh-seh-tah

Please go to the drugstore and pick up this prescription.
Favor de ir a la farmacia para recoger esta receta.
fah-bohr deh eer ah lah fahr-mah-see-ah pah-rah rreh-koh-hehr ehs-tah rreh-seh-tah

Please put potpourri in a bowl on the counter.
Favor de poner popurrí en un tazón sobre el mostrador.
fah-bohr deh poh-nehr poh-poo-rree ehn oon tah-sohn soh-breh ehl mohs-trah-dohr

In the Linen Closet

Look for _____ in the linen closet.
Favor de buscar _____ en la lencería.
fah-bohr deh boos-kahr _____ ehn lah lehn-seh-ree-ah

a bath towel	**una toalla**	*oo-nah toh-ah-yah*
a beach towel	**una toalla de playa**	*oo-nah toh-ah-yah deh plah-yah*
a blanket	**una manta**	*oo-nah mahn-tah*
a face towel	**una toalla de mano**	*oo-nah toh-ah-yah deh mah-noh*

a floor mat	**una alfombrilla**	*oo-nah ahl-fohm-bree-yah*
a hand towel	**una toalla de mano**	*oo-nah toh-ah-yah deh mah-noh*
a pillowcase	**una funda de almohada**	*oo-nah foon-dah deh ahl-moh-ah-dah*
sheets (flat, fitted)	**las sábanas (planas, elásticas)**	*lahs sah-bah-nahs (plah-nahs, eh-lahs-tee-kahs)*
a washcloth	**una toallita**	*oo-nah toh-ah-yee-tah*

Please wash the _____ once a day (a week, a month).
Favor de lavar el/la _____ una vez al día (a la semana, al mes).
fah-bohr deh lah-bahr ehl/lah _____ oo-nah behs ahl dee-ah (ah lah seh-mah-nah, ahl mehs)

Please fold the _____ like this (this way).
Favor de doblar el/la _____ de esta manera (así).
fah-bohr deh doh-blahr ehl/lah _____ deh ehs-tah mah-neh-rah (ah-see)

Please stack the _____ neatly.
Favor de colocar el/la _____ en orden.
fah-bohr deh koh-loh-kahr ehl/lah _____ ehn ohr-dehn

In the Bedroom

Furniture and Electrics

> **Note**
> When de is followed by a masculine singular noun (one
> that uses the pronoun el), as in the first sentence that
> follows, use the contraction del (de + el).

Please clean (dust) _____.
Favor de limpiar (quitar el polvo de[l]) _____.
fah-bohr deh leem-pee-ahr (kee-tahr ehl pohl-boh deh[l]) _____

Please handle _____ gently.
Favor de tener cuidado con _____.
fah-bohr deh teh-nehr koo-ee-dah-doh kohn _____

Please don't touch _____.
Favor de no tocar _____.
fah-bohr deh noh toh-kahr _____

the air bed	**la cama de aire**	*lah kah-mah deh ah-ee-reh*
the alarm clock	**el despertador**	*ehl dehs-pehr-tah-dohr*
the armoire	**el armario**	*ehl ahr-mah-ree-oh*
the bed	**la cama**	*lah kah-mah*

the bench	**el banco**	*ehl bahn-koh*
the cable box	**la caja del cable**	*lah kah-hah dehl kah-bleh*
the canopy	**el baldaquín**	*ehl bahl-dah-keen*
the CD player	**el reproductor de discos compactos**	*ehl rreh-proh-dook-tohr deh dees-kohs kohm-pahk-tohs*
the ceiling fan	**el ventilador de techo**	*ehl behn-tee-lah-dohr deh teh-choh*
the chair	**la silla**	*lah see-yah*
the dresser	**el vestidor**	*ehl behs-tee-dohr*
the DVD player	**el reproductor de videodiscos**	*ehl rreh-proh-dook-tohr deh bee-deh-oh-dees-kohs*
the entertain-ment unit	**el módulo de entretenimiento**	*ehl moh-doo-loh deh ehn-treh-teh-nee-mee-ehn-toh*
the headboard	**la cabecera**	*lah kah-beh-seh-rah*
the high hats	**las luces de techo**	*lahs loo-sehs deh teh-choh*
the keys	**las llaves**	*lahs yah-behs*
the lamp	**la lámpara**	*lah lahm-pah-rah*
the mirror	**el espejo**	*ehl ehs-peh-hoh*
the night light	**la luz de noche**	*lah loos deh noh-cheh*
the night table	**la mesa de noche**	*lah meh-sah deh noh-cheh*
the photographs	**las fotos**	*lahs foh-tohs*
the picture frames	**los marcos**	*lohs mahr-kohs*
the pictures	**los cuadros**	*lohs koo-ah-drohs*
the plants	**las plantas**	*lahs plahn-tahs*
the radio (clock)	**el radio (reloj)**	*ehl rrah-dee-oh (rreh-loh)*
the remote control	**el control remoto**	*ehl kohn-trohl rreh-moh-toh*
the sofa bed	**el sofa-cama**	*ehl soh-fah-kah-mah*
the stereo	**el estéreo**	*ehl ehs-teh-reh-oh*
the television	**la televisión**	*lah teh-leh-bee-see-ohn*
the wardrobe	**el armario**	*ehl ahr-mah-ree-oh*
the water bed	**la cama de agua**	*lah kah-mah deh ah-goo-ah*

Don't touch the buttons (the cords, the switches, the connections).
Favor de no tocar los botones (los cordones, los interruptores, las conexiones).
fah-bohr deh noh toh-kahr lohs boh-toh-nehs (lohs kohr-doh-nehs, lohs een-teh-rroop-toh-rehs, lahs koh-nehk-see-oh-nehs)

Please don't touch any of the electronic equipment.
Favor de no tocar el equipo eléctronico.
fah-bohr deh noh toh-kahr ehl eh-kee-poh eh-lehk-troh-nee-koh

Please drape the clothing on the chair.
Favor de colgar la ropa sobre la silla.
fah-bohr deh kohl-gahr lah rroh-pah soh-breh lah see-yah

Please (don't) wax the wood furniture.
Favor de (no) encerar los muebles de madera.
fah-bohr deh (noh) ehn-seh-rahr lohs moo-eh-blehs deh mah-deh-rah

Have you seen the TV remote control (portable telephone, my keys)?
¿Ha visto usted el control remoto, (el teléfono portátil, mis llaves)?
ah bees-toh oo-stehd ehl kohn-trohl rreh-moh-toh (ehl teh-leh-foh-noh pohr-tah-teel, mees yah-behs)

On the Bed

Please wash _____.
Favor de lavar _____.
fah-bohr deh lah-bahr _____

Please take (send) _____ to the dry cleaner.
Favor de llevar (mandar) _____ a la tintorería.
fah-bohr deh yeh-bahr (mahn-dahr) _____ ah lah teen-toh-reh-ree-ah

the bed skirt	**el volado para la cama**	*ehl boh-lah-doh pah-rah lah kah-mah*
the blanket	**la manta**	*lah mahn-tah*
the bolster	**el almohadón**	*ehl ahl-moh-ah-dohn*
the comforter	**la colcha**	*lah kohl-chah*
the fitted sheet	**la sábana ajustable**	*lah sah-bah-nah ah-hoos-tah-bleh*

the flat sheet	**la sábana encimera**	*lah sah-bah-nah ehn-see-meh-rah*
the linens	**la ropa de cama**	*lah rroh-pah deh kah-mah*
the mattress	**el colchón**	*ehl kohl-chohn*
the mattress pad	**el cobertor**	*ehl koh-behr-tohr*
the pillow (decorative)	**la almohada (decorativa)**	*lah ahl-moh-ah-dah (deh-koh-rah-tee-bah)*
the pillow sham	**la funda de almohada**	*lah foon-dah deh ahl-moh-ah-dah*
the pillowcase	**la funda de almohada**	*lah foon-dah deh ahl-moh-ah-dah*
the quilt	**la colcha**	*lah kohl-chah*
the sheets	**las sábanas**	*lahs sah-bah-nahs*

Please change the sheets.
Favor de cambiar las sábanas.
fah-bohr deh kahm-bee-ahr lahs sah-bah-nahs

Please make the bed.
Favor de tender la cama.
fah-bohr deh tehn-dehr lah kah-mah

We are having overnight guests. Please make up the guest room.
Tenemos invitados esta noche. Favor de arreglar la habitación de huéspedes.
teh-neh-mohs een-bee-tah-dohs ehs-tah noh-cheh fah-bohr deh ah-rreh-glahr lah ah-bee-tah-see-ohn deh oo-ehs-peh-dehs

Please straighten the children's rooms.
Favor de arreglar los cuartos de los niños.
fah-bohr deh ah-rreh-glahr lohs koo-ahr-tohs deh lohs nee-nyohs

Please put flowers in the vase.
Favor de poner las flores en el florero.
fah-bohr deh poh-nehr lahs floh-rehs ehn ehl floh-reh-roh

Please take (send) the dirty sheets to the laundry (dry cleaner).
Favor de llevar (mandar) las sábanas sucias a la lavandería (tintorería).
fah-bohr deh yeh-bahr (mahn-dahr) lahs sah-bah-nahs soo-see-ahs ah lah lah-bahn-deh-ree-ah (teen-toh-reh-ree-ah)

In the Closet or Dresser

Please put the hangers (the sachet, the potpourri) in the closet (drawer).

Favor de poner las perchas (el sobrecito, el popurrí) en el armario (cajón).

fah-bohr deh poh-nehr lahs pehr-chahs (ehl soh-breh-see-toh, ehl poh-poo-rree) ehn ehl ahr-mah-ree-oh

Please put the shoes on the shelves (in boxes).

Favor de poner los zapatos en los estantes (en las cajas).

fah-bohr deh poh-nehr lohs sah-pah-tohs ehn lohs ehs-tahn-tehs (ehn lahs kah-hahs)

Please put the ties on the tie rack.

Favor de poner las corbatas en el estirador de corbatas.

fah-bohr deh poh-nehr lahs kohr-bah-tahs ehn ehl ehs-tee-rah-dohr deh kohr-bah-tahs

Articles of Clothing and Jewelry

English	Spanish	Pronunciation
the bathing suit	**el traje de baño**	*ehl trah-heh deh bah-nyoh*
the belt	**el cinturón**	*ehl seen-too-rohn*
the blazer	**la chaqueta deportiva**	*lah chah-keh-tah deh-pohr-tee-bah*
the blouse	**la blusa**	*lah bloo-sah*
the boots	**las botas**	*lahs boh-tahs*
the bracelet	**el bracelete**	*ehl brah-seh-leh-teh*
the cap	**la gorra**	*lah goh-rrah*
the chain	**la cadena**	*lah kah-deh-nah*
the clothing	**la ropa**	*lah rroh-pah*
the coat	**el abrigo**	*ehl ah-bree-goh*
the dress	**el vestido**	*ehl behs-tee-doh*
the earrings	**los aretes**	*lohs ah-reh-tehs*
the evening gown	**el vestido de noche**	*ehl behs-tee-doh deh noh-cheh*

continued

English	Spanish	Pronunciation
the fur coat	**el abrigo de piel**	*ahl ah-bree-goh deh pee-ehl*
the glasses	**los espejuelos**	*lohs ehs-peh-hoo-eh-lohs*
the gloves	**los guantes**	*lohs goo-ahn-tehs*
the handkerchief	**el pañuelo**	*ehl pah-nyoo-eh-loh*
the hat	**el sombrero**	*ehl sohm-breh-roh*
the jacket	**la chaqueta**	*lah chah-keh-tah*
the jeans	**los vaqueros**	*lohs bah-keh-rohs*
the lingerie	**la lencería**	*lah lehn-seh-ree-ah*
the mittens	**los mitones**	*lohs mee-toh-nehs*
the necklace	**el collar**	*ehl koh-yahr*
the nightgown	**la ropa de dormir**	*lah rroh-pah deh dohr-meer*
the night shirt	**la camisa de dormir**	*lah kah-mee-sah deh dohr-meer*
the overalls	**el overol**	*ehl oh-beh-rohl*
the pajamas	**las pijamas**	*lahs pee-hah-mahs*
the pants	**los pantalones**	*lohs pahn-tah-loh-nehs*
the pantsuit	**el traje pantalón**	*ehl trah-heh pahn-tah-lohn*
the pantyhose	**las medias**	*lahs meh-dee-ahs*
the pin	**el broche**	*ehl broh-cheh*
the pocketbook	**la cartera**	*lah kahr-teh-rah*
the pullover	**el jersey**	*ehl hehr-seh*
the raincoat	**el impermeable**	*ehl eem-pehr-meh-ah-bleh*
the ring	**el anillo**	*ehl ah-nee-yoh*
the robe	**la bata**	*lah bah-tah*
the sandals	**las sandalias**	*lahs sahn-dah-lee-ahs*
the scarf	**la bufanda**	*lah boo-fahn-dah*
the shirt	**la camisa**	*lah kah-mee-sah*

English	Spanish	Pronunciation
the shoe rack	el zapatero	ehl sah-pah-teh-roh
the shoes	los zapatos	lohs sah-pah-tohs
the shorts	los pantalones cortos	lohs pahn-tah-loh-nehs kohr-tohs
the skirt	la falda	lah fahl-dah
the slip (half, full)	la combinación (corta, larga)	lah kohm-bee-nah-see-ohn (kohr-tah, lahr-gah)
the slippers	las chancletas	lahs chahn-kleh-tahs
the sneakers	los tenis	lohs teh-nees
the socks	los calcetines	lohs kahl-seh-tee-nehs
the sports coat	la chaqueta deportiva	lah chah-keh-tah deh-pohr-tee-bah
the stockings	las medias	lahs meh-dee-ahs
the suit	el traje	ehl trah-heh
the suspenders	los tirantes	lohs tee-rahn-tehs
the sweater	el suéter	ehl soo-eh-tehr
the sweatsuit	el chándal	ehl chahn-dahl
the T-shirt	la camiseta	lah kah-mee-seh-tah
the tie	la corbata	lalh kohr-bah-tah
the tie rack	el estirador de corbatas	ehl ehs-tee-rah-dohr deh kohr-bah-tahs
the tights	los leotardos	lohs leh-oh-tahr-dohs
the umbrella	el paraguas	ehl pah-rah-goo-ahs
the underwear	la ropa interior	lah rroh-pah een-teh-ree-ohr
the uniform	el uniforme	ehl oo-nee-fohr-meh
the vest	el chaleco	ehl chah-leh-koh
the wallet	la cartera	lah kahr-teh-rah
the watch	el reloj	ehl rreh-loh
the windbreaker	la cazadora	la kah-sah-doh-rah

Colors

English	Spanish	Pronunciation
beige	**beige**	*beh-ee-heh*
black	**negro**	*neh-groh*
blue	**azul**	*ah-sool*
brown	**pardo**	*pahr-doh*
green	**verde**	*behr-deh*
gray	**gris**	*grees*
orange	**anaranjado**	*ah-nah-rahn-hah-doh*
pink	**rosado**	*rroh-sah-doh*
purple	**púrpura**	*poor-poo-rah*
red	**rojo**	*rroh-hoh*
white	**blanco**	*blahn-koh*
yellow	**amarillo**	*ah-mah-ree-yoh*

Note

The masculine plural, feminine singular, and feminine plural forms of adjectives are given, respectively, in parentheses. They must agree with the nouns they modify. *Example:* negro (negra, negros, negras)

My dress (My skirt) is black.

Mi vestido (Mi falda) es negro (negra).

My dresses (My skirts) are black.

Mis vestidos (Mis faldas) son negros (negras).

When no feminine singular form is indicated, the feminine adjective has the same form as the masculine adjective.

My dress (My skirt) is gray.

Mi vestido (Mi falda) es gris.

My dresses (My skirts) are gray.

Mis vestidos (Mis faldas) son grises.

I have (He/She has) misplaced my (his/her) black shirt.

He (Ha) colocado en un lugar equivocado mi (su) camisa negra.

eh (ah) koh-loh-kah-doh ehn oon loo-gahr eh-kee-boh-kah-doh mee (soo) kah-mee-sah neh-grah

I have (He/She has) misplaced my (his/her) gray pants.

He (Ha) colocado en un lugar equivocado mis (sus) pantalones grises.

eh (ah) koh-loh-kah-doh ehn oon loo-gahr eh-kee-boh-kah-doh mees (soos) pahn-tah-loh-nehs gree-sehs

Have you seen my red dress?

¿Ha visto mi vestido rojo?

ah bees-toh mee behs-tee-doh rroh-hoh

Have you seen my gold (silver) bracelet?

¿Ha visto mi bracelete de oro (de plata)?

ah bees-toh mee brah-seh-leh-teh deh oh-roh (deh plah-tah)

In the Laundry Room

Here is the washing machine (dryer).

Aquí está la lavadora (secadora).

ah-kee ehs-tah lah lah-bah-doh-rah (seh-kah-doh-rah)

You will find _____ in this closet (in this cabinet, on this shelf).

Usted encontrará _____ en este armario (en este gabinete, en este estante).

oo-stehd ehn-kohn-trah-rah _____ ehn ehs-teh ahr-mah-ree-oh (ehn ehs-teh gah-bee-neh-teh, ehn ehs-teh ehs-tahn-teh)

the bleach	**el blanqueador**	*ehl blahn-keh-ah-dohr*
the cleaning agents	**los limpiadores**	*lohs leem-pee-ah-doh-rehs*
the detergent (liquid, powder)	**el detergente (líquido, en polvo)**	*ehl deh-tehr-hehn-teh (lee-kee-doh, ehn pohl-boh)*
the drying rack	**la rejilla de secado**	*lah rreh-hee-yah deh seh-kah-doh*

the fabric softener	**el suavizador**	*ehl soo-ah-bee-sah-dohr*
the hand vacuum	**la aspiradora de mano**	*lah ahs-pee-rah-doh-rah deh mah-noh*
the iron	**la plancha**	*lah plahn-chah*
the ironing board	**la tabla de planchar**	*lah tah-blah deh plahn-chahr*
the ironing-board cover	**el forro de la tabla de planchar**	*ehl foh-rroh deh lah tah-blah deh plahn-chahr*
the laundry	**la ropa sucia**	*lah rroh-pah soo-see-ah*
the laundry basket	**la cesta de la ropa sucia**	*lah sehs-tah deh lah rroh-pah soo-see-ah*
the sink	**el lavamanos**	*ehl lah-bah-mah-nohs*
the soap	**el jabón**	*ehl hah-bohn*
the stain remover	**el quitamanchas**	*ehl kee-tah-mahn-chahs*
the starch (spray)	**el almidón (en espray)**	*ehl ahl-mee-dohn (ehn ehs-preh-ee)*

The dirty clothes are in the hamper/laundry basket.
La ropa sucia está en la cesta.
lah rroh-pah soo-see-ah ehs-tah ehn lah sehs-tah

Please do the laundry when the hamper/laundry basket is full.
Favor de lavar la ropa sucia cuando la cesta esté llena.
fah-bohr deh lah-bahr lah rroh-pah soo-see-ah koo-ahn-doh lah sehs-tah ehs-teh yeh-nah

Please allow these clothes to soak.
Favor de dejar que la ropa se remoje.
fah-bohr deh deh-hahr keh lah rroh-pah seh rreh-moh-heh

Here is a stain.
Aquí está una mancha.
ah-kee ehs-tah oo-nah mahn-chah

Please try to remove it, but don't rub too hard.
Favor de quitarla, pero no restregue mucho.
fah-bohr deh kee-tahr-lah peh-roh noh rrehs-treh-geh moo-choh

Please pretreat these clothes with stain remover.
Favor de usar el quitamanchas en esta ropa.
fah-bohr deh oo-sahr ehl kee-tah-mahn-chahs ehn ehs-tah rroh-pah

These clothes need the gentle (permanent press, normal) cycle.
Esta ropa necesita el ciclo delicado (de planchado permanente, normal).
ehs-tah rroh-pah neh-seh-see-tah ehl see-cloh deh lee-kah-doh (deh plahn chah-doh pehr-mah-nehn-teh, nohr-mahl)

Please use the cold (warm, hot) rinse (wash) cycle.
Favor de usar el ciclo frío (tibio, caliente) de enjuagar (lavar).
fah-bohr deh oo-sahr ehl see-kloh free-oh (tee-bee-oh, kah-lee-ehn-teh) deh ehn-hoo-ah-gahr (lah-bahr)

Please set the machine by pressing (turning) this button.
Favor de poner la máquina oprimiendo (dando vueltas a) este botón.
fah-bohr deh poh-nehr lah mah-kee-nah oh-pree-mee-ehn-doh (dahn-doh boo-ehl-tahs ah) ehs-teh boh-tohn

Please choose the wash time.
Favor de escoger la duración del ciclo.
fah-bohr deh ehs-koh-hehr lah doo-rah-see-ohn dehl see-kloh

Please do not put my (his/her) _____ in the washer (dryer).
Favor de no poner mi (su) _____ en la lavadora (secadora).
fah-bohr deh noh poh-nehr mee (soo)   ehn lah lah-bah-doh-rah (seh-kah-doh-rah)

Please wash these clothes by hand and rinse them well.
Favor de lavar esta ropa a mano y enjuagarla bién.
fah-bohr deh lah-bahr ehs-tah rroh-pah ah mah-noh ee ehn-hoo-ah-gahr-lah bee-ehn

If the clothes become unbalanced, the washing machine will shake and move.
Si la ropa está desbalanceada, la lavadora temblará y se moverá.
see lah rroh-pah ehs-tah dehs-bah-lahn-seh-ah-dah, lah lah-bah-doh-rah tehm-blah-rah ee seh moh-beh-rah

Please stop the machine and rearrange the clothes.
Favor de parar la máquina y arreglar la ropa.
fah-bohr deh pah-rahr lah mah-kee-nah ee ah-rreh-glahr lah rroh-pah

Please add fabric softener to every wash.
Favor de añadir suavizante a cada lavado.
fah-bohr deh ah-nyah-deer soo-ah-bee-sahn-teh ah kah-dah lah-bah-doh

Please add bleach to the white wash.
Favor de añadir blanqueador a la ropa blanca.
fah-bohr deh ah-nyah-deer blahn-keh-ah-dohr ah lah rroh-pah blahn-kah

Please don't launder whites with darks.
Favor de no lavar lo oscuro con lo claro.
fah-bohr deh noh lah-bahr loh ohs-koo-roh kohn loh klah-roh

Separate them carefully.
Favor de separarlos con cuidado.
fah-bohr deh seh-pah-rahr-lohs kohn koo-ee-dah-doh

Please don't overload the washer (dryer).
Favor de no poner demasiada ropa en la lavadora (secadora).
fah-bohr deh noh poh-nehr deh-mah-see-ah-dah rroh-pah ehn lah lah-bah-doh-rah (seh-kah-doh-rah)

Please wash towels separately one time (two times) per week (per day).
Favor de lavar las toallas aparte una vez (dos veces) a la semana (al día).
fah-bohr deh lah-bahr lahs toh-ah-yahs ah-pahr-teh oo-nah behs (dohs beh-sehs) ah lah seh-mah-nah (ahl dee-ah)

The beeper tells you when the washer (dryer) is finished.
El bíper le avisa cuando la lavadora (secadora) termine.
ehl bee-pehr leh ah-bee-sah koo-ahn-doh lah lah-bah-doh-rah (seh-kah-doh-rah) tehr-mee-neh

Please read the labels on all of the clothing.
Favor de leer las etiquetas en toda la ropa.
fah-bohr deh leh-ehr lahs eh-tee-keh-tahs ehn toh-dah lah rroh-pah

The washing machine (dryer) is broken.
La lavadora (secadora) está rota.
lah lah-bah-doh-rah (seh-kah-doh-rah) ehs-tah rroh-tah

You must go to the laundromat.
Usted debe ir a la lavandería.
oo-stehd deh-beh eer ah lah lah-bahn-deh-ree-ah

Please don't leave the clothes unattended.
Favor de no dejar la ropa desatendida.
fah-bohr deh noh deh-hahr lah rroh-pah dehs-ah-tehn-dee-dah

Don't put anything made of _____ in the washing machine (dryer).
Favor de no poner cosas de _____ en la lavadora (secadora).
fah-bohr deh noh poh-nehr koh-sahs deh _____ ehn lah lah-bah-doh-rah (seh-kah-doh-rah)

Clothing made of _____ may go in the washing machine (dryer).
La ropa hecha de _____ se puede poner en la lavadora (secadora).
lah rroh-pah eh-chah deh _____ seh poo-eh-deh poh-nehr ehn lah lah-bah-doh-rah (seh-kah-doh-rah)

cashmere	**cachemira**	*kah-cheh-mee-rah*
corduroy	**pana**	*pah-nah*
cotton	**algodón**	*ahl-goh-dohn*
denim	**dril**	*dreel*
flannel	**franela**	*frah-neh-lah*
fur	**piel**	*pee-ehl*
lace	**encaje**	*ehn-kah-heh*
leather	**cuero**	*koo-eh-roh*
linen	**lino**	*lee-noh*
nylon	**nilón**	*nee-lohn*
polyester	**poliéster**	*poh-lee-ehs-tehr*
satin	**raso**	*rrah-soh*
silk	**seda**	*seh-dah*
suede	**gamuza**	*gah-moo-sah*
velvet	**terciopelo**	*tehr-see-oh-peh-loh*
wool	**lana**	*lah-nah*

Please dry the clothes immediately.
Favor de secar la ropa inmediatamente.
fah-bohr deh seh-kahr lah rroh-pah een-meh-dee-ah-tah-mehn-teh

Please hang the clothes on the clothesline outside.
Favor de colgar la ropa afuera en el tendedero.
fah-bohr deh kohl-gahr lah rroh-pah ah-foo-eh-rah ehn ehl tehn-deh-deh-roh

Here are the clothespins.
Aquí están las pinzas para tender.
ah-kee ehs-tahn lahs peen-sahs pah-rah tehn-dehr

Please iron these clothes.
Favor de planchar esta ropa.
fah-bohr deh plahn-chahr ehs-tah rroh-pah

Please set the iron on low (medium, high, permanent press).
Favor de poner la plancha en temperatura baja (media, alta, de planchado permanente).
fah-bohr deh poh-nehr lah plahn-chah ehn tehm-peh-rah-too-rah bah-hah (meh-dee-ah, ahl-tah, deh plahn-chah-doh pehr-mah-nehn-teh)

Please spray the clothes with water (spray starch) before ironing them.
Favor de rociar la ropa con agua (almidón en espray) antes de plancharla.
fah-bohr deh rroh-see-ahr lah rroh-pah kohn ah-goo-ah (ahl-mee-dohn ehn ehs-preh-ee) ahn-tehs deh plahn-chahr-lah

Please don't use (too much) spray starch.
Favor de no usar (demasiado) almidón.
fah-bohr deh noh oo-sahr (deh-mah-see-ah-doh) ahl-mee-dohn

Please fold the clothes neatly and put them away.
Favor de doblar la ropa ordenadamente y guardarla.
fah-bohr deh doh-blahr lah rroh-pah ohr-deh-nah-dah-mehn-teh ee goo-ahr-dahr-lah

You may stack the clothes and I will put them away.
Usted puede encimar la ropa y yo la voy a guardar.
oo-stehd poo-eh-deh ehn-see-mahr lah rroh-pah ee yoh lah boh-ee ah goo-ahr-dahr

This is how I fold.
Así es como yo la doblo.
ah-see ehs koh-moh yoh lah doh-bloh

Do you know how to sew?
¿Sabe coser?
sah-beh koh-sehr

I have a sewing machine.
Yo tengo una máquina de coser.
yoh tehn-goh oo-nah mah-kee-nah deh koh-sehr

My _____ is (are) torn.
Mi (Mis) _____ está (están) roto/rota (rotos/rotas).
mee (mees) _____ ehs-tah (ehs-tahn) rroh-toh/rroh-tah (rroh-tohs/rroh-tahs)

The sewing box is in the laundry room.
El costurero está en la lavandería.
ehl kohs-too-reh-roh ehs-tah ehn lah lah-bahn-deh-ree-ah

In it you will find a needle, pins, scissors, and thread.
Allí, usted encontrará una aguja de coser, alfileres, tijeras e hilo de coser.
ah-yee oo-stehd ehn-kohn-trah-rah oo-nah ah-goo-hah deh koh-sehr, ahl-fee-leh-rehs, tee-heh-rahs eh ee-loh deh koh-sehr

Here is my sewing kit.
Aquí está mi costurero.
ah-kee ehs-tah mee kohs-too-reh-roh

Here is a tape measure.
Aquí está una cinta métrica.
ah-kee ehs-tah oo-nah seen-tah meh-tree-kah

Can you mend my _____?
¿Puede usted remendar mi (mis) _____?
poo-eh-deh oo-stehd rreh-mehn-dahr mee (mees) _____

Can you sew on a button?
¿Puede usted coser un botón?
poo-eh-deh oo-stehd koh-sehr oon boh-tohn

Can you hem my skirt (my pants)?
¿Puede usted hacer un dobladillo en mi falda (mis pantalones)?
poo-eh-deh oo-stehd ah-sehr oon doh-blah-dee-yoh ehn mee fahl-dah (mees pahn-tah-loh-nehs)

Can you replace this zipper?
¿Puede usted cambiar esta cremallera?
poo-eh-deh oo-stehd kahm-bee-ahr ehs-tah kreh-mah-yeh-rah

Will you please take my _____ to the tailor?

¿Me puede hacer el favor de llevar mi (mis) _____ al sastre?

meh poo-eh-deh ah-sehr ehl fah-bohr deh yeh-bahr mee (mees) _____ ahl sahs-treh

Will you please take these shoes (these boots, these sandals) to the shoemaker?

¿Me puede hacer el favor de llevar estos zapatos (estas botas, estas sandalias) al zapatero?

meh poo-eh-deh ah-sehr ehl fah-bohr deh yeh-bahr ehs-tohs sah-pah-tohs (ehs-tahs boh-tahs, ehs-tahs sahn-dah-lee-ahs) ahl sah-pah-teh-roh

10

In the Living Room, Home Office, Basement, and Attic

In the Living Room

> **Note**
>
> When de is followed by a masculine singular noun
> (one that uses the pronoun el), use the contraction del
> (de + el).

Please clean (dust) the _____.

Favor de limpiar (quitar el polvo de[l]) _____.

fah-bohr deh leem-pee-ahr (kee-tahr ehl pohl-boh deh[l]) _____

armchair	**la butaca**	*lah boo-tah-kah*
bar	**el bar**	*ehl bahr*
bookcase	**la estantería**	*lah ehs-tahn-teh-ree-ah*
bookshelves	**los estantes**	*lohs ehs-tahn-tehs*
carpet	**la alfombra**	*lah ahl-fohm-brah*
CD player	**el reproductor**	*ehl rreh-proh-dook-tohr*
	de discos	*deh dees-kohs*
	compactos	*kohm-pahk-tohs*
chair (lounge)	**el sillón**	*ehl see-yohn*

cushion	el cojín	ehl koh-heen
DVD player	el reproductor de videodiscos	ehl rreh-proh-dook-tohr deh bee-deh-oh-dees-kohs
entertainment unit	la unidad de entretenimiento	lah oo-nee-dahd deh ehn-treh-teh-nee-mee-ehn-toh
figurines	las figuritas	lahs fee-goo-ree-tahs
fireplace	la chimenea	lah chee-meh-neh-ah
fireplace screen	la pantalla de la chimenea	lah pahn-tah-yah deh lah chee-meh-neh-ah
fireplace tools	las herramientas de la chimenea	lahs eh-rrah-mee-ehn-tahs deh lah chee-meh-neh-ah
flowers (artificial)	las flores (artificiales)	lahs floh-rehs (ahr-tee-fee-see-ah-lehs)
footrest	el descanso para el pie	ehl dehs-kahn-soh pah-rah ehl pee-eh
high hats	las luces de techo	lahs loo-sehs deh teh-choh
knickknacks	el cachivache	ehl kah-chee-bah-cheh
lamp (floor, table)	la lámpara (de piso, de mesa)	lah lahm-pah-rah (deh pee-soh, deh meh-sah)
love seat	el sofá de dos plazas	ehl soh-fah deh dohs plah-sahs
mantel	la repisa	lah rreh-pee-sah
mirror	el espejo	ehl ehs-peh-hoh
picture	el cuadro	ehl koo-ah-droh
picture frame	el marco	ehl mahr-koh
pillow (decorative)	el cojín	ehl koh-heen
plants	las plantas	lahs plahn-tahs
pottery	la cerámica	lah seh-rah-mee-kah
recliner	el sillón reclinable	ehl see-yohn rreh-klee-nah-bleh
rug	la alfombra	lah ahl-fohm-brah
sculpture	la escultura	lah ehs-kool-too-rah
sliding doors	las puertas corredizas	lahs poo-ehr-tahs koh-rreh-dee-sahs
sofa (couch)	el sofá	ehl soh-fah

stereo	**el estéreo**	*ehl ehs-teh-reh-oh*
table (coffee, end)	**la mesa (de café, la mesita auxiliaria de salón)**	*lah meh-sah (deh kah-feh, lah meh-see-tah ah-ok-see-lee-ah-ree-ah deh sah-lohn)*
television (large-screen)	**el televisor (de pantalla grande)**	*ehl teh-leh-bee-sohr (deh pahn-tah-yah grahn-deh)*
vase	**el florero**	*ehl floh-reh-roh*
wall unit	**la unidad de pared**	*lah oo-nee-dahd deh pah-rehd*

Please move the furniture when you clean.
Favor de mover los muebles cuando limpie.
fah-bohr deh moh-behr lohs moo-eh-blehs koo-ahn-doh leem-pee-eh

Please straighten the books on the bookshelves.
Favor de arreglar los libros en los estantes.
fah-bohr deh ah-rreh-glahr lohs lee-brohs ehn lohs ehs-tahn-tehs

Please dust behind (under, on top of) the books.
Favor de quitar el polvo detrás de (debajo de, encima de) los libros.
fah-bohr deh kee-tahr ehl pohl-boh deh-trahs deh (deh-bah-hoh deh, ehn-see-mah deh) lohs lee-brohs

Please vacuum (clean) the carpet /rug.
Favor de pasar la aspiradora en (limpiar) la alfombra.
fah-bohr deh pah-sahr lah ahs-pee-rah-doh-rah ehn (leem-pee-ahr) lah ahl-fohm-brah

Please don't put water on the leather couch.
Favor de no echar agua sobre el sofá de cuero.
fah-bohr deh noh eh-chahr ah-goo-ah soh-breh ehl soh-fah deh koo-eh-roh

Please clean it with a soft rag and this product.
Favor de limpiarlo con este trapo suave y este producto.
fah-bohr deh leem-pee-ahr-loh kohn ehs-teh trah-poh soo-ah-beh ee ehs-teh proh-dook-toh

Please don't touch anything in the entertainment unit (in the bar).
Favor de no tocar nada en la unidad de entretenimiento (en el bar).
fah-bohr deh noh toh-kahr nah-dah ehn lah oo-nee-dahd deh ehn-treh-teh-nee-mee-ehn-toh (ehn ehl bahr)

Please sweep the ashes from the fireplace.
Favor de barrer las cenizas de la chimenea.
fah-bohr deh bah-rrehr lahs seh-nee-sahs deh lah chee-meh-neh-ah

Please fluff the pillows (cushions).
Favor de sacudir las almohadas de plumas (los cojines).
fah-bohr deh sah-koo-deer lahs ahl-moh-ah-dahs deh ploo-mahs (lohs koh-hee-nehs)

Please water the plants.
Favor de regar las plantas
fah-bohr deh rreh-gahr lahs plahn-tahs

Please open (close) the sliding doors.
Favor de abrir (cerrar) las puertas corredizas.
fah-bohr deh ah-breer (seh-rrahr) lahs poo-ehr-tahs koh-rreh-dee-sahs

Please clean the television screen with an antistatic rag.
Favor de limpiar la pantalla del televisor con un trapo antiestático.
fah-bohr deh leem-pee-ahr lah pahn-tah-yah dehl teh-leh-bee-sohr kohn oon trah-poh ahn-tee-ehs-tah-tee-koh

Please put fresh water in the vases.
Favor de poner agua fresca en los floreros.
fah-bohr deh poh-nehr ah-goo-ah frehs-kah ehn lohs floh-reh-rohs

Please (don't) wax the wood furniture.
Favor de (no) encerar los muebles de madera.
fah-bohr deh (noh) ehn-seh-rahr lohs moo-eh-blehs deh mah-deh-rah

Please throw out the old newspapers and magazines.
Favor de botar los periódicos y las revistas viejas.
fah-bohr deh boh-tahr lohs peh-ree-oh-dee-kohs ee lahs rreh-bees-tahs bee-eh-hahs

This is an antique (heirloom).
Esto es una antigüedad (reliquia).
ehs-toh ehs oo-nah ahn-tee-goo-eh-dahd (rreh-lee-kee-ah)

Be careful. Please don't touch it.
Tenga cuidado. Favor de no tocarlo (tocarla).
tehn-gah koo-ee-dah-doh fah-bohr deh noh toh-kahr-loh (toh-kahr-lah)

There is firewood in the backyard. Please bring some logs inside.
Hay leña en el patio. Favor de traer algunos troncos adentro.
ah-ee leh-nyah ehn ehl pah-tee-oh fah-bohr deh trah-ehr ahl-goo-nohs trohn-kohs ah-dehn-troh

In the Home Office

Please clean (dust) the _____.
Favor de limpiar (quitar el polvo de[l]) _____.
fah-bohr deh leem-pee-ahr (kee-tahr ehl pohl-boh deh[l]) _____

Please don't touch (unplug) the _____.
Favor de no tocar (desenchufar) _____.
fah-bohr deh noh toh-kahr (dehs-ehn-choo-fahr) _____

You may (not) use _____.
Usted (no) puede usar _____.
oo-stehd (noh) poo-eh-deh oo-sahr _____

the answering machine	el contestador automático	ehl kohn-tehs-tah-dohr ah-oo-toh-mah-tee-koh
the BlackBerry	el aparato BlackBerry	ehl ah-pah-rah-toh blahk-beh-ree
the bookcase	la estantería	lah ehs-tahn-teh-ree-ah
the bookshelves	los estantes	lohs ehs-tahn-tehs
the cable box	la caja del cable	lah kah-hah deh kah-bleh
the chair	la silla	lah see-yah
the computer	la computadora	lah kohm-poo-tah-doh-rah
the copy machine	la fotocopiadora	lah foh-toh-koh-pee-ah-doh-rah
the CPU	la unidad central	lah oo-nee-dah sehn-trahl
the desk	el escritorio	ehl ehs-kree-toh-ree-oh

the fax machine	**la máquina fax**	*lah mah-kee-nah fahks*
the file cabinet	**el fichero**	*ehl fee-cheh-roh*
the keyboard	**el teclado**	*ehl teh-klah-doh*
the monitor	**la pantalla del monitor**	*lah pahn-tah-yah dehl moh-nee-tohr*
the mouse	**el ratón**	*ehl rrah-tohn*
the pencil sharpener	**el sacapuntas**	*ehl sah-kah-poon-tahs*
the printer	**la impresora**	*lah eem-preh-soh-rah*
the scanner	**el escáner**	*ehl ehs-kah-nehr*
the screen	**la pantalla**	*lah pahn-tah-yah*
the shredder	**la trituradora**	*lah tree-too-rah-doh-rah*
the speakers	**los altavoces**	*lohs ahl-tah-boh-sehs*
the table	**la mesa**	*lah meh-sah*
the telephone	**el teléfono**	*ehl teh-leh-foh-noh*
the wastebasket	**la papelera**	*lah pah-peh-leh-rah*
the workstation	**el terminal**	*ehl tehr-mee-nahl*

You can find _____ in this drawer (cabinet) [on these shelves].
Usted puede encontrar _____ en este cajón (gabinete) [en estos estantes].
oo-stehd poo-eh-deh ehn-kohn-trahr _____ ehn ehs-teh kah-hohn (gah-bee-neh-teh) [ehn ehs-tohs ehs-tahn-tehs]

the calculator	**la calculadora**	*lah kahl-koo-lah-doh-rah*
the calendar	**el calendario**	*ehl kah-lehn-dah-ree-oh*
the cards	**las fichas**	*lahs fee-chahs*
the dictionary	**el diccionario**	*ehl deek-see-oh-nah-ree-oh*
envelopes (legal, letter, manila)	**los sobres (legales, regulares, manilas)**	*lohs soh-brehs (leh-gah-lehs, rreh-goo-lah-rehs, mah-nee-lahs)*
the encyclopedia	**la enciclopedia**	*lah ehn-see-kloh-peh-dee-ah*
the eraser	**la goma**	*lah goh-mah*
the folder	**la carpeta**	*lah kahr-peh-tah*
the highlighter (the highlighters)	**el marcador (los marcadores)**	*ehl mahr-kah-dohr (lohs mahr-kah-doh-rehs)*
the labels (address)	**las etiquetas (de correo)**	*lahs eh-tee-keh-tahs (deh koh-rreh-oh)*

the notepad (the notepads)	el bloc (los bloques)	*ehl blohk (lohs bloh-kehs)*
the paper	el papel	*ehl pah-pehl*
the paper clips	los sujetapapeles	*lohs soo-heh-tah-pah-peh-lehs*
the paperweight	el pisapapeles	*ehl pee-sah-pah-peh-lehs*
the pen	el bolígrafo	*ehl boh-lee-grah-foh*
the pencil sharpener	el sacapuntas	*ehl sah-kah-poon-tahs*
the pencil(s)	el lápiz (los lápices)	*ehl lah-pees (lohs lah-pee-sehs)*
the reference book	el libro de referencias	*ehl lee-broh deh rreh-feh-rehn-see-ahs*
the rubber bands	las gomas elásticas	*lahs goh-mahs eh-lahs-tee-kahs*
the ruler	la regla	*lah rreh-glah*
the tape (such as Scotch brand)	la cinta adhesiva	*lah seen-tah ahd-eh-see-bah*
the stamps	los sellos	*lohs seh-yohs*
the staple remover	el quitagrapas	*ehl kee-tah-grah-pahs*
the stapler	la grapadora	*lah grah-pah-doh-rah*
the staples	las grapas	*lahs grah-pahs*
the stationery	los artículos de papelería	*lohs ahr-tee-koo-lohs deh pah-peh-leh-ree-ah*
the stickpins	los alfileres	*lohs ahl-fee-leh-rehs*
the thesaurus	el tesauro	*ehl teh-sah-oo-roh*
the thumbtacks	las tachuelas	*lahs tah-choo-eh-lahs*
the wrapping paper	el papel de envolver	*ehl pah-pehl deh ehn-bohl-behr*

Use what you need.
Use lo que necesite.
oo-seh loh keh neh-seh-see-teh

Please go to the stationery store (office supply store).
Favor de ir a la papelería (la tienda de artículos de oficina).
fah-bohr deh eer ah lah pah-peh-leh-ree-ah (lah tee-ehn-dah deh ahr-tee-koo-los deh oh-fee-see-nah)

Please pick up a (some, a box of) _____.
Favor de comprar un/una (unos/unas, una caja de) _____.
fah-bohr deh kohm-prahr oon/oo-nah (oo-nohs/oo-nahs, oo-nah kah-hah deh) _____

Please put a stamp on these letters.
Favor de poner un sello en estas cartas.
fah-bohr deh poh-nehr oon seh-yoh ehn ehs-tahs kahr-tahs

Please put these letters in the mailbox.
Favor de echar estas cartas en el buzón.
fah-bohr deh eh-chahr ehs-tahs kahr-tahs ehn ehl boo-sohn

In the Basement and Attic

_____ is (are) located in the basement.
_____ está (están) en el sótano.
_____ ehs-tah (ehs-tahn) ehn ehl soh-tah-noh

The air-conditioning condenser	**El condensador del aire acondicionado**	*ehl kohn-dehn-sah-dohr dehl ah-ee-reh ah-kohn-dee-see-oh-nah-doh*
The boiler	**La caldera**	*lah kahl-deh-rah*
The circuit breakers	**Los cortacircuitos**	*lohs kohr-tah-seer-koo-ee-tohs*
The dryer	**La secadora**	*lah seh-kah-doh-rah*
The electric meter	**El contador de electricidad**	*ehl kohn-tah-dohr deh eh-lehk-tree-see-dahd*
The fuse box	**La caja de los fusibles**	*lah kah-hah deh lohs foo-see-blehs*
The gas meter	**El contador de gas**	*ehl kohn-tah-dohr deh gahs*
The heating unit	**El calentador**	*ehl kah-lehn-tah-dohr*
The oil burner	**El quemador de petróleo**	*ehl keh-mah-dohr deh peh-troh-leh-oh*
The washing machine	**La lavadora**	*lah lah-bah-doh-rah*
The water heater	**El calentador del agua**	*ehl kah-lehn-tah-dohr dehl ah-goo-ah*

Please do not touch these machines.
Favor de no tocar estas máquinas.
fah-bohr deh noh toh-kahr ehs-tahs mah-kee-nahs

If there is a problem, please call me.
Si hay un problema, favor de llamarme.
see ah-ee oon proh-bleh-mah fah-bohr deh yah-mahr-meh

The electric (gas) company comes to read the meter at the beginning
(end) of the month.
**La compañía de electricidad (gas) viene a revisar el contador
al principio (fin) del mes.**
*lah kohm-pah-nyee ah doh oh lehk-tree-see-dahd (gahs) bee-eh-neh ah
rreh-bee-sahr ehl kohn-tah-dohr ahl preen-see-pee-oh (feen) dehl mehs*

The electric (gas) meter is over here.
El contador de electricidad (gas) está aquí.
ehl kohn-tah-dohr deh eh-lehk-tree-see-dahd (gahs) ehs-tah ah-kee

Please ask the meter reader for his/her I.D.
**Favor de pedirle la identificación a quien venga a leer el
contador.**
*fah-bohr deh peh-deer-leh lah ee-dehn-tee-fee-kah-see-ohn ah kee-ehn
behn-gah ah leh-ehr ehl kohn-tah-dohr*

Please do not allow him/her in the house without identification.
Favor de no permitirle entrar en la casa sin la identificación.
*fah-bohr doh noh pohr-mee-teer-leh ohn-trahr ehn lah kah-sah seen
ee-dehn-tee-fee-kah-see-ohn*

Please dust the pool table (jukebox, Ping-Pong table).
**Favor de desempolvar la mesa de billar (la máquina de discos,
la mesa de pimpón).**
*fah-bohr deh deh-sehm-pohl-bahr lah meh-sah deh bee-yahr (lah mah-kee-nah
deh dees-kohs, lah meh-sah deh peem-pohn)*

The basement (attic) is used for storage (odds and ends).
**El sótano (el desván) se usa para almacenar (los artículos
misceláneos).**
*ehl soh-tah-noh (ehl dehs-bahn) seh oo-sah pah-rah ahl-mah-seh-nahr (lohs
ahr-tee-koo-lohs mees-eh-lah-neh-ohs)*

I (We) don't use these things anymore.
Yo (Nosotros) ya no uso (usamos) estas cosas.
yoh (noh-soh-trohs) yah noh oo-soh (oo-sah-mohs) ehs-tahs koh-sahs

Please help me put these things in the basement (attic).
Favor de ayudarme a poner estas cosas en el sótano (desván).
fah-bohr deh ah-yoo-dahr-meh ah poh-nehr ehs-tahs koh-sahs ehn ehl soh-tah-noh (dehs-bahn)

Please dust the boxes (cartons, containers, crates).
Favor de quitar el polvo de las cajas (de las cajas grandes, de los contenedores, de los cajones).
fah-bohr deh kee-tahr ehl pohl-boh deh lahs kah-hahs (deh lahs kah-hahs grahn-dehs, deh lohs kohn-teh-neh-doh-rehs, deh lohs kah-hoh-nehs)

Please don't move anything.
Favor de no mover nada.
fah-bohr deh noh moh-behr nah-dah

11

Caring for Loved Ones

Please keep the doors locked at all times.
Favor de mantener las puertas cerradas con llave todo el tiempo.
fah-bohr deh mahn-teh-nehr lahs poo-ehr-tahs seh-rrah-dahs kohn yah-beh toh-doh ehl tee-ehm-poh

Please read all labels carefully.
Favor de leer todas las etiquetas cuidadosamente.
fah-bohr deh lee-ehr toh-dahs lahs eh-tee-keh-tahs koo-ee-dah-doh-sah-mehn-teh

Child Care

I have (We have) _____ son/sons (_____ daughter/daughters).
Yo tengo (Nosotros tenemos) _____ hijo/hijos (_____ hija/hijas).
yoh tehn-goh (noh-soh-trohs teh-neh-mohs) _____ ee-hoh/ee-hohs (_____ ee-hah/ee-hahs)

I don't have (We don't have) any sons (daughters).
No tengo (No tenemos) hijos (hijas).
noh tehn-goh (noh teh-neh-mohs) ee-hohs (ee-hahs)

_____ is _____ years old.
_____ tiene _____ años.
_____ tee-eh-neh _____ ah-nyohs

Note

The following sections are organized by age group—infants and toddlers, children, and adolescents. There may be overlap, so if you don't find what you're looking for in one section, check the other sections. For example, we place sentences dealing with sports teams and musical instruments in the section on adolescents, but your younger child may play some of those sports or instruments, too.

Infants and Toddlers

Here is (are) the baby's _____.
Aquí está (están) _____ del bebé.
ah-kee ehs-tah (ehs-tahn) _____ dehl beh-beh

bassinet	**el bacinete**	*ehl bah-see-neh-teh*
bathtub	**la bañerita**	*lah bah-nyeh-ree-tah*
bib	**el babero**	*ehl bah-beh-roh*
blanket	**la cobija**	*lah koh-bee-hah*
booties	**los escarpines**	*lohs ehs-kahr-pee-nehs*
bottle	**el biberón**	*ehl bee-beh-rohn*
bottle warmer	**el calentador de botellas**	*ehl kah-lehn-tah-dohr deh boh-teh-yahs*
car seat	**el asiento de seguridad para niños**	*ehl ah-see-ehn-toh deh seh-goo-ree-dahd pah-rah nee-nyohs*
carriage	**el cochecito**	*ehl koh-cheh-see-toh*
carrier	**el portabebés**	*ehl pohr-tah-beh-behs*
changing table	**la mesa de muda**	*lah meh-sah deh moo-dah*
clothing	**la ropa**	*lah rroh-pah*
crib	**la cuna**	*lah koo-nah*
diaper	**el pañal**	*ehl pah-nyahl*
diaper bag	**la pañalera**	*lah pah-nyah-leh-rah*
doll	**la muñeca**	*lah moo-nyeh-kah*
dressing table	**la cómoda**	*lah koh-moh-dah*
feeding dish	**el plato**	*ehl plah-toh*
food	**la comida**	*lah koh-mee-dah*

highchair	la silla alta para niños	lah see-yah ahl-tah pah-rah nee-nyohs
lotion	la loción	lah loh-see-ohn
milk	la leche	lah leh-cheh
oil	el aceite	ehl ah-seh-ee-teh
pacifier	el chupete	ehl choo-peh-teh
plastic pants	los pantalones plásticos	lohs pahn-tah-loh-nehs plahs-tee-kohs
playpen	el corral	ehl koh-rrahl
potty	el orinal de niño	ehl oh-ree-nahl deh nee-nyoh
powder	el talco	ehl tahl-koh
rattle	el sonajero	ehl soh-nah-heh-roh
rubber sheet	la sábana de goma	lah sah-bah-nah deh goh-mah
safety pins	los imperdibles	lohs eem-pehr-dee-blehs
shampoo	el champú	ehl chahm-poo
soap	el jabón	ehl hah-bohn
stroller	el cochecillo	ehl koh-cheh-see-yoh
stuffed animal	el animal de peluche	ehl ah-nee-mahl deh peh-loo-cheh
swing	el columpio	ehl koh-loom-pee-oh
toy	el juguete	ehl hoo-geh-teh
training pants	los calzones para entrenar	lohs kahl-soh-nehs pah-rah ehn-treh-nahr
walker	el andador	ehl ahn-dah-dohr
wipes	las toallitas desechables	lahs toh-ah-yee-tahs deh-seh-chah-blehs

Please bathe him (her).
Favor de bañarlo (bañarla).
fah-bohr deh bah-nyahr-loh (bah-nyahr-lah)

Please burp him (her).
Favor de hacerlo (hacerla) eructar.
fah-bohr deh ah-sehr-loh (ah-sehr-lah) eh-rook-tahr

Please change his/her diaper frequently.
Favor de cambiar el pañal regularmente.
fah-bohr deh kahm-bee-ahr ehl pah-nyahl rreh-goo-lahr-mehn-teh

Please don't let him (her) put foreign objects in his/her mouth.
Favor de no dejarlo (dejarla) ponerse objetos en la boca.
fah-bohr deh noh deh-hahr-loh (deh-hahr-lah) poh-nehr-seh ohb-heh-tohs ehn lah boh-kah

Please dress him (her).
Favor de vestirlo (vestirla).
fah-bohr deh behs-teer-loh (behs-teer-lah)

Please feed him/her.
Favor de darle de comer.
fah-bohr deh dahr-leh deh koh-mehr

Please (do not) give him/her his/her pacifier all the time.
Favor de (no) darle el chupete todo el tiempo.
fah-bohr deh (noh) dahr-leh ehl choo-peh-teh toh-doh ehl tee-ehm-poh

Please hold him (her) when he/she cries.
Favor de cogerlo (cogerla) al hombro cuando llore.
fah-bohr deh koh-hehr-loh (koh-hehr-lah) ahl ohm-broh koo-ahn-doh yoh-reh

Please keep all dangerous substances out of his/her reach.
Favor de mantener todas las sustancias peligrosas fuera de su alcance.
fah-bohr deh mahn-teh-nehr toh-dahs lahs soos-tahn-see-ahs peh-lee-groh-sahs foo-eh-rah deh soo ahl-kahn-seh

Please (don't) let him (her) suck his/her thumb.
Favor de (no) dejarlo (dejarla) chuparse el dedo.
fah-bohr deh (noh) deh-hahr-loh (deh-hahr-lah) choo-pahr-seh ehl deh-doh

Please put him/her to sleep on his/her back (on his/her side).
Favor de acostarlo/acostarla boca arriba (de lado).
fah-bohr deh ah-kohs-tahr-loh/ah-kohs-tahr-lah boh-kah ah-rree-bah (deh lah-doh)

Please rock him (her) in a rocking chair.
Favor de mecerlo (mecerla) en la mecedora.
fah-bohr deh meh-sehr-loh (meh-sehr-lah) ehn lah meh-seh-doh-rah

Please (don't) wake him (her).
Favor de (no) despertarlo (despertarla).
fah-bohr deh (noh) dehs-pehr-tahr-loh (dehs-pehr-tahr-lah)

Please wash his/her clothing with a gentle detergent.
Favor de lavar la ropa con un detergente suave.
fah-bohr deh lah-bahr lah rroh-pah kohn oon deh-tehr-gehn-teh soo-ah-beh

Please watch him (her) very carefully.
Favor de vigilarlo (vigilarla) con cuidado.
fah-bohr deh bee-hee-lahr-loh (bee-hee-lahr-lah) kohn koo-ee-dah-doh

He (She) needs to be toilet trained.
Él (Ella) necesita aprender a usar el inodoro.
ehl (eh-yah) neh-seh-see-tah ah-prehn-dehr ah oo-sahr ehl een-oh-doh-roh

Children

> **Note**
>
> Use the direct object pronoun **lo** to express *him* when
> you are speaking about one male. Use **los** to express
> *them* when you are speaking about more than one
> male or a group of females and males. Use the direct
> object pronoun **la** to express *her* when you are speaking
> about one female. Use **las** to express *them* when you are
> speaking about more than one female. Use the indirect
> object **le** to express *to/for him/her*. And use **les** to express
> *to/for them* when speaking about more than one person,
> whether male or female.

Please keep chemicals (cleaning agents, matches, pills, plastic bags)
out of his/her reach.
**Favor de mantener los productos químicos (los limpiadores,
los fósforos, las píldoras, las bolsas plásticas) fuera de su
alcance.**
*fah-bohr deh mahn-teh-nehr lohs proh-dook-tohs kee-mee-kohs (lohs leem-
pee-ah-doh-rehs, lohs fohs-foh-rohs, lahs peel-doh-rahs, lahs bohl-sahs plahs-
tee-kahs) foo-eh-rah deh soo ahl-kahn-seh*

He (She) must not touch (use) the (microwave) oven.
Él (Ella) no debe tocar (usar) el microondas.
ehl (eh-yah) noh deh-beh toh-kahr (oo-sahr) ehl mee-kroh-ohn-dahs

Please keep him (her, them) away from electrical outlets.
Favor de mantenerlo (mantenerla, mantenerlos, mantenerlas) alejado (alejada, alejados, alejadas) de los enchufes.
fah-bohr deh mahn-teh-nehr-loh (mahn-teh-nehr-lah, mahn-teh-nehr-lohs, mahn-teh-nehr-lahs) ah-leh-hah-doh (ah-leh-hah-dah, ah-leh-hah-dohs, ah-leh-hah-dahs) deh lohs ehn-choo-fehs

He (She) must (always) play quietly.
Él (Ella) (siempre) debe jugar tranquilamente.
ehl (eh-yah) (see-ehm-preh) deh-beh hoo-gahr trahn-kee-lah-mehn-teh

He (She) must (always) put away his/her toys.
Él (Ella) (siempre) debe guardar los juguetes.
ehl (eh-yah) (see-ehm-preh) deh-beh goo-ahr-dahr lohs hoo-geh-tehs

He (She) must (always) share.
Él (Ella) (siempre) debe compartir sus cosas.
ehl (eh-yah) (see-ehm-preh) deh-beh kohm-pah-teer soos koh-sahs

He (She) must (always) wash his/her hands after using the bathroom.
Él (Ella) (siempre) debe lavarse las manos después de usar el baño.
ehl (eh-yah) (see-ehm-preh) deh-beh lah-bahr-seh lahs mah-nohs dehs-poo-ehs deh oo-sahr ehl bah-nyoh

He (She) must (always) brush his/her teeth after breakfast and before bed.
Él (Ella) (siempre) debe cepillarse los dientes después de desayunarse y antes de acostarse.
ehl (eh-yah) (see-ehm-preh) deh-beh seh-pee-yahr-seh lohs dee-ehn-tehs dehs-poo-ehs deh deh-sah-yoo-nahr-seh ee ahn-tehs deh ah-kohs-tahr-seh

He (She) must (always) take a bath or a shower every day.
Él (Ella) (siempre) debe bañarse o ducharse todos los días.
ehl (eh-yah) (see-ehm-preh) deh-beh bah-nyahr-seh oh doo-chahr-seh toh-dohs lohs dee-ahs

Please supervise him (her) when he (she) takes a bath.
Favor de supervisarlo (supervisarla) cuando él (ella) se bañe.
fah-bohr deh soo-pehr-bee-sahr-loh (soo-pehr-bee-sahr-lah) koo-ahn-doh ehl (eh-yah) seh bah-nyeh

Please supervise him (her) when he (she) takes a shower.
Favor de supervisarlo (supervisarla) cuando él (ella) se duche.
fah-bohr deh soo-pehr-bee-sahr-loh (soo-pehr-bee-sahr-lah) koo-ahn-doh ehl
(eh-yah) seh doo-cheh

He (She) must (always) do his/her homework before (after) dinner.
Él (Ella) (siempre) debe hacer la tarea antes (después) de cenar.
ehl (eh-yah) (see-ehm-preh) deh-beh ah-sehr lah tah-reh-ah ahn-tehs (dehs-
poo ehs) doh soh nahr

Please supervise him (her) when he (she) does his/her homework.
Favor de supervisarlo (supervisarla) cuando él (ella) haga su
tarea.
fah-bohr deh soo-pehr-bee-sahr-loh (soo-pehr-bee-sahr-lah) koo-ahn-doh ehl
(eh-yah) ah-gah soo tah-reh-ah

He (She) must (always) go to bed at _____ on school nights
(weekends).
Él (Ella) (siempre) debe acostarse a las _____ los días
laborables (los fines de semana).
ehl (eh-yah) (see-ehm-preh) deh-beh ah-kohs-tahr-seh ah lahs _____ lohs
dee-ahs lah-boh-rah-blehs (lohs fee-nehs deh seh-mah-nah)

He (She) must (always) ask permission.
Él (Ella) (siempre) debe pedir permiso.
ehl (eh-yah) (see-ehm-preh) deh-beh peh-deer pehr-mee-soh

He (She) must (always) have good manners.
Él (Ella) (siempre) debe tener buenos modales.
ehl (eh-yah) (see-ehm-preh) deh-beh teh-nehr boo-eh-nohs moh-dah-lehs

He (She) must (always) finish his/her chores.
Él (Ella) (siempre) debe terminar los quehaceres.
ehl (eh-yah) (see-ehm-preh) deh-beh tehr-mee-nahr lohs keh-ah-seh-rehs

He (She) must (always) keep his/her room neat (clean).
Él (Ella) (siempre) debe mantener ordenado (limpio) su cuarto.
ehl (eh-yah) (see-ehm-preh) deh-beh mahn-teh-nehr ohr-dehn-ah-doh (leem-
pee-oh) soo koo-ahr-toh

He (She) must (always) make his/her bed.
Él (Ella) (siempre) debe tender la cama.
ehl (eh-yah) (see-ehm-preh) deh-beh tehn-dehr lah kah-mah

He (She) must (always) pick up his/her clothes.
Él (Ella) (siempre) debe recoger la ropa.
ehl (eh-yah) (see-ehm-preh) deh-beh rreh-koh-hehr lah rroh-pah

He (She) must (always) wake up by _____ on school days (weekends).
Él (Ella) (siempre) debe despertarse a las _____ los días laborables (los fines de semana).
ehl (eh-yah) (see-ehm-preh) deh-beh dehs-pehr-tahr-seh ah lahs _____ lohs dee-ahs lah-boh-rah-blehs (lohs fee-nehs deh seh-mah-nah)

He (She) must not misbehave.
Él (Ella) no debe portarse mal.
ehl (eh-yah) noh deh-beh pohr-tahr-seh mahl

He (She) must not bite.
Él (Ella) no debe morder.
ehl (eh-yah) noh deh-beh mohr-dehr

He (She) must not hit.
Él (Ella) no debe golpear.
ehl (eh-yah) noh deh-beh gohl-peh-ahr

He (She) must not kick.
Él (Ella) no debe patear.
ehl (eh-yah) noh deh-beh pah-teh-ahr

He (She) must not push.
Él (Ella) no debe empujar.
ehl (eh-yah) noh deh-beh ehm-poo-hahr

He (She) must not scream.
Él (Ella) no debe gritar.
ehl (eh-yah) noh deh-beh gree-tahr

He (She) must not run.
Él (Ella) no debe correr.
ehl (eh-yah) noh deh-beh koh-rrehr

He (She) must not ride his/her bike without a helmet.
Él (Ella) no debe montar en bicicleta sin casco.
ehl (eh-yah) noh deh-beh mohn-tahr ehn bee-see-kleh-tah seen kahs-koh

He (She) must not make a mess.
Él (Ella) no debe ensuciar nada.
ehl (eh-yah) noh deh-beh ehn-soo-see-ahr nah-dah

He (She) must not eat too many sweets.
Él (Ella) no debe comer demasiados dulces.
ehl (eh-yah) noh deh-beh koh-mehr deh-mah-see-ah-dohs dool-sehs

He (She) must not argue.
Él (Ella) no debe discutir.
ehl (eh-yah) noh deh-beh dees-koo-teer

He (She) must not fight.
Él (Ella) no debe pelear.
ehl (eh-yah) noh deh-beh peh-leh-ahr

He (She) likes to swim.
A él (ella) le gusta nadar.
ah ehl (eh-yah) leh goos-tah nah-dahr.

He (She) must not swim by himself (herself).
Él (Ella) no debe nadar solo (sola).
ehl (eh-yah) noh deh-beh nah-dahr soh-loh (soh-lah)

He (She) likes to go to the park (the playground).
A él (ella) le gusta ir al parque (al patio de recreo).
ah ehl (eh-yah) leh goos-tah eer ahl pahr-keh (ahl pah-tee-oh deh rreh-kreh-oh)

Please supervise him (her) when he (she) plays in the playground.
Favor de supervisarlo (supervisarla) cuando él (ella) juegue en el patio de recreo.
fah-bohr deh soo-pehr-bee-sahr-loh (soo-pehr-bee-sahr-lah) koo-ahn-doh ehl (eh-yah) hoo-eh-geh ehn ehl pah-tee-oh deh rreh-kreh-oh

He (She) must not talk to strangers.
Él (Ella) no debe hablar con desconocidos.
ehl (eh-yah) noh deh-beh ah-blahr kohn dehs-koh-noh-see-dohs

Please check on him (her, them).
Favor de supervisarlo (supervisarla, supervisarlos, supervisarlas).
fah-bohr deh soo-pehr-bee-sahr-loh (soo-pehr-bee-sahr-lah, soo-pehr-bee-sahr-lohs, soo-pehr-bee-sahr-lahs)

Please don't leave him (her, them) alone.
Favor de no dejarlo (dejarla, dejarlos, dejarlas) solo (sola, solos, solas).
fah-bohr deh noh deh-hahr-loh (deh-hahr-lah, deh-hahr-lohs, deh-hahr-lahs)
soh-loh (soh-lah, soh-lohs, soh-lahs)

He (She) likes to color.
A él (ella) le gusta colorear.
ah ehl (eh-yah) leh goos-tah koh-loh-reh-ahr

He (She) likes to do puzzles.
A él (ella) le gusta hacer rompecabezas.
ah ehl (eh-yah) leh goos-tah ah-sehr rrohm-peh-kah-beh-sahs

He (She) likes to jump rope.
A él (ella) le gusta saltar la cuerda.
ah ehl (eh-yah) leh goos-tah sahl-tahr lah koo-ehr-dah

He (She) likes to fly a kite.
A él (ella) le gusta volar cometas.
ah ehl (eh-yah) leh goos-tah boh-lahr koh-meh-tahs

He (She) likes to make model cars (airplanes).
A él (ella) le gusta hacer modelos de coches (aviones).
ah ehl (eh-yah) leh goos-tah ah-sehr moh-deh-lohs deh koh-chehs
(ah-bee-oh-nehs)

He (She) likes to play _____.
A él (ella) le gusta jugar _____.
ah ehl (eh-yah) leh goos-tah hoo-gahr _____

with blocks	**con bloques**	*kohn bloh-kehs*
board games	**juegos de mesa**	*hoo-eh-gohs deh meh-sah*
cards	**a los naipes**	*ah lohs nah-ee-pehs*
checkers	**a las damas**	*ah lahs dah-mahs*
chess	**al ajedrez**	*ahl ah-heh-drehs*
computer games	**juegos de computadora**	*hoo-eh-gohs deh kohm-poo-tah-doh-rah*
with dolls	**con muñecas**	*kohn moo-nyeh-kahs*
dominoes	**a los dominós**	*ah lohs doh-mee-nohs*
with toy cars (trains, trucks)	**con coches (trenes, camiones) de juguete**	*kohn koh-chehs (treh-nehs, kah-mee-oh-nehs) deh hoo-geh-teh*
video games	**juegos de video**	*hoo-eh-gohs deh bee-deh-oh*

He (She) likes to play sports.
A él (ella) le gusta practicar deportes.
ah ehl (eh-yah) leh goos-tah prahk-tee-kahr deh-pohr-tehs

He (She) likes to read.
A él (ella) le gusta leer.
ah ehl (eh-yah) leh goos-tah leh-ehr

He (She) likes to ride a bicycle.
A él (ella) le gusta montar en bicicleta.
ah ehl (eh-yah) leh goos-tah mohn-tahr ehn bee-see-kleh-tah

He (She) likes to rollerskate (iceskate, rollerblade).
A él (ella) le gusta patinar sobre ruedas (patinar sobre hielo, patinar con patines de ruedas en línea).
ah ehl (eh-yah) leh goos-tah pah-tee-nahr soh-breh rroo-eh-dahs (pah-tee-nahr soh-breh ee-eh-loh, pah-tee-nahr kohn pah-tee-nehs ehn lee-neh-ah)

He (She) likes to watch television (movies).
A él (ella) le gusta mirar la tele (las películas).
ah ehl (eh-yah) leh goos-tah mee-rahr lah teh-leh (lahs peh-lee-koo-lahs)

He (She) likes to watch cartoons.
A él (ella) le gusta mirar los dibujos animados.
ah ehl (eh-yah) leh goos-tah mee-rahr lohs dee-boo-hohs ah-nee-mah-dohs

He (She) must not watch _____ on TV.
Él (Ella) no debe mirar _____ en la televisión.
ehl (eh-yah) noh deh-beh mee-rahr _____ ehn lah teh-leh-bee-see-ohn

Please pick him (her) up after school at _____ o'clock.
Favor de recogerlo (recogerla) después de la escuela a las _____.
fah-bohr deh rreh-koh-hehr-loh (rreh-koh-hehr-lah) dehs-poo-ehs deh lah ehs-koo-eh-lah ah lahs _____

Please supervise him (her) when he (she) plays on the computer.
Favor de supervisarlo (supervisarla) cuando él (ella) juegue en la computadora.
fah-bohr deh soo-pehr-bee-sahr-loh (soo-pehr-bee-sahr-lah) koo-ahn-doh ehl (eh-yah) hoo-eh-geh ehn lah kohm-poo-tah-doh-rah

Please supervise him (her) when he (she) plays video games.
Favor de supervisarlo (supervisarla) cuando él (ella) juegue los videojuegos.
fah-bohr deh soo-pehr-bee-sahr-loh (soo-pehr-bee-sahr-lah) koo-ahn-doh ehl (eh-yah) hoo-eh-geh lohs bee-deh-oh-hoo-eh-gohs

Please leave the nightlight on in his/her room.
Favor de dejar la luz de noche encendida en su cuarto.
fah-bohr deh deh-hahr lah loos deh noh-cheh ehn-sehn-dee-dah ehn soo koo-ahr-toh

Please pack his/her lunch in his/her lunchbox every day (except ____).
Favor de poner su almuerzo en su fiambrera cada día (menos ____).
fah-bohr deh poh-nehr soo ahl-moo-ehr-soh ehn soo fee-ahm-breh-rah kah-dah dee-ah (meh-nohs ____)

Adolescents

He (She) has a ____ o'clock curfew on school nights (weekends).
Él (Ella) tiene toque de queda a las ____ los días laborables (los fines de semana).
ehl (eh-yah) tee-eh-neh toh-que deh keh-dah ah lahs ____ lohs dee-ahs lah-boh-rah-blehs (lohs fee-nehs deh seh-mah-nah)

He (She) must not curse.
Él (Ella) no debe maldecir.
ehl (eh-yah) noh deh-beh mahl-deh-seer

He (She) must not smoke.
Él (Ella) no debe fumar.
ehl (eh-yah) noh deh-beh foo-mahr

He (She) must not drink alcohol.
Él (Ella) no debe beber alcohol.
ehl (eh-yah) noh deh-beh beh-behr ahl-koh-ohl

He (She) must not use drugs.
Él (Ella) no debe usar drogas.
ehl (eh-yah) no deh-beh oo-sahr droh-gahs

He/She must (always) treat others with respect.
Él/Ella (siempre) debe tratar a los demás con respeto.
ehl/eh-yah (see-ehm-preh) deh-beh trah-tahr ah lohs deh-mahs kohn
rrehs-peh-toh

He (She) plays _____.
Él (Ella) juega al _____.
ehl (eh-yah) hoo-eh-gah ahl _____

baseball	**béisbol**	*beh-ees-bohl*
basketball	**básquetbol**	*bahs-keht-bohl*
field hockey	**hockey**	*oh-kee*
football	**fútbol americano**	*foot-bohl ah-meh-ree-kah-noh*
golf	**golf**	*gohlf*
ice hockey	**hockey sobre hielo**	*oh-kee soh-breh ee-eh-loh*
lacrosse	**lacrosse**	*lah-krohs*
rugby	**rugby**	*rroog-bee*
soccer	**fútbol**	*foot-bohl*
softball	**sófbol**	*sohf-bohl*
tennis	**tenis**	*teh-nees*
volleyball	**voleibol**	*boh-leh-ee-bohl*
water polo	**polo acuático**	*poh-loh ah-koo-ah-tee-koh*

He (She) participates in _____.
Él (Ella) participa en _____.
ehl (eh-yah) pahr-tee-see-pah ehn _____

cheerleading	**echar porras**	*eh-chahr poh-rrahs*
cross-country	**carrera a campo traviesa**	*kah-rreh-rah ah kahm-poh trah-bee-eh-sah*
swimming	**natación**	*nah-tah-see-ohn*
track	**atletismo**	*aht-leh-tees-moh*
wrestling	**lucha libre**	*loo-chah lee-breh*

He (She) plays _____.
Él (Ella) toca _____.
ehl (eh-yah) toh-kah _____

the bassoon	**el fagote**	*ehl fah-goh-teh*
the cello	**el violonchelo**	*ehl bee-oh-leen-cheh-loh*
the clarinet	**el clarinete**	*ehl klah-ree-neh-teh*

the bass	**el violón**	*ehl bee-oh-lohn*
the drums	**la batería**	*lah bah-teh-ree-ah*
the flute	**la flauta**	*lah flah-oo-tah*
the French horn	**la trompa**	*lah trohm-pah*
the guitar	**la guitarra**	*lah gee-tah-rrah*
the harp	**el arpa**	*ehl ahr-pah*
the oboe	**el oboe**	*ehl oh-boh-eh*
percussion instruments	**los instrumentos de percusión**	*lohs een-stroo-mehn-tohs deh pehr-koo-see-ohn*
the piano	**el piano**	*ehl pee-ah-noh*
the piccolo	**el flautín**	*ehl flah-oo-teen*
the saxophone	**el saxofón**	*ehl sahk-soh-fohn*
the trombone	**el trombón**	*ehl trohm-bohn*
the trumpet	**la trompeta**	*lah trohm-peh-tah*
the tuba	**la tuba**	*lah too-bah*
the viola	**la viola**	*lah bee-oh-lah*
the violin	**el violín**	*ehl bee-oh-leen*

He (She) likes to paint.
A él (ella) le gusta pintar.
ah ehl (eh-yah) leh goos-tah peen-tahr

He (She) likes to draw.
A él (ella) le gusta dibujar.
ah ehl (eh-yah) leh goos-tah dee-boo-hahr

He (She) likes to skateboard.
A él (ella) le gusta montar en monopatín.
ah ehl (eh-yah) leh goos-tah mohn-tahr ehn moh-noh-pah-teen

Elder Care

My mother (father, grandmother, grandfather, aunt, uncle, sister, brother) needs constant care (help).
Mi madre (padre, abuela, abuelo, tía, tío, hermana, hermano) necesita cuidado (ayuda) constante.
mee mah-dreh (pah-dreh, ah-boo-eh-lah, ah-boo-eh-loh, tee-ah, tee-oh, ehr-mah-nah, ehr-mah-noh) neh-seh-see-tah koo-ee-dah-doh (ah-yoo-dah) kohn-stahn-teh

He (She) has just undergone surgery.
Él (Ella) acaba de tener cirugía.
ehl (eh-yah) ah-kah-bah deh teh-nehr see-roo-hee-ah

He (She) is very weak.
Él (Ella) está muy débil.
ehl (eh-yah) ehs-tah moo-ee deh-beel

He (She) is immobile.
Él (Ella) está inmóvil.
ehl (eh-yah) ehs-tah een-moh-beel

He (She) can't get around well.
Él (Ella) no puede moverse bien.
ehl (eh-yah) noh poo-eh-deh moh-behr-seh bee-ehn

He (She) has a restricted diet.
Él (Ella) tiene una dieta restringida.
ehl (eh-yah) tee-eh-neh oo-nah dee-eh-tah rrehs-treen-gee-dah

He (She) takes pills for high blood pressure (cholesterol).
Él (Ella) toma píldoras para la hipertensión (el colesterol).
ehl (eh-yah) toh-mah peel-doh-rahs pah-rah lah ee-pehr-tehn-see-ohn (ehl koh-lehs-teh-rohl)

He (She) takes heart medication.
Él (Ella) toma medicina para el corazón.
ehl (eh-yah) toh-mah meh-dee-see-nah pah-rah ehl koh-rah-sohn

Why are you interested in providing home care?
¿Por qué le interesa prestar cuidado doméstico?
pohr keh leh een-teh-reh-sah prehs-tahr koo-ee-dah-doh doh-mehs-tee-koh

What kind of training have you had?
¿Qué clase de entrenamiento ha recibido usted?
keh klah-seh deh ehn-treh-nah-mee-ehn-toh ah rreh-see-bee-doh oo-stehd

Why did you leave your last position?
¿Por qué dejó usted su último empleo?
pohr-keh deh-hoh oo-stehd soo ool-tee-moh ehm-pleh-oh

Do you currently provide care for others?
Actualmente, ¿está usted cuidando a otras personas?
ahk-too-ahl-mehn-teh ehs-tah oo-stehd koo-ee-dahn-doh ah oh-trahs pehr-soh-nahs

For how long will you commit to this position?
¿Por cuánto tiempo puede usted comprometerse a este empleo?
pohr koo-ahn-toh tee-ehm-poh poo-eh-deh oo-stehd kohm-proh-meh-tehr-seh ah ehs-teh ehm-pleh-oh

Do you have any medical conditions?
¿Tiene usted alguna condición médica?
tee-eh-neh oo-stehd ahl-goo-nah kohn-dee-see-ohn meh-dee-kah

Are you willing to cook and (or) do light housekeeping?
¿Está dispuesto (dispuesta) a cocinar y (o) hacer la limpieza ligera de la casa?
ehs-tah dees-poo-ehs-toh (dees-poo-ehs-tah) ah koh-see-nahr ee (oh) ah-sehr lah leem-pee-eh-sah lee-heh-rah deh lah kah-sah

Can you run errands?
¿Puede hacer recados?
poo-eh-deh ah-sehr rreh-kah-dohs

Are you willing to drive my mother (father, grandmother, grandfather, aunt, uncle, sister, brother) to appointments?
¿Está dispuesto (dispuesta) a llevar a mi madre (padre, abuela, abuelo, tía, tío, hermana, hermano) a las citas?
ehs-tah dees-poo-ehs-toh (dees-poo-ehs-tah) ah yeh-bahr ah mee mah-dreh (pah-dreh, ah-boo-eh-lah, ah-boo-eh-loh, tee-ah, tee-oh, ehr-mah-nah, ehr-mah-noh) ah lahs see-tahs

Are you willing to stay overnight if necessary?
¿Está dispuesto (dispuesta) a pasar la noche si es necesario?
ehs-tah dees-poo-ehs-toh (dees-poo-ehs-tah) ah pah-sahr lah noh-cheh see ehs neh-seh-sah-ree-oh

What will you do if you are ill and cannot come to work?
¿Qué hará si está enfermo (enferma) y no puede venir a trabajar?
keh ah-rah see ehs-tah ehn-fehr-moh (ehn-fehr-mah) ee noh poo-eh-deh beh-neer ah trah-bah-hahr

What will you do in case of an emergency?
¿Qué hará en caso de emergencia?
keh ah-rah ehn kah-soh deh eh-mehr-hehn-see-ah

Is your schedule flexible?
¿Es flexible su horario?
ehs flehk-see-bleh soo oh-rah-ree-oh

Please dress him (dress her).
Favor de vestirlo (vestirla).
fah-bohr deh behs-teer-loh (behs-teer-lah)

Please undress him (undress her).
Favor de desvestirlo (desvestirla).
fah-bohr deh dehs-behs-teer-loh (dehs-beh-teer-lah)

Please bathe him (bathe her).
Favor de bañarlo (bañarla).
fah-bohr deh bah-nyahr-loh (bah-nyahr-lah)

Please change his/her diaper frequently.
Favor de cambiarle el pañal a menudo.
fah-bohr deh kahm-bee-ahr-leh ehl pah-nyahl ah meh-noo-doh

Please feed him/her.
Favor de darle de comer.
fah-bohr deh dahr-leh deh koh-mehr

Please give him/her his/her medicine (pills, vitamins).
Favor de darle la medicina (las píldoras, las vitaminas).
*fah-bohr deh dahr-leh lah meh-dee-see-nah (lahs peel-doh-rahs, lahs
bee-tah-mee-nahs)*

Please help him (her) to the bathroom.
Favor de ayudarlo (ayudarla) a ir al baño.
fah-bohr deh ah-yoo-dahr-loh (ah-yoo-dahr-lah) ah eer ahl bah-nyoh

Please help him (her) take a shower.
Favor de ayudarlo (ayudarla) a ducharse.
fah-bohr deh ah-yoo-dahr-loh (ah-yoo-dahr-lah) ah doo-chahr-seh

Please help him (her) walk upstairs (downstairs).
Favor de ayudarlo (ayudarla) a subir (bajar) la escalera.
*fah-bohr deh ah-yoo-dahr-loh (ah-yoo-dahr-lah) ah soo-beer (bah-hahr) lah
ehs-kah-leh-rah*

Please let him (her) sleep (watch TV, listen to the radio).
Favor de dejarlo (dejarla) dormir (mirar la tele, escuchar la radio).
fah-bohr deh deh-hahr-loh (deh-hahr-lah) dohr-meer (mee-rahr lah teh-leh, ehs-koo-chahr lah rrah-dee-oh)

Please prepare his/her meals.
Favor de prepararle las comidas.
fah-bohr deh preh-pah-rahr-leh lahs koh-mee-dahs

Please send me his (her) bills.
Favor de mandarme sus cuentas.
fah-bohr deh mahn-dahr-meh soos koo-ehn-tahs

Please shave him.
Favor de afeitarlo.
fah-bohr deh ah-feh-ee-tahr-loh

Please take him (her) for a walk.
Favor de llevarlo (llevarla) a caminar.
fah-bohr deh yeh-bahr-loh (yeh-bahr-lah) ah kah-mee-nahr

Please take him (her) shopping.
Favor de llevarlo (llevarla) de compras.
fah-bohr deh yeh-bahr-loh (yeh-bahr-lah) deh kohm-prahs

Please take him (her) to the doctor.
Favor de llevarlo (llevarla) al médico.
fah-bohr deh yeh-bahr-loh (yeh-bahr-lah) ahl meh-dee-koh

He (She) eats breakfast at _____ o'clock.
Él (Ella) se desayuna a las _____.
ehl (eh-yah) seh deh-sah-yoo-nah ah lahs _____

He (She) eats lunch at _____ o'clock.
Él (Ella) almuerza a las _____.
ehl (eh-yah) ahl-moo-ehr-sah ah lahs _____

He (She) eats dinner at _____ o'clock.
Él (Ella) cena a las _____.
ehl (eh-yah) seh-nah ah lahs _____

Please call me if you need me.
Favor de llamarme si me necesita.
fah-bohr deh yah-mahr-meh see meh neh-seh-see-tah

Medical Care

My (Our) son (father, brother) is sick.
Mi (Nuestro) hijo (padre, hermano) está enfermo.
mee (noo-ehs-troh) ee-hoh (pah-dreh, ehr-mah-noh) ehs-tah ehn-fehr-moh

My (Our) daughter (mother, sister) is sick.
Mi (Nuestra) hija (madre, hermana) está enferma.
mee (noo-ehs-trah) ee-hah (mah-dreh, erh-mah-nah) ehs-tah ehn-fehr-mah

Symptoms

He (She) has the following symptoms:
Él (Ella) tiene los siguientes síntomas:
ehl (eh-yah) tee-eh-neh lohs see-gee-ehn-tehs seen-toh-mahs

> ### Note
> Most symptoms are talked about without the use of an
> indefinite article expressing *a* or *an*. If the symptom is
> modified by an adjective—for example **crónico
> (crónica)** — then the definite article is needed: **una
> tos crónica (a chronic cough)**. In the following list, all
> genders are indicated after the noun with an *m.* (mas-
> culine) or *f.* (feminine).

a cavity	**una caries** *(f.)*	*oo-nah kah-ree-ehs*
chills	**escalofríos** *(m. pl.)*	*ehs-kah-loh-free-ohs*
colic	**cólico** *(m.)*	*koh-lee-koh*
constipation	**estreñimiento** *(m.)*	*ehs-treh-nyee-mee-ehn-toh*
convulsions	**convulsiones** *(f. pl.)*	*kohn-bool-see-oh-nehs*
a cough	**tos** *(f.)*	*tohs*
depression	**depresión** *(f.)*	*deh-preh-see-ohn*
diarrhea	**diarrea** *(f.)*	*dee-ah-rreh-ah*
dizziness	**mareo** *(m.)*	*mah-reh-oh*
an earache	**dolor de oído** *(m.)*	*doh-lohr deh oh-ee-doh*
fatigue	**fatiga** *(f.)*	*fah-tee-gah*
a fever	**fiebre** *(f.)*	*fee-eh-breh*
a headache	**dolor de cabeza** *(m.)*	*doh-lohr deh kah-beh-sah*
high blood pressure	**presión alta** *(f.)*	*preh-see-ohn ahl-tah*

high cholesterol	colesterol alto (m.)	koh-lehs-teh-rohl ahl-toh
indigestion	indigestión (f.)	een-dee-hehs-tee-ohn
an infection	infección (f.)	een-fehk-see-ohn
nausea	náusea (f.)	nah-oo-seh-ah
pain	dolor (m.)	doh-lohr
phlegm	flema (m.)	fleh-mah
a rash	erupción (f.)	eh-roop-see-ohn
a sore throat	dolor (m.) de garganta	doh-lohr deh gahr-gahn-tah
a stomachache	dolor (m.) de estómago	doh-lohr deh ehs-toh-mah-goh
a toothache	dolor (m.) de muela	doh-lohr deh moo-eh-lah

He/She needs to see a doctor (dentist, surgeon).
Necesita ver al médico (dentista, cirujano).
neh-seh-see-tah behr ahl meh-dee-koh (dehn-tees-tah, see-roo-hah-noh)

He (She) is weak.
Él (Ella) está débil.
ehl (eh-yah) ehs-tah deh-beel

He (She) is unconscious (in shock).
Él (Ella) está inconsciente (en estado de conmoción).
ehl (eh-yah) ehs-tah een-kohn-see-ehn-teh (ehn ehs-tah-doh deh kohn-moh-see-ohn)

He (She) is vomiting (choking, gasping for air).
Él (Ella) está vomitando (asfixiándose, jadeando).
ehl (eh-yah) ehs-tah boh-mee-tahn-doh (ahs-feek-see-ahn-doh-seh, hah-deh-ahn-doh)

He (She) sneezes (coughs, wheezes) a lot.
Él (Ella) estornuda (tose, resuella) mucho.
ehl (eh-yah) ehs-tohr-noo-dah (toh-seh, rreh-soo-eh-yah) moo-choh

He (She) has an infection.
Él (Ella) tiene una infección.
ehl (eh-yah) tee-eh-neh oo-nah een-fehk-see-ohn

He (She) is (not) contagious.
Él (Ella) (no) está contagioso (contagiosa).
ehl (eh-yah) (noh) ehs-tah kohn-tah-hee-oh-soh (kohn-tah-hee-oh-sah)

He (She) has a heart condition (seizures).
Él (Ella) tiene una insuficiencia cardíaca (convulsiones).
ehl (eh-yah) tee-eh-neh oo-nah een-soo-fee-see-ehn-see-ah kahr-dee-ah-kah (kohn-bool-see-oh-nehs)

He (She) needs surgery.
Él (Ella) necesita cirugía.
ehl (eh-yah) neh-seh-see-tah see-roo-hee-ah

He (She) needs to have a cavity filled.
Él (Ella) necesita empastar una caries.
ehl (eh-yah) neh-seh-see-tah ehm-pahs-tahr oo nah kah-ree-ehs

He (She) needs to have a (wisdom) tooth pulled.
Él (Ella) necesita sacarse (una muela de juicio) un diente.
ehl (eh-yah) neh-seh-see-tah sah-kahr-seh (oo-nah moo-eh-lah deh hoo-ee-see-oh) oon dee-ehn-teh

He (She) has trouble _____.
Él (Ella) tiene problemas _____.
ehl (eh-yah) tee-eh-neh proh-bleh-mahs _____

English	Spanish	Pronunciation
breathing	**respirando**	*rrehs-pee-rahn-doh*
concentrating	**concentrándose**	*kohn-sehn-trahn-doh-seh*
eating (solid foods)	**comiendo (comidas sólidas)**	*koh-mee-ehn-doh (koh-mee-dahs soh-lee-dahs)*
expressing himself/herself	**expresándose**	*ehks-preh-sahn-doh-seh*
focusing	**enfocándose**	*ehn-foh-kahn-doh-seh*
going to the bathroom alone	**yendo al baño solo (sola)**	*yehn-doh ahl bah-nyoh soh-loh (soh-lah)*
hearing	**oyendo**	*oh-yehn-doh*
moving his/her arms (legs)	**moviéndo los brazos (las piernas)**	*moh-bee-ehn-doh lohs brah-sohs (lahs pee-ehr-nahs)*
paying attention	**prestando atención**	*prehs-tahn-doh ah-tehn-see-ohn*
remembering	**recordando**	*rreh-kohr-dahn-doh*
seeing	**viendo**	*bee-ehn-doh*
sleeping	**durmiendo**	*door-mee-ehn-doh*
speaking	**hablando**	*ah-blahn-doh*

spelling	**deletreando**	*deh-leh-treh-ahn-doh*
swallowing	**tragando**	*trah-gahn-doh*
thinking clearly	**pensando claramente**	*pehn-sahn-doh klah-rah-mehn-teh*
understanding	**comprendiendo**	*kohm-prehn-dee-ehn-doh*
walking	**caminando**	*kah-mee-nahn-doh*

His (Her) whole body hurts.
A él (ella) le duele todo el cuerpo.
ah ehl (eh-yah) leh doo-eh-leh toh-doh ehl koo-ehr-poh

He (She) needs physical therapy.
Él (Ella) necesita fisioterapia.
ehl (eh-yah) neh-seh-see-tah fee-see-oh-teh-rah-pee-ah

Allergies

He (She) has had an allergic reaction (a heart attack, a stroke).
Él (Ella) ha tenido una reacción alérgica (un ataque cardíaco, una apoplejía).
ehl (eh-yah) ah teh-nee-doh oo-nah rreh-ahk-see-ohn ah-lehr-hee-kah (oon ah-tah-keh kahr-dee-ah-koh, oo-nah ah-poh-pleh-hee-ah)

He/She may go into anaphylactic shock.
Es posible que tenga un choque anafiláctico.
ehs poh-see-bleh keh tehn-gah oon choh-keh ah-nah-fee-lahk-tee-koh

Let's go to the hospital.
Vamos al hospital.
bah-mohs ahl ohs-pee-tahl

He (She) is allergic _____.
Él (Ella) es alérgico (alérgica) _____.
ehl (eh-yah) ehs ah-lehr-hee-koh (ah-lehr-hee-kah) _____

to antibiotics	**a los antibióticos**	*ah lohs ahn-tee-bee-oh-tee-kohs*
to bee stings	**a las picaduras de abejas**	*ah lahs pee-kah-doo-rahs deh ah-beh-hahs*
to cats	**a los gatos**	*ah lohs gah-tohs*

to dogs	**a los perros**	*ah lohs peh-rrohs*
to dust	**al polvo**	*ahl pohl-boh*
to grass	**a la hierba**	*ah lah ee-ehr-bah*
to milk	**a la leche**	*ah lah leh-cheh*
to mold	**al moho**	*ahl moh-hoh*
to peanuts	**a los cacahuetes**	*ah lohs kah-kah-hoo-eh-tehs*
to penicillin	**a la penicilina**	*ah lah peh-nee-see-lee-nah*
to perfume	**al perfume**	*ahl pehr-foo-meh*
to pollen	**al polen**	*ahl poh-lehn*
to shellfish	**a los mariscos**	*ah lohs mah-rees-kohs*
to strawberries	**a las fresas**	*ah lahs freh-sahs*

Parts of the Body

He (She) has had an accident (an illness).
Él (Ella) ha tenido un accidente (una enfermedad).
ehl (eh-yah) ah teh-nee-doh oon ahk-see-dehn-teh (oo-nah ehn-fehr-meh-dahd)

He (She) fell and hit his/her _____.
Él (Ella) se cayó y se golpeó _____.
ehl (eh-yah) seh kah-yoh ee seh gohl-peh-oh _____

He (She) has a rash on his/her _____.
Él (Ella) tiene una erupción en _____.
ehl (eh-yah) tee-eh-neh oo-nah eh-roop-see-ohn ehn _____

His (Her) _____ hurt (hurts).
A él (ella) le duele (duelen) _____.
ah ehl (eh-yah) leh doo-eh-leh (doo-eh-lehn) _____

He (She) burned (cut) his/her _____.
Él (Ella) se quemó (se cortó) _____.
ehl (eh-yah) seh keh-moh (seh kohr-toh) _____

His/Her _____ is broken (sprained, swollen, bruised, infected).
Se rompió (torció, se hinchó, golpeó, infectó) _____.
seh rrohm-pee-oh (tohr-see-oh, seh een-choh, gohl-peh-oh, een-fehk-toh) _____

Parts of the Body

English	Spanish	Pronunciation
ankle	**el tobillo**	*ehl toh-bee-yoh*
arm	**el brazo**	*ehl brah-soh*
back	**la espalda**	*lah ehs-pahl-dah*
body	**el cuerpo**	*ehl koo-ehr-poh*
brain	**el cerebro**	*ehl seh-reh-broh*
cheek	**la mejilla**	*lah meh-hee-yah*
chest	**el pecho**	*ehl peh-choh*
chin	**la barbilla**	*lah bahr-bee-yah*
ear	**el oído**	*ehl oh-ee-doh*
elbow	**el codo**	*ehl koh-doh*
eye	**el ojo**	*ehl oh-hoh*
face	**la cara**	*lah kah-rah*
finger	**el dedo**	*ehl deh-doh*
foot	**el pie**	*ehl pee-eh*
forehead	**la frente**	*lah frehn-teh*
hand	**la mano**	*lah mah-noh*
head	**la cabeza**	*lah kah-beh-sah*
hip	**la cadera**	*lah kah-deh-rah*
knee	**la rodilla**	*lah rroh-dee-yah*
leg	**la pierna**	*lah pee-ehr-nah*
lip	**el labio**	*ehl lah-bee-oh*
mouth	**la boca**	*lah boh-kah*
neck	**el cuello**	*ehl koo-eh-yoh*
nose	**la nariz**	*lah nah-rees*
shoulder	**el hombro**	*ehl ohm-broh*
skin	**la piel**	*lah pee-ehl*
spine	**la espina dorsal**	*lah ehs-pee-nah dohr-sahl*
stomach	**el estómago**	*ehl ehs-toh-mah-goh*

English	Spanish	Pronunciation
throat	**la garganta**	*lah gahr-gahn-tah*
toe	**el dedo de pie**	*ehl deh-doh deh pee-eh*
tongue	**la lengua**	*lah lehn-goo-ah*
tooth	**el diente**	*ehl dee-ehn-teh*
wrist	**la muñeca**	*lah moo-nyeh-kah*

Please bandage (clean) the wound.
Favor de vendar (limpiar) la herida.
fah-bohr deh behn-dahr (leem-pee-ahr) lah eh-ree-dah

A dog (bat, raccoon) bit him (her).
Un perro (murciélago, mapache) lo (la) mordió.
oon peh-rroh (moor-see-eh-lah-goh, mah-pah-cheh) loh (lah) mohr-dee-oh

He (She) needs a tetanus (rabies) shot.
Él (Ella) necesita una vacuna contra el tétano (la rabia).
ehl (eh-yah) neh-seh-see-tah oo-nah bah-koo-nah kohn-trah ehl teh-tah-noh (lah rrah-bee-ah)

Medical Necessities

He (She) needs _____.
Él (Ella) necesita _____.
ehl (eh-yah) neh-seh-see-tah

a bandage	**una venda**	*oo-nah behn-dah*
books written in Braillle	**libros escritos en Braille**	*lee-brohs ehs-kree-tohs ehn Braille*
braces (for the teeth)	**frenillos**	*freh-nee-yohs*
a cane	**un bastón**	*oon bahs-tohn*
a cast	**un yeso**	*oon yeh-soh*
contact lenses	**lentes de contacto**	*lehn-tehs deh kohn-tahk-toh*
crutches	**muletas**	*moo-leh-tahs*
glasses	**gafas**	*gah-fahs*
a hearing aid	**un audífono**	*oon ah-oo-dee-foh-noh*
large-type books	**libros escritos con letra grande**	*lee-brohs ehs-kree-tohs kohn leh-trah grahn-deh*

a leg brace	un aparato ortopédico para la pierna	*oon ah-pah-rah-toh ohr-toh-peh-dee-koh pah-rah lah pee-ehr-nah*
a Seeing Eye dog	un perro guía	*oon peh-rroh gee-ah*
stitches	puntos	*poon-tohs*
a walker	un andador	*oon ahn-dah-dohr*
a wheelchair	una silla de ruedas	*oo-nah see-yah deh rroo-eh-dahs*

He (She) is blind (deaf, mute, paralyzed).
Él (Ella) es ciego (ciega) (sordo [sorda], mudo [muda], paralítico [paralítica]).
ehl (eh-yah) ehs see-eh-goh (see-eh-gah) (sohr-doh [sohr-dah], moo-doh [moo-dah], pah-rah-lee-tee-koh [pah-rah-lee-tee-kah])

Do you know sign language?
¿Conoce usted el lenguaje de señas?
koh-noh-seh oo-stehd ehl lehn-goo-ah-heh deh seh-nyahs

Illness and Ailments

My child has special needs.
Mi hijo (hija) tiene necesidades especiales.
mee ee-hoh (ee-hah) tee-eh-neh neh-seh-see-dah-dehs ehs-peh-see-ah-lehs

He (She) has _____.
Él (Ella) tiene _____.
ehl (eh-yah) tee-eh-neh _____

Have you had experience caring for a child (person) with _____?
¿Ha tenido usted experiencia cuidando a niños (a gente) con _____?
ah teh-nee-doh oo-stehd ehks-peh-ree-ehn-see-ah koo-ee-dahn-doh ah nee-nyohs (ah hehn-teh) kohn _____

> ## Note
> Many of the following illnesses wouldn't normally rquire a definite article expressing *the* or an indefinite article expressing *a* or *an*. Where necessary, the article is used. All genders are indicated after the noun with an *m.* (masculine) or *f.* (feminine).

appendicitis	**apendicitis (f.)**	*ah-pehn-dee-see-tees*
asthma	**asma (f. but takes m. article)**	*ahs-mah*
an attention deficit disorder (with hyperactivity)	**un desorden de déficit de atención (con hiperactividad) (m.)**	*oon deh-sohr-dehn deh deh-fee-seet deh ah-tehn-see-ohn (kohn ee-pehr-ahk-tee-bee-dahd)*
autism	**autismo (m.)**	*ah-oo-tees-moh*
bipolar disorder	**un trastorno bipolar (m.)**	*oon trahs-tohr-noh bee-poh-lahr*
bronchitis	**bronquitis (f.)**	*brohn-kee-tees*
cancer	**cancer (m.)**	*kahn-sehr*
cerebral palsy	**parálisis cerebral (f.)**	*pah-rah-lee-sees seh-reh-brahl*
chicken pox	**varicela (f.)**	*bah-ree-seh-lah*
a cold	**un catarro (m.)**	*oon kah-tah-rroh*
a concussion	**una conmoción (f.) cerebral**	*oo-nah kohn-moh-see-ohn seh-reh-brahl*
cystic fibrosis	**fibrosis cística (f.)**	*fee-broh-sees sees-tee-kah*
diabetes	**diabetes (f.)**	*dee-ah-beh-tehs*
Down syndrome	**síndrome (m.) de Down**	*ehl seen-droh-meh deh down*
dyslexia	**dislexia (f.)**	*dees-lehk-see-ah*
epilepsy	**epilepsia (f.)**	*eh-pee-lehp-see-ah*
the flu	**gripe (f.)**	*gree-peh*
a genetic disease	**una enfermedad (f.) genética**	*oo-nah ehn-fehr-meh-dahd heh-neh-tee-kah*
gout	**gota (f.)**	*goh-tah*
hay fever	**fiebre del heno (f.)**	*fee-eh-breh dehl eh-noh*
hepatitis	**hepatitis (f.)**	*eh-pah-tee-tees*
hyperactivity	**hiperactividad (f.)**	*ee-pehr-ahk-tee-bee-dahd*
leukemia	**leucemia (f.)**	*leh-oo-seh-mee-ah*
measles	**sarampión (m.)**	*ehl sah-rahm-pee-ohn*
mononucleosis	**mononucleosis (f.)**	*moh-noh-noo-kleh-oh-sees*
multiple sclerosis	**esclerosis múltiple (f.)**	*ehs-kleh-roh-sees mool-tee-pleh*
the mumps	**paperas (f., pl.)**	*pah-peh-rahs*
muscular dystrophy	**distrofia muscular (f.)**	*dees-troh-fee-ah moos-koo-lahr*

a neurological disease	**una enfermedad (f.) neurológica**	*oo-nah ehn-fehr-meh-dahd neh-oo-roh-loh-hee-kah*
a personality disorder	**un trastorno (m.) de la personalidad**	*oon trahs-tohr-noh deh lah pehr-soh-nah-lee-dahd*
pneumonia	**pulmonía (f.)**	*pool-moh-nee-ah*
rubella	**rubiola (f.)**	*rroo-bee-oh-lah*
a sore throat	**un dolor (m.) de garganta**	*oon doh-lohr deh gahr-gahn-tah*
tonsilitis	**amigdalitis (f.)**	*ah-meeg-dah-lee-tees*
an ulcer	**una úlcera (f.)**	*oo-nah ool-seh-rah*
a virus	**un virus (m.)**	*oon bee-roos*

Treatments

Please give him/her _____.
Favor de darle _____.
fah-bohr deh dahr-leh _____

this antacid	**este antiácido**	*ehs-teh ahn-tee-ah-see-doh*
this antibiotic	**este antibiótico**	*ehs-teh an-tee-bee-oh-tee-koh*
this antihistamine	**este antihistamínico**	*ehs-teh ahn-tee-ees-tah-mee-nee-koh*
this aspirin	**esta aspirina**	*ehs-tah ahs-pee-ree-nah*
this capsule	**esta cápsula**	*ehs-tah kahp-soo-lah*
this cough syrup	**este jarabe para la tos**	*ehs-teh hah-rah-beh pah-rah lah tohs*
this lozenge	**esta pastilla**	*ehs-tah pahs-tee-yah*
this inhaler	**este inhalador**	*ehs-teh een-ah-lah-dohr*
this nasal spray	**este spray nasal**	*ehs-teh ehspreh-ee nah-sahl*
this pill	**esta píldora**	*ehs-tah peel-doh-rah*
this tablet	**esta pastilla**	*ehs-tah pahs-tee-yah*

Please cut the pill (tablet) in half.
Favor de cortar la píldora (la pastilla) en dos.
fah-bohr deh kohr-tahr lah peel-doh-rah (lah pahs-tee-yah) ehn dohs

Please apply _____.
Favor de aplicar _____.
fah-bohr deh ah-plee-kahr _____

antiseptic	**este antiséptico**	*ehs-teh ahn-tee-sehp-tee koh*
cream	**esta crema**	*ehs-tah kreh-mah*
gel	**este gel**	*ehs-teh hehl*
lotion	**esta loción**	*ehs-tah loh-see-ohn*
ointment	**esta pomada**	*ehs-tah poh-mah-dah*
powder	**este polvo**	*ehs-teh pohl-boh*

Please give him/her a lot of liquids.
Favor de darle muchos líquidos.
fah-bohr deh dahr-leh moo-chohs lee-kee-dohs

He (She) needs to take _____.
Él (Ella) necesita tomar _____.
ehl (eh-yah) neh-seh-see-tah toh-mahr _____

Please give him/her one pill (two pills, a teaspoonful, a tablespoonful) _____.
Favor de darle una píldora (dos píldoras, una cucharadita, una cucharada) _____.
fah-bohr deh dahr-leh oo-nah peel-doh-rah (dohs peel-doh-rahs, oo-nah koo-chah-rah-dee-tah, oo-nah koo-chah-rah-dah) _____

every _____ hours	**cada _____ horas**	*kah-dah _____ oh-rahs*
once a day	**una vez al día**	*oo-nah behs ahl dee-ah*
_____ times a day	**_____ veces al día**	*_____ beh-sehs ahl dee-ah*
_____ times a week	**_____ veces a la semana**	*_____ beh-sehs ah lah seh-mah-nah*
in the morning	**por la mañana**	*pohr lah mah-nyah-nah*
in the afternoon	**por la tarde**	*pohr lah tahr-deh*
at night	**por la noche**	*pohr lah noh-cheh*
at bedtime	**antes de acostarse**	*ahn-tehs deh ah-kohs-tahr-seh*
with food	**con comida**	*kohn koh-mee-dah*
before breakfast (lunch, dinner)	**antes del desayuno (del almuerzo, de la cena)**	*ahn-tehs dehl dehs-ah-yoo-noh (dehl ahl-moo-ehr-soh, deh lah seh-nah)*
between meals	**entre comidas**	*ehn-treh koh-mee-dahs*

Are you CPR certified?

¿Está usted certificado (certificada) en CPR?

ehs-tah oo-stehd sehr-tee-fee-kah-doh (sehr-tee-fee-kah-dah) ehn seh peh eh-reh?

Please get this prescription filled at the pharmacy as soon as possible.

Favor de llenar esta receta en la farmacia lo más pronto posible.

fah-bohr deh yeh-nahr ehs-tah rreh-seh-tah ehn lah fahr-mah-see-ah loh mahs prohn-toh poh-see-bleh

Please take him (her) to the doctor (dentist, hospital).

Favor de llevarlo (llevarla) al médico (dentista, hospital).

fah-bohr deh yeh-bahr-loh (yeh-bahr-lah) ahl meh-dee-koh (dehn-tees-tah, ohs-pee-tahl)

Please come with us to the doctor (dentist, hospital).

Favor de venir con nosotros al médico (dentista, hospital).

fah-bohr deh beh-neer kohn noh-soh-trohs ahl meh-dee-koh (dehn-tees-tah, ohs-pee-tahl)

In case of an emergency, call me (my husband, my wife) immediately.

En caso de emergencia, favor de llamarme (llamar a mi esposo, a mi esposa) en seguida.

ehn kah-soh deh eh-mehr-heh-see-ah, fah-bohr deh yah-mahr-meh (yah-mahr a mee ehs-poh-soh, ah mee ehs-poh-sah) ehn seh-gee-dah

Please call for an ambulance.

Favor de llamar una ambulancia.

fah-bohr de yah-mahr oo-nah ahm-boo-lahn-see-ah

Please dial 911.

Favor de llamar al nueve once.

fah-bohr deh yah-mahr ahl noo-eh-beh ohn-seh

Pet Care

Do you like animals?

¿A usted le gustan los animales?

ah oo-stehd leh goos-tahn lohs ah-nee-mah-lehs

I have (We have) _____.
Tengo (Tenemos) _____.
tehn-goh (teh-neh-mohs) _____

a bird	**un pájaro**	*oon pah-hah-roh*
a canary	**un canario**	*oon kah-nah-ree-oh*
a cat	**un gato**	*oon gah-toh*
a dog	**un perro**	*oon peh-rroh*
a fish	**un pez**	*oon pehs*
a gerbil	**un jerbo**	*oon hehr-boh*
a goldfish	**un pez de colores**	*oon pehs deh koh-loh-rehs*
a guinea pig	**una cobaya**	*oo-nah koh-bah-yah*
a hamster	**un hámster**	*oon ahm-stehr*
a horse	**un caballo**	*oon kah-bah-yoh*
a lizard	**una lagartija**	*oo-nah lah-gahr-tee-hah*
a mouse	**un ratón**	*oon rrah-tohn*
a parakeet	**un perico**	*oon peh-ree-koh*
a parrot	**un loro**	*oon loh-roh*
a rabbit	**un conejo**	*oon koh-neh-hoh*
a snake	**una serpiente**	*oo-nah sehr-pee-ehn-teh*
a turtle	**una tortuga**	*oo-nah tohr-too-gah*

His/Her name is _____.
Se llama _____.
seh yah-mah _____

It is a male (female).
Es macho (hembra).
ehs mah-choh (ehm-brah)

He/She is _____ months (years) old.
Tiene _____ meses (años).
tee-eh-neh _____ *meh-sehs (ah-nyohs)*

He (She) is (not) friendly (tame).
(No) es amistoso (amistosa) (manso [mansa]).
(noh) ehs ah-mees-toh-soh (ah-mees-toh-sah) (mahn-soh [mahn-sah])

Don't be afraid.
No tenga miedo.
noh tehn-gah mee-eh-doh

He (She) bites (doesn't bite).
Él (Ella) muerde (no muerde).
ehl (eh-yah) moo-ehr-deh (noh moo-ehr-deh)

He (She) won't hurt you.
Él (Ella) no le hará daño.
ehl (eh-yah) noh leh ah-rah dah-nyoh

You may pet him (her).
Usted puede acariciarlo (acariciarla).
oo-stehd poo-eh-deh ah-kah-ree-see-ahr-loh (ah-kah-ree-see-ahr-lah)

His/Her food is in this closet (drawer, cabinet).
Su comida está en este armario (cajón, gabinete).
soo koh-mee-dah ehs-tah ehn ehs-teh ahr-mah-ree-oh (kah-hohn, gah-bee-neh-teh

He (She) eats _____.
Él (Ella) come _____.
ehl (eh-yah) koh-meh _____

anything	**cualquier cosa**	*koo-ahl-kee-ehr koh-sah*
birdseed	**semillas**	*seh-mee-yahs*
cat food	**comida de gato**	*koh-mee-dah deh gah-toh*
dog food	**comida de perro**	*koh-mee-dah deh peh-rroh*
fish food	**comida de pez**	*koh-mee-dah deh pehs*
food pellets	**bolitas de comida**	*boh-lee-tahs deh koh-mee-dah*
grain	**grano**	*grah-noh*
insects	**insectos**	*een-sehk-tohs*
leaves	**hojas**	*oh-hahs*
seeds	**semillas**	*seh-mee-yahs*

Please leave him (her) in (on) his/her _____.
Favor de dejarlo (dejarla) en (sobre) su _____.
fah-bohr deh deh-hahr-loh (deh-hahr-lah) ehn (soh-breh) soo _____

aquarium	**acuario**	*ah-koo-ah-ree-oh*
basket	**cesta**	*sehs-tah*
bowl	**tazon**	*tah-sohn*
box	**caja**	*kah-hah*
cage	**jaula**	*hah-oo-lah*
doghouse	**casita**	*kah-see-tah*

fish tank	**pecera**	*peh-seh-rah*
leash	**traílla**	*trah-ee-yah*
terrarium	**terrario**	*teh-rrah-ree-oh*

Please (do not) remove his/her collar.
Favor de (no) quitarle el collar.
fah-bohr deh (noh) kee-tahr-leh ehl koh-yahr

Please feed him/her at _____ o'clock (_____ times per day).
Favor de darle de comer a la (las) _____ (_____ veces al día).
fah-bohr deh dahr-leh deh koh-mehr ah lah (lahs) _____ (_____ beh-sehs ahl dee-ah)

Please walk him (her) at _____ o'clock (_____ times per day).
Favor de caminarlo (caminarla) a la (las) _____ (_____ veces al día).
fah-bohr deh kah-mee-nahr-loh (kah-mee-nahr-lah) ah lah (lahs) _____ (_____ beh-sehs ahl dee-ah)

Please give him/her fresh water (milk).
Favor de darle agua (leche) fresca.
fah-bohr deh dahr-leh ah-goo-ah (leh-cheh) frehs-kah

Please fill his/her bowl with food (water, milk).
Favor de llenarle el tazón con comida (agua, leche).
fah-bohr deh yeh-nahr-leh ehl tah-sohn kohn koh-mee-dah (ah-goo-ah, leh-cheh)

Please don't forget to give him/her his/her pills (vitamins).
Favor de no olvidar darle sus píldoras (vitaminas).
fah-bohr deh noh ohl-bee-dahr dahr-leh soos peel-doh-rahs (bee-tah-mee-nahs)

Please empty his/her litter box (cage, basket, bowl).
Favor de vaciar su caja de arena (jaula, cesta, tazón).
fah-bohr deh bah-see-ahr soo kah-hah deh ah-reh-nah (hah-oo-lah, sehs-tah, tah-sohn)

Please clean the aquarium (the doghouse, the fish tank, the terrarium).
Favor de limpiar el acuario (la casita, la pecera, el terrario).
fah-bohr deh leem-pee-ahr ehl ah-koo-ah-ree-oh (lah kah-see-tah, lah peh-seh-rah, ehl teh-rrah-ree-oh)

Please give him/her a bath.
Favor de darle un baño.
fah-bohr deh dahr-leh oon bah-nyoh

Please brush him (her).
Favor de cepillarlo (cepillarla).
fah-bohr deh seh-pee-yahr-loh (seh-pee-yahr-lah)

Please take him (her) to the veterinarian (groomer).
Favor de llevarlo (llevarla) al veterinario (peluquero canino).
fah-bohr deh yeh-bahr-loh (yeh-bahr-lah) ahl beh-teh-ree-nah-ree-oh
(peh-loo-keh-roh kah-nee-noh)

12

Outside the House

In the Garage

I (do not) keep my car (cars) in the garage.
Yo (no) guardo el coche (los coches) en el garaje.
yoh (noh) goo-ahr-doh ehl koh-cheh (lohs koh-chehs) ehn ehl gah-rah-heh

We (do not) keep our car (cars) in the garage.
Nosotros (no) guardamos el coche (los coches) en el garaje.
noh-soh-trohs (noh) goo-ahr-dah-mohs ehl koh-cheh (lohs koh-chehs) ehn ehl gah-rah-heh

I (We) use the garage for storage.
Yo uso (Nosotros usamos) el garaje para almacenar.
yoh oo-soh (noh-soh-trohs oo-sah-mohs) ehl gah-rah-heh pah-rah ahl-mah-seh-nahr

Please check the tire pressure.
Favor de revisar la presión de las gomas.
fah-bohr deh rreh-bee-sahr lah preh-see-ohn deh lahs goh-mahs

Please clean the car (shine the hubcaps) with this product.
Favor de limpiar el coche (sacar brillo a los tapacubos) con este producto.
fah-bohr deh leem-pee-ahr ehl koh-cheh (sah-kahr bree-yoh ah lohs tah-pah-koo-bohs) kohn ehs-teh proh-dook-toh

Please replenish the windshield-washer fluid.
Favor de rellenar el líquido del parabrisas.
fah-bohr deh rreh-yeh-nahr ehl lee-kee-doh dehl pah-rah-bree-sahs

Please use a soft, damp cloth to clean (dry) the car.
Favor de usar un paño suave y húmedo para limpiar (secar) el coche.
fah-bohr deh oo-sahr oon pah-nyoh soo-ah-beh ee oo-meh-doh pah-rah leem-pee-ahr (seh-kahr) ehl koh-cheh

Please vacuum the interior of the car.
Favor de pasar la aspiradora dentro del coche.
fah-bohr deh pah-sahr lah ahs-pee-rah-doh-rah dehn-troh dehl koh-cheh

Please vacuum the floormats.
Favor de pasar la aspiradora por los tapetes.
fah-bohr deh pah-sahr lah ahs-pee-rah-doh-rah pohr lohs tah-peh-tehs

Please wash (wax) the car (the cars) in the shade.
Favor de lavar (encerar) el coche (los coches) en la sombra.
fah-bohr deh lah-bahr (ehn-seh-rahr) ehl koh-cheh (lohs koh-chehs) ehn lah sohm-brah

Please paint the garage.
Favor de pintar el garaje.
fah-bohr deh peen-tahr ehl gah-rah-heh

Please put new batteries in the garage remote.
Favor de poner baterías nuevas en el control remoto del garaje.
fah-bohr deh poh-nehr bah-tah-ree-ahs noo-eh-bahs ehn ehl kohn-trohl rreh-moh-toh dehl gah-rah-heh

There are tools and gardening (pool) equipment in the garage.
Hay herramientas y equipo de jardinería (para la piscina) en el garaje.
ah-ee eh-rrah-mee-ehn-tahs ee eh-kee-poh deh hahr-dee-neh-ree-ah (pah-rah lah pee-see-nah) ehn ehl gah-rah-heh

Tools and Miscellaneous Equipment

You may use any of the tools.
Usted puede usar cualquier herramienta.
oo-stehd poo-eh-deh oo-sahr koo-ahl-kee-ehr eh-rrah-mee-ehn-tah

Please call a handyman.
Favor de llamar a un reparador.
fah-bohr deh yah-mahr ah oon rreh-pah-rah-dohr

Please show him where the tools are if he needs them.
Favor de enseñarle dónde están las herramientas si las necesita.
*fah-bohr deh ehn-seh-nyahr-leh dohn-deh ehs-tahn lahs eh-rrah-mee-ehn-tahs
see lahs neh-seh-see-tah*

_____ is (are) hanging on the wall (on the shelf, in the cabinet).
**_____ está (están) colgando en la pared (en el estante, en el
gabinete).**
*_____ ehs-tah (ehs-tahn) kohl-gahn-doh ehn lah pah-rehd (ehn ehl ehs tahn
teh, ehn ehl gah-bee-neh-teh)*

_____ is (are) in that corner.
_____ está (están) en esa esquina.
_____ ehs-tah (ehs-tahn) ehn eh-sah ehs-kee-nah

The antifreeze	**El anticongelante**	*ehl ahn-tee-kohn-heh-lahn-teh*
The bicycle (bicycles)	**La bicicleta (Las bicicletas)**	*lah bee-see-kleh-tah (lahs bee-see-kleh-tahs)*
The bolts	**Los pernos**	*lohs pehr-nohs*
The bricks	**Los ladrillos**	*lohs lah-dree-yohs*
The cement	**El cemento**	*ehl seh-mehn-toh*
The chainsaw	**El serrucho**	*ehl seh-rroo-choh*
The chisel	**El cincel**	*ehl seen-sehl*
The crowbar	**La pata de cabra**	*lah pah-tah deh kah-brah*
The drill	**El taladro**	*ehl tah-lah-droh*
The drill bits	**Las brocas**	*lahs broh-kahs*
The dropcloths	**Las lonas protectoras**	*lahs loh-nahs proh-tehk-toh-rahs*
The fire extinguisher	**El extinguidor**	*ehl ehks-teen-gee-dohr*
The hammer	**El martillo**	*ehl mahr-tee-yoh*
The hatchet	**El hacha**	*ehl ah-chah*
The ladder	**La escalera**	*lah ehs-kah-leh-rah*
The lawn mower	**El cortacésped**	*ehl kohr-tah-sehs-pehd*
The level	**El nivel**	*ehl nee-behl*
The nails	**Los clavos**	*lohs klah-bohs*
The nozzle	**La boquilla**	*lah boh-kee-yah*
The nuts	**Las tuercas**	*lahs too-ehr-kahs*
The oil	**El aceite**	*ehl ah-seh-ee-teh*
The paint pans	**Las bandejas de pintura**	*lahs bahn-deh-hahs deh peen-too-rah*
The paint remover	**El quitapintura**	*ehl kee-tah-peen-too-rah*

English	Spanish	Pronunciation
The paint rollers	**Los rodillos para pintar**	lohs rroh-dee-yohs pah-rah peen-tahr
The paint stirrers	**Los agitadores de pintura**	lohs ah-hee-tah-doh-rehs deh peen-too-rah
The plane	**El cepillo**	ehl seh-pee-yoh
The plaster	**El enlucido**	ehl ehn-loo-see-doh
The pliers	**Las pinzas**	lahs peen-sahs
The sandpaper	**El papel de lija**	ehl pah-pehl deh lee-hah
The saw	**El serrucho**	ehl seh-rroo-choh
The screwdriver	**El destornillador**	ehl dehs-tohr-nee-yah-dohr
The screws	**Los tornillos**	lohs tohr-nee-yohs
The snow shovel	**La pala de nieve**	lah pah-lah deh nee-eh-beh
The sockets	**Los enchufes**	lohs ehn-choo-fehs
The spare tires	**Los neumáticos de repuesto**	lohs neh-oo-mah-tee-kohs deh rreh-poo-ehs-toh
The spray gun	**La pistola rociadora**	lah pees-toh-lah rroh-see-ah-doh-rah
The tape measure	**La cinta métrica**	lah seen-tah meh-tree-kah
The tiles	**Las baldosas**	lahs bahl-doh-sahs
The toolbox	**La caja de herramientas**	lah kah-hah deh eh-rrah-mee-ehn-tahs
The wire	**El alambre**	ehl ah-lahm-breh
The wire cutters	**El cortalambres**	ehl kohr-tah-lahm-brehs
The workbench	**El banco de trabajo**	ehl bahn-koh deh trah-bah-hoh
The wrench	**La llave inglesa**	lah yah-beh een-gleh-sah
The yardstick	**La regla de una yarda**	lah reh-glah deh oo-nah yahr-dah

Gardening Tools and Equipment

When you do the gardening, you may use _____.
Cuando trabaje en el jardín, usted puede usar _____.
koo-ahn-doh trah-bah-heh ehn ehl hahr-deen oo-stehd poo-eh-deh oo-sahr _____

English	Spanish	Pronunciation
the blower	**el soplahojas**	ehl soh-plah-oh-hahs
the broom	**la escoba**	lah ehs-koh-bah
the compost	**el abono**	ehl ah-boh-noh
the containers	**los recipientes**	lohs rreh-see-pee-ehn-tehs

the edger	**la bordeadora**	*lah bohr-deh-ah-doh-rah*
the fertilizer	**el abono**	*ehl ah-boh-noh*
the flower pots	**las macetas/**	*lahs mah-seh-tahs/*
	los tiestos	*lohs tee-ehs-tohs*
the gloves	**los guantes**	*lohs goo-ahn-tehs*
the hedge	**las tijeras**	*lahs tee-heh-rahs*
clippers	**podadoras**	*poh-dah-doh-rahs*
the hoe	**el azadón**	*ehl ah-sah-dohn*
the hose	**la manguera**	*lah mahn-geh-rah*
the insecticide	**el insecticida**	*ehl een-sehk-tee-see-dah*
the ladder	**la escalera**	*lah ehs-kah-leh-rah*
the lawn mower	**el cortacésped**	*ehl kohr-tah-sehs-pehd*
the manure	**el estiércol**	*ehl ehs-tee-ehr-kohl*
the mulch	**el mantillo**	*ehl mahn-tee-yoh*
the pail	**el cubo**	*ehl koo-boh*
the pick	**el pico**	*ehl pee-koh*
the potting soil	**la tierra abonada**	*lah tee-eh-rrah*
		ah-boh-nah-dah
the pruner	**la podadera**	*lah poh-dah-deh-rah*
the rake	**el rastrillo**	*ehl rrahs-tree-yoh*
the rope	**la soga**	*lah soh-gah*
the rotary tiller	**el rototiller**	*ehl rroh-toh-tee-yehr*
the seeds	**las semillas**	*lahs seh-mee-yahs*
the shovel	**la pala**	*lah pah-lah*
the spade	**la pala**	*lah pah-lah*
the sprayer	**el rociador**	*ehl rroh-see-ah-dohr*
the spreader	**el esparcidor**	*ehl ehs-pahr-see-dohr*
the trash bags	**las bolsas**	*lahs bohl-sahs deh*
	de basura	*bah-soo-rah*
the trimmer	**la podadera**	*lah poh-dah-deh-rah*
the trowel	**la paleta**	*lah pah-leh-tah*
the twine	**el cordel**	*ehl kohr-dehl*
the watering can	**la regadera**	*ehl rreh-gah-deh-rah*
the weed killer	**el herbicida**	*ehl ehr-bee-see-dah*
the wheelbarrow	**la carretilla**	*lah kah-rreh-tee-yah*

Pool Equipment

When you take care of the pool you will need _____.

Cuando usted limpie la piscina, necesitará _____.

koo-ahn-doh oo-stehd leem-pee-eh lah pee-see-nah neh-seh-see-tah-rah _____

the acid	**el ácido**	*ehl ah-see-doh*
the brushes	**los cepillos**	*lohs seh-peh-yohs*
the chemicals	**los compuestos químicos**	*lohs kohm-poo-ehs-tohs kee-mee-kohs*
the chlorine	**el cloro**	*ehl kloh-roh*
the cover	**la cubierta**	*lah koo-bee-ehr-tah*
the hook	**el gancho**	*ehl-gahn-choh*
the net	**la red**	*lah rrehd*
the test kit	**el estuche de prueba**	*ehl ehs-too-cheh deh proo-eh-bah*
the thermometer	**el termómetro**	*ehl tehr-moh-meh-troh*
the vacuum	**la aspiradora**	*lah ahs-pee-rah-doh-rah*

In the Backyard

Maintaining the Garden

Please aerate the soil with a rotary tiller.
Favor de airear la tierra con un rototiller.
fah-bohr deh ah-ee-reh-ahr lah tee-eh-rrah kohn oon rroh-toh-tee-yehr

Please clean the birdbath (the fountain).
Favor de limpiar la bañera de aves (la fuente).
fah-bohr deh leem-pee-ahr lah bah-nyeh-rah deh ah-behs (lah foo-ehn-teh)

Please clip these hedges.
Favor de podar estos setos.
fah-bohr deh poh-dahr ehs-tohs seh-tohs

Please cut the grass.
Favor de cortar el césped.
fah-bohr deh kohr-tahr ehl sehs-pehd

Please dig a hole.
Favor de excavar un hoyo.
fah-bohr deh ehks-kah-bahr oon oh-yoh

Please fertilize the lawn.
Favor de abonar el césped.
fah-bohr deh ah-boh-nahr ehl sehs-pehd

Please fill the birdfeeder.
Favor de llenar el comedero para pájaros.
fah-bohr deh yeh-nahr ehl koh-meh-deh-roh pah-rah pah-hah-rohs

Please fix the fence.
Favor de arreglar la cerca.
fah-bohr deh ah-rreh-glahr lah sehr-kah

Please maintain the correct temperature in the greenhouse (solarium).
Favor de mantener la temperatura correcta en el invernadero (solario).
fah-bohr deh mahn-teh-nehr lah tehm-peh-rah-too-rah koh-rrehk-tah ehn ehl een-behr-nah-deh-roh (soh-lah-ree-oh)

Please mow the lawn.
Favor de cortar el césped.
fah-bohr deh kohr-tahr ehl sehs-pehd

Please plant these seeds (flowers).
Favor de plantar estas semillas (flores).
fah-bohr deh plahn-tahr ehs-tahs seh-mee-yahs (floh-rehs)

Please plant these bulbs (bushes/shrubs).
Favor de plantar estos bulbos (arbustos).
fah-bohr deh plahn-tahr ehs-tohs bool-bohs (ahr-boos-tohs)

Please prune the branches.
Favor de podar las ramas.
fah-bohr deh poh-dahr lahs rrah-mahs

Please pull the weeds.
Favor de arrancar las malas hierbas.
fah-bohr deh ah-rrahn-kahr lahs mah-lahs ee-ehr-bahs

Please put down more soil.
Favor de echar más tierra.
fah-bohr deh eh-chahr mahs tee-eh-rrah

Please put flowers in the flower boxes.
Favor de poner flores en el cantero.
fah-bohr deh poh-nehr floh-rehs ehn ehl kahn-teh-roh

Please put mulch in the flower beds.
Favor de poner mantillo en los canteros.
fah-bohr deh poh-nehr mahn-tee-yoh ehn lohs kahn-teh-rohs

Please rake the leaves.
Favor de rastrillar las hojas.
fah-bohr deh rrahs-tree-yahr lahs oh-hahs

Please spray for insects.
Favor de rociar insecticida.
fah-bohr deh rroh-see-ahr een-sehk-tee-see-dah

Please turn the flower beds.
Favor de voltear los canteros.
fah-bohr deh bohl-teh-ahr lohs kahn-teh-rohs

Please turn on the sprinklers to water the lawn.
Favor de prender las rociadoras para regar el césped.
fah-bohr deh prehn-dehr lahs rroh-see-ah-doh-rahs pah-rah rreh-gahr ehl sehs-pehd

Please use weed control.
Favor de usar herbicidas.
fah-bohr deh oo-sahr ehr-bee-see-dahs

Please water the garden _____ times a week.
Favor de regar el jardín _____ veces a la semana.
fah-bohr deh rreh-gahr ehl hahr-deen _____ beh-sehs ah lah seh-mah-nah

This plant (This bush, This tree) is _____.
Esta planta (Este arbusto, Este árbol) está _____.
ehs-tah plahn-tah (ehs-teh ahr-boos-toh, ehs-teh ahr-bohl) ehs-tah _____

alive	**viva (vivo)**	*bee-bah (bee-boh)*
on its last legs	**casi muerta (muerto)**	*kah-see moo-ehr-tah (moo-ehr-too)*
dead	**muerta (muerto)**	*moo-ehr-tah (moo-ehr-toh)*
too dry	**demasiada seca (seco)**	*deh-mah-see-ah-dah seh-kah (seh-kah-koh)*
too wet	**demasiada mojada (mojado)**	*deh-mah-see-ah-dah moh-hah-dah (moh-hah-doh)*

Please plant some new flowers (plants) in the garden (greenhouse, solarium).
Favor de plantar algunas flores nuevas (plantas) en el jardín (invernadero, solario).
fah-bohr deh plahn-tahr ahl-goo-nahs floh-rehs noo-eh-bahs (plahn-tahs) ehn ehl hahr-deen (een-behr-nah-deh-roh, soh-lah-ree-oh)

Please plant some new bushes in the garden (greenhouse, solarium).
Favor de plantar algunos arbustos nuevos en el jardín (invernadero, solario).
fah-bohr deh plahn-tahr ahl-goo-nohs ahr-boos-tohs noo-eh-bohs ehn ehl hahr-deen (een-behr-nah-deh-roh, soh-lah-ree-oh)

I prefer _____.
Yo prefiero _____.
yoh preh-fee-eh-roh _____

annuals	**las anuales**	*lahs ah-noo-ah-lehs*
azaleas	**las azaleas**	*lahs ah-sah-leh-ahs*
cacti	**los cactos**	*lohs kahk-tohs*
carnations	**los claveles**	*lohs klah-beh-lehs*
chrysanthemums	**los crisantemos**	*lohs kree-sahn-teh-mohs*
crocuses	**los azafranes**	*lohs ah-sah-frah-nehs*
daffodils	**los narcisos**	*lohs nahr-sees-kohs*
dahlias	**las dalias**	*lahs dah-lee-ahs*
daisies	**las margaritas**	*lahs mahr-gah-ree-tahs*
forsythia	**las forsitias**	*lahs fohr-see-tee-ahs*
geraniums	**los geranios**	*lohs heh-rah-nee-ohs*
gladioluses	**las gladiolas**	*lahs glah-dee-oh-lahs*
hibiscuses	**los hibiscos**	*lohs ee-bees-kohs*
hyacinths	**los jacintos**	*lohs hah-seen-tohs*
hydrangeas	**las hortensias**	*lahs ohr-tehn-see-ahs*
irises	**los lirios**	*lohs lee-ree-ohs*
lilacs	**las lilas**	*lahs lee-lahs*
lilies	**los lirios**	*lohs lee-ree-ohs*
magnolias	**las magnolias**	*lahs mahg-noh-lee-ahs*
marigolds	**las maravillas**	*lahs mah-rah-bee-yahs*
orchids	**las orquídeas**	*lahs ohr-kee-deh-ahs*
pansies	**los pensamientos**	*lohs pehn-sah-mee-ehn-tohs*
peonies	**las peonías**	*lahs peh-oh-nee-ahs*
perennials	**las perennes**	*lahs peh-reh-nehs*
poppies	**las petunias**	*lahs peh-too-nee-ahs*
rhododendrons	**los rododendros**	*lohs rroh-doh-dehn-drohs*
roses	**las rosas**	*lahs rroh-sahs*
sunflowers	**los girasoles**	*lohs hee-rah-soh-lehs*
tulips	**los tulipanes**	*lohs too-lee-pah-nehs*
violets	**las violetas**	*lahs bee-oh-leh-tahs*

Please go to the garden center and buy _____ tree.
Favor de ir al centro de jardinería y comprar _____.
fah-bohr deh eer ahl sehn-troh deh har-dee-neh-ree-ah ee kohm-prahr _____

an apple	**un manzano**	*oon mahn-sah-noh*
a birch	**un abedul**	*oon ah-beh-dool*
a cedar	**un cedro**	*oon seh-droh*
a cherry	**un cerezo**	*oon seh-reh-soh*
a cypress	**un ciprés**	*oon see-prehs*
an elm	**un olmo**	*oon ohl-moh*
a fig	**una higuera**	*oo-nah ee-goo-eh-rah*
a fir	**un pino noruego**	*oon pee-noh noh-roo-eh-goh*
a maple	**un arce**	*oon ahr-seh*
an oak	**un roble/ una encina**	*oon rroh-bleh/ oo-nah ehn-see-nah*
an olive	**un olivo**	*oon oh-lee-boh*
a palm	**una palmera**	*oo-nah pahl-meh-rah*
a peach	**un melocotonero**	*oon meh-loh-koh-toh-neh-roh*
a pear	**un peral**	*oon peh-rahl*
a pine	**un pino**	*oon pee-noh*
a poplar	**un álamo/ un chopo**	*oon ah-lah-moh/ oon choh-poh*
a spruce	**un abeto**	*oon ah-beh-toh*
a weeping willow	**un sauce llorón**	*oon sah-oo-seh yoh-rohn*

Maintaining the Pool and the Tennis Court

Please cover (uncover) the pool.
Favor de cubrir (destapar) la piscina.
fah-bohr deh koo-breer (dehs-tah-pahr) lah pee-see-nah

Please add any necessary chemicals (chlorine).
Favor de añadir los químicos (el cloro) necesarios (necesario).
fah-bohr deh ah-nyah-deer lohs kee-mee-kohs (ehl kloh-roh) neh-seh-sah-ree-ohs (neh-seh-sah-ree-oh)

Please check the pH of the pool.
Favor de revisar el pH de la piscina.
fah-bohr deh rreh-bee-sahr ehl peh ah-cheh deh lah pee-see-nah

Please check the pool's temperature.
Favor de revisar la temperatura de la piscina.
fah-bohr deh rreh-bee-sahr lah tehm-peh-rah-too-rah deh lah pee-see-nah

Please clean the pool (the drain, the filter, the cabana).
Favor de limpiar la piscina (el desagüe, el filtro, la cabaña).
fah-bohr deh leem-pee-ahr lah pee-see-nah (ehl dehs-ah-goo-eh, ehl feel-troh, lah kah-bah-nyah)

Please scrub the diving board.
Favor de fregar el trampolín.
fah-bohr deh freh-gahr ehl trahm-poh-leen

Please tell me if you notice any cracks (algae).
Favor de decirme si ve grietas (algas).
fah-bohr deh deh-seer-meh see beh gree-eh-tahs (ahl-gahs)

Please vacuum the pool.
Favor de pasar la aspiradora en la piscina.
fah-bohr deh pah-sahr lah ahs-pee-rah-doh-rah ehn lah pee-see-nah

Please wash (sweep) the pool deck.
Favor de lavar (barrer) la terraza de la piscina.
fah-bohr deh lah-bahr (bah-rrehr) lah teh-rrah-sah deh lah pee-see-nah

Please put the balls in the bag.
Favor de poner las pelotas en la bolsa.
fah-bohr deh poh-nehr lahs peh-loh-tahs ehn lah bohl-sah

Please replace the net.
Favor de reponer la red.
fah-bohr deh rreh-poh-nehr lah rrehd

Please sweep the tennis court.
Favor de barrer la cancha de tenis.
fah-bohr deh bah-rrehr lah kahn-chah deh teh-nees

The pool pump (the heater) is broken.
La bomba de la piscina (el calentador) está rota (roto).
lah bohm-bah deh lah pee-see-nah (ehl kah-lehn-tah-dohr) ehs-tah rroh-tah (rroh-toh)

Please call a repairman.
Favor de llamar a un mecánico.
fah-bohr deh yah-mahr ah oon meh-kah-nee-koh

Please fix it.
Favor de arreglarlo.
fah-bohr deh ah-rreh-glahr-loh

You may (not) use the pool (the tennis court) when we aren't home.
Usted (no) puede usar la piscina (la cancha de tenis) cuando no estemos en casa.
oo-stehd (noh) poo-eh-deh oo-sahr lah pee-see-nah (lah kahn-chah deh teh-nees) koo-ahn-doh noh ehs-teh-mohs ehn kah-sah

On the Patio

Please clean _____.
Favor de limpiar _____.
fah-bohr deh leem-pee-ahr _____

the barbecue	**la barbacoa**	*lah bahr-bah-koh-ah*
the barbecue fork	**el tenedor de la barbacoa**	*ehl teh-neh-dohr deh lah bahr-bah-koh-ah*
the barbecue tongs	**las pinzas de la barbacoa**	*lahs peen-sahs deh lah bahr-bah-koh-ah*
the chairs	**las sillas**	*lahs see-yahs*
the deck	**la terraza**	*lah teh-rrah-sah*
the hammock	**la hamaca**	*lah ah-mah-kah*
the lights	**las luces**	*lahs loo-sehs*
the lounge chairs	**los sillones**	*lohs see-yoh-nehs*
the rotisserie	**el asador**	*ehl ah-sah-dohr*
the screen door	**la puerta con tela metálica**	*lah poo-ehr-tah kohn teh-lah meh-tah-lee-kah*
the screens	**los tamices metálicos**	*lohs tah-mee-sehs meh-tah-lee-kohs*
the spit	**el asador**	*ehls ah-sah-dohr*
the table	**la mesa**	*lah meh-sah*
the umbrella	**el paraguas**	*ehl pah-rah-goo-ahs*

Please light the grill.
Favor de prender la parrilla.
fah-bohr deh prehn-dehr lah pah-rree-yah

English-Spanish Dictionary

> **Note**
> Except where noted, nouns ending in –o are masculine
> and nouns ending in –a are feminine. The gender for
> nouns ending in –e or a consonant is marked by m. or f.

English	Spanish	Pronunciation
accident	**accidente** *(m.)*	*ahk-see-dehn-teh*
acid	**ácido**	*ah-see-doh*
add, to	**añadir**	*ah-nyah-deer*
address	**dirección** *(f.)*	*dee-rehk-see-ohn*
aerate, to	**airear**	*ah-ee-reh-ahr*
afraid, to be	**tener miedo (de)**	*teh-nehr mee-eh-doh (deh)*
after	**después**	*dehs-poo-ehs*
aftershave lotion	**loción** *(f.)* **para después de afeitarse**	*loh-see-ohn pah-rah dehs-poo-ehs deh ah-feh-ee-tahr-seh*
afternoon	**tarde** *(f.)*	*tahr-deh*
ago	**hace**	*ah-seh*
air-conditioning unit	**climatizador** *(m.)*	*klee-mah-tee-sah-dohr*

continued

English	Spanish	Pronunciation
air-conditioning condenser	**condensador** (*m.*) **del aire acondicionado**	*kohn-dehn-sah-dohr dehl ah-ee-reh ah-kohn-dee-see-oh-nah-doh*
air freshener	**ambientador** (*m.*)	*ahm-bee-ehn-tah-dohr*
alarm clock	**despertador** (*m.*)	*dehs-pehr-tah-dohr*
alcohol	**alcohol** (*m.*)	*ahl-koh-ohl*
algae	**alga** (*f., but takes m. article*)	*ahl-gah*
alive	**vivo (viva)**	*bee-boh (bee-bah)*
allergic to	**alérgico (alérgica) a**	*ah-lehr-hee-koh (ah-lehr-hee-kah) ah*
allergy	**alergia**	*ah-lehr-hee-ah*
allow, to	**permitir**	*pehr-mee-teer*
almond	**almendra** (*f.*)	*ahl-mehn-drah*
aloe	**aloe** (*m.*)	*ah-loh-eh*
aluminum foil	**papel de aluminio** (*m.*)	*pah-pehl deb ah-loo-mee-nee-oh*
always	**siempre**	*see-ehm-preh*
ammonia	**amoníaco**	*ah-moh-nee-ah-koh*
anchovy	**anchoa**	*ahn-choh-ah*
ankle	**tobillo**	*toh-bee-yoh*
annuals	**anuales** (*m., pl.*)	*ah-noo-ah-lehs*
answer, to	**contestar**	*kohn-tehs-tahr*
answering machine	**contestador automático** (*m.*)	*kohn-tehs-tah-dohr ah-oo-toh-mah-tee-koh*
antacid	**antiácido**	*ahn-tee-ah-see-doh*
antibacterial soap	**jabón antibacteriano** (*m.*)	*hah-bohn ahn-tee-bahk-teh-ree-ah-noh*
antibiotic	**antibiótico**	*ahn-tee-bee-oh-tee-koh*
antifreeze	**anticongelante** (*m.*)	*ahn-tee-kohn-heh-lahn-teh*
antihistamine	**antihistamínico**	*ahn-tee-ees-tah-mee-nee-koh*
antique	**antigüedad** (*f.*)	*ahn-tee-goo-eh-dahd*

English	Spanish	Pronunciation
antiseptic	**antiséptico**	*ahn-tee-sehp-tee-koh*
antistatic	**antiestático** (antiestática)	*ahn-tee-ehs-tah-tee-koh (ahn-tee-ehs-tah-tee-kah)*
appendicitis	**apendicitis** (f.)	*ah-pehn-dee-see-tees*
appetizer	**aperitivo**	*ah-peh-ree-tee-boh*
apple	**manzana**	*mahn-sah-nah*
apply/put on, to	**aplicar**	*ah-plee-kahr*
apply (for a job), to	**solicitar**	*soh-lee-see-tahr*
appointment	**cita**	*see-tah*
apricot	**durazno**	*doo-rahs-noh*
April	**abril**	*ah-breel*
apron	**delantal** (m.)	*deh-lahn-tahl*
aquarium	**acuario**	*ah-koo-ah-ree-oh*
argue, to	**discutir**	*dees-koo-teer*
arm	**brazo**	*brah-soh*
armchair	**butaca**	*boo-tah-kah*
armoire	**armario**	*ahr-mah-ree-oh*
arrange, to	**arreglar**	*ah-rreh-glahr*
arrive, to	**llegar**	*yeh-gahr*
artichoke	**alcachofa**	*ahl-kah-choh-fah*
ashtray	**cenicero**	*seh-nee-seh-roh*
ask (a question), to	**preguntar**	*preh-goon-tahr*
ask for, to	**pedir**	*peh-deer*
asparagus	**espárragos** (m., pl.)	*ehs-pah-rrah-gohs*
aspirin	**aspirina**	*ahs-pee-ree-nah*
assure	**asegurar**	*ah-seh-goo-rahr*
attention deficit disorder (with hyperactivity)	**desorden** (m.) **de déficit de atención (con hiperactividad)**	*deh-sohr-dehn deh deh-fee-seet deh ah-tehn-see-ohn (kohn ee-pehr-ahk-tee-bee-dahd)*
attic	**desván** (m.)	*dehs-bahn*
August	**agosto**	*ah-gohs-toh*

continued

English	Spanish	Pronunciation
aunt	**tía**	*tee-ah*
autism	**autismo**	*ah-oo-tees-moh*
autumn	**otoño**	*oh-toh-nyoh*
available	**disponible**	*dees-poh-nee-bleh*
avocado	**aguacate** *(m.)*	*ah-goo-ah-kah-teh*
avoid, to	**evitar**	*eh-bee-tahr*
azalea	**azalea**	*ah-sah-leh-ah*
back	**espalda**	*ehs-pahl-dah*
backyard	**jardín** *(m.)*	*hahr-deen*
bacon	**tocino**	*toh-see-noh*
bag (paper, plastic)	**bolsa (de papel, de plástico)**	*bohl-sah (deh pah-pehl, deh plahs-tee-koh)*
bake, to	**hornear**	*ohr-neh-ahr*
bakery	**panadería**	*pah-nah-deh-ree-ah*
bakeware	**fuentes para el horno** *(f., pl.)*	*foo-ehn-tehs pah-rah ehl ohr-noh*
baking dish	**molde de hornear** *(m.)*	*mohl-deh deh ohr-neh-ahr*
baking powder	**polvo de hornear** *(m.)*	*pohl-boh deh ohr-neh-ahr*
baking soda	**bicarbonato de soda** *(m.)*	*bee-kahr-boh-nah-toh deh soh-dah*
ball	**pelota**	*peh-loh-tah*
banana	**banana**	*bah-nah-nah*
bandage	**venda**	*behn-dah*
bandage, to	**vendar**	*behn-dahr*
Band-Aid	**curita**	*koo-ree-tah*
bannister	**pasamanos** *(m., sing. and pl.)*	*pah-sah-mah-nohs*
bar	**barra**	*bah-rrah*
bar (serving drinks)	**bar** *(m.)*	*bahr*
barbecue	**barbacoa**	*bahr-bah-koh-ah*
barbecue fork (tongs)	**tenedor** *(m.)* **de barbacoa (pinzas)**	*teh-neh-dohr deh bahr-bah-koh-ah (peen-sahs)*

English	Spanish	Pronunciation
barbecue sauce	**salsa de barbacoa**	*sahl-sah deh bahr-bah-koh-ah*
barbecue, to	**asar a la parrilla**	*ah-sahr ah lah pah-ree-yah*
baseball	**béisbol** *(m.)*	*beh ees-bohl*
baseboard	**zócalo**	*soh-kah-loh*
basement	**sótano**	*soh-tah-noh*
basil	**albahaca**	*ahl-bah-ah-kah*
basket	**cesta**	*sehs-tah*
basketball	**básquetbol** *(m.)*	*bahs-keht-bohl*
bass	**lubina**	*loo-bee-nah*
bassinet	**bacinete** *(m.)*	*bah-see-neh-teh*
bat (animal)	**murciélago**	*moor-see-eh-lah-goh*
bathmat	**alfombrilla**	*ahl-fohm-bree-yah*
bath oil	**aceite** *(m.)* **para el baño**	*ah-seh-ee-teh pah-rah ehl bah-nyoh*
bathe, to	**bañar**	*bah-nyahr*
bathing suit	**traje de baño** *(m.)*	*trah-heh deh bah-nyoh*
bathtub	**bañera**	*bah-nyeh-rah*
bathtub mat	**alfombrilla del baño**	*ahl-fohm-bree-yah dehl bah-nyoh*
battery	**batería**	*bah-teh-ree-ah*
bay leaf	**hoja de laurel**	*oh-hah deh lah-oo-rehl*
be careful, to	**tener cuidado**	*teh-nehr koo-ee-dah-doh*
be willing to, to	**estar dispuesto (dispuesta) a**	*ehs-tahr dees-poo-ehs-toh (dees-poo-ehs-tah) ah*
bean	**frijol** *(m.)*	*free-hohl*
beat, to	**batir**	*bah-teer*
bed (sofa, air, water)	**cama (el sofá-cama, la cama de aire, la cama de agua)**	*kah-mah (ehl soh-fah-kah-mah, lah kah-mah deh ah-ee-reh, lah kah-mah deh ah-goo-ah)*
bed skirt	**volado para la cama**	*boh-lah-doh pah-rah lah kah-mah*

continued

English	Spanish	Pronunciation
bee sting	**picadura de abeja**	*pee-kah-doo-rah deh ah-beh-hah*
beef	**carne (f.) de vaca**	*kahr-neh deh bah-kah*
beeper	**biper (m.)**	*bee-pehr*
beer (light, domestic, imported))	**cerveza (ligera, doméstica, importada)**	*sehr-beh-sah (lee-heh-rah, doh-mehs-tee-kah, eem-pohr-tah-dah)*
beet	**remolacha**	*rreh-moh-lah-chah*
begin, to	**empezar**	*ehm-peh-sahr*
beige	**beige**	*beh-ee-heh*
belt	**cinturón (m.)**	*seen-too-rohn*
bench	**banco**	*bahn-koh*
bib	**babero**	*bah-beh-roh*
bicycle	**bicicleta**	*bee-see-kleh-tah*
bidet	**bidé (m.)**	*bee-deh*
bipolar disorder	**trastorno bipolar**	*trahs-tohr-noh bee-poh-lahr*
birch	**abedul (m.)**	*ah-beh-dool*
bird	**pájaro**	*pah-hah-roh*
birdbath	**bañera**	*bah-nyeh-rah*
birdfeeder	**comedero para pájaros**	*koh-meh-deh-roh pah-rah pah-hah-rohs*
bite, to	**morder**	*mohr-dehr*
bitter	**amargo (amarga)**	*ah-mahr-goh (ah-mahr-gah)*
black	**negro (negra)**	*neh-groh (neh-grah)*
blackberry (fruit)	**mora**	*moh-rah*
BlackBerry (wireless e-mail device)	**aparato blackberry**	*ah-pah-rah-toh blahk-beh-ree*
blade	**hoja**	*oh-hah*
blanch, to	**blanquear**	*blahn-keh-ahr*
blanket	**manta**	*mahn-tah*
blazer	**americana**	*ah-meh-ree-kah-nah*
bleach	**blanqueador (m.)**	*blahn-keh-ah-dohr*

English	Spanish	Pronunciation
blend, to	**mezclar**	*mahs-klahr*
blender	**licuadora**	*lee-koo-ah-doh-rah*
blind	**ciego (ciega)**	*see-eh-goh (see-eh-gah)*
blinds	**persianas**	*pehr-see-ah-nahs*
blocks	**bloques** *(m., pl.)*	*bloh-kehs*
blouse	**blusa**	*bloo-sah*
blower	**sopladora**	*soh-plah-doh-rah*
blue	**azul**	*ah-sool*
blueberry	**arándano**	*ah-rahn-dah-noh*
board game	**juego de mesa**	*hoo-eh-goh deh meh-sah*
body	**cuerpo**	*koo-ehr-poh*
boil, to (vegetables, meat, eggs)	**hervir (los vegetales, la carne, los huevos)**	*ehr-beer (lohs beh-heh-tah-lehs, lah kahr-neh, lohs oo-eh-bohs)*
boiler	**caldera**	*kahl-deh-rah*
bolster	**almohadón** *(m.)*	*ahl-moh-ah-dohn*
bolt	**perno**	*pehr-noh*
bookcase	**estantería**	*ehs-tahn-teh-ree-ah*
booties	**escarpines** *(m., pl.)*	*ehs-kahr-pee-nehs*
boots	**botas**	*boh-tahs*
bottle	**botella**	*boh-teh-yah*
bottle (baby)	**biberón** *(m.)*	*bee-beh-rohn*
bottle opener	**abre botellas** *(m.)*	*ah-breh boh-teh-yahs*
bottle warmer	**calentador** *(m.)* **de botellas**	*kah-lehn-tah-dohr deh boh-teh-yahs*
bourbon	**whisky americano**	*oo-ees-kee ah-meh-ree-kah-noh*
bowl	**bol** *(m.)*	*bohl*
box	**caja**	*kah-hah*
brace (leg)	**aparato ortopédico para la pierna**	*ah-pah-rah-toh ohr-toh-peh-dee-koh pah-rah lah pee-ehr-nah*

continued

English	Spanish	Pronunciation
bracelet	**brazalete** *(m.)*	*brah-sah-leh-teh*
braces (teeth)	**frenillos**	*freh-nee-yohs*
brain	**cerebro**	*seh-reh-broh*
branch	**rama**	*rrah-mah*
brand	**marca**	*mahr-kah*
brandy	**coñac** *(m.)*	*koh-nyahk*
bread (white, rye, whole wheat)	**pan** *(m.)* **(blanco, de centeno, integral)**	*pahn (blahn-koh, deh sehn-teh-noh, een-teh-grahl)*
bread, to	**empanizar**	*ehm-pah-nee-sahr*
breadbasket	**canasta**	*kah-nahs-tah*
breadcrumbs	**pan** *(m.)* **rallado**	*pahn rrah-yah-doh*
break, to	**romperse**	*rrohm-pehr-seh*
breakfast	**desayuno**	*deh-sah-yoo-noh*
breathe, to	**respirar**	*rrehs-pee-rahr*
brick	**ladrillo**	*lah-dree-yoh*
bring, to	**traer**	*trah-ehr*
broccoli	**bróculi** *(m.)*	*broh-koo-lee*
broil, to	**asar a la parrilla**	*ah-sahr ah lah pah-rree-yah*
broken	**roto (rota)**	*rroh-toh (rroh-tah)*
bronchitis	**bronquitis** *(f.)*	*brohn-kee-tees*
broom	**escoba**	*ehs-koh-bah*
broth	**caldo**	*kahl-doh*
brother	**hermano**	*ehr-mah-noh*
brown	**pardo (parda)**	*pahr-doh (pahr-dah)*
brown, to	**dorar**	*doh-rahr*
brush	**cepillo**	*seh-pee-yoh*
brush, to (oneself)	**cepillar (cepillarse)**	*seh-pee-yahr (seh-pee-yahr-seh)*
Brussels sprouts	**repollitos de Bruselas**	*rreh-poh-yee-tohs deh broo-seh-lahs*

English	Spanish	Pronunciation
bucket	**cubo**	*koo-boh*
buffet server	**aparador** *(m.)*	*ah-pah-rah-dohr*
building	**edificio**	*eh-dee-fee-see-oh*
bulb	**bulbo**	*bool-boh*
bunch	**atado**	*ah-tah-doh*
bundt pan	**caserola de bundt**	*kah seh roh-lah deh bunht*
burn, to (oneself)	**quemar (quemarse)**	*keh-mahr (keh-mahr-seh)*
burned	**quemado (quemada)**	*keh-mah-doh (keh-mah-dah)*
burner	**quemador** *(m.)*	*keh-mah-dohr*
burp, to	**hacer eructar**	*ah-sehr eh-rook-tahr*
bush	**matorral** *(m.)*	*mah-toh-rrahl*
butcher shop	**carnicería**	*kahr-nee-seh-ree-ah*
butter	**mantequilla**	*mahn-teh-kee-yah*
butter dish	**mantequillera**	*mahn-teh-kee-yeh-rah*
buttermilk	**suero de leche**	*soo-eh-roh deh leh-cheh*
button	**botón** *(m.)*	*boh-tohn*
buy, to	**comprar**	*kohm-prahr*
cabana	**cabaña**	*kah-bah-nyah*
cabbage	**col** *(f.)*	*kohl*
cabinet	**gabinete** *(m.)*	*gah-bee-neh-teh*
cable box	**caja del cable**	*kah-hah dehl kah-bleh*
cactus	**cacto**	*kahk-toh*
cage	**jaula**	*hah-oo-lah*
cake	**torta**	*tohr-tah*
cake pan	**molde** *(m.)* **para torta**	*mohl-deh pah-rah tohr-tah*
calculator	**calculadora**	*kahl-koo-lah-doh-rah*
calendar	**calendario**	*kah-lehn-dah-ree-oh*
call, to	**llamar**	*yah-mahr*
can	**lata**	*lah -tah*

continued

English	Spanish	Pronunciation
can opener	**abrelatas** *(m., sing. and pl.)*	*ah-breh-lah-tahs*
canary	**canario**	*kah-nah-ree-oh*
cancer	**cáncer** *(m.)*	*kahn-sehr*
candle	**vela**	*beh-lah*
candlestick holder	**candelero**	*kahn-deh-leh-roh*
candlesticks	**candeleros**	*kahn-deh-leh-rohs*
candy	**dulce** *(m.)*	*dool-seh*
candy store	**confitería**	*kohn-fee-teh-ree-ah*
cane	**bastón** *(m.)*	*bahs-tohn*
canopy	**baldaquín** *(m.)*	*bahl-dah-keen*
cap	**gorra**	*goh-rrah*
capers	**alcaparras**	*ahl-kah-pah-rrahs*
cappucino	**capuchino**	*kah-poo-chee-noh*
capsule	**cápsula**	*kahp-soo-lah*
car	**coche** *(m.)*	*koh-cheh*
car seat	**asiento de seguridad para niños**	*ah-see-ehn-toh deh seh-goo-ree-dahd pah-rah nee-nyohs*
carafe	**garrafa**	*gah-rrah-fah*
caramel custard	**flan** *(m.)*	*flahn*
card	**tarjeta**	*tahr-heh-tah*
cards (playing)	**naipes** *(m., pl.)*	*nah-ee-pehs*
care, to	**cuidar**	*koo-ee-dahr*
carnation	**clavel** *(m.)*	*klah-behl*
carpet	**alfombra**	*ahl-fohm-brah*
carriage	**cochecito**	*koh-cheh-see-toh*
carrier	**portabebés** *(m.)*	*pohr-tah-beh-behs*
carrot	**zanahoria**	*sah-nah-oh-ree-ah*
carry, to	**llevar**	*yeh-bahr*
cartoons	**dibujos animados**	*dee-boo-hohs ah-nee-mah-dohs*

English	Spanish	Pronunciation
carving knife (fork)	**cuchillo de cortar (tenedor)**	*koo-chee-yoh deh kohr-tahr (teh-neh-dohr)*
cashmere	**cachemira**	*kah-cheh-mee-rah*
casserole	**caserola**	*kah-seh-roh-lah*
cast	**yeso**	*yeh-soh*
cat	**gato**	*gah-toh*
cauliflower	**coliflor** *(f.)*	*koh-lee-flohr*
cavity	**caries** *(f., sing. and pl.)*	*kah-ree-ehs*
CD player	**reproductor** *(m.)* **de discos compactos**	*rreh proh dook tohr deh dees-kohs kohm-pahk-tohs*
cedar	**cedro**	*seh-droh*
ceiling	**techo**	*teh-choh*
ceiling fan	**ventilador** *(m.)* **de techo**	*behn-tee-lah-dohr deh teh-choh*
celery	**apio**	*ah-pee-oh*
cement	**cemento**	*seh-mehn-toh*
cereal	**cereal** *(m.)*	*seh-reh-ahl*
cerebral palsy	**parálisis cerebral** *(f.)*	*pah-rah-lee-sees seh-reh-brahl*
chain	**cadena**	*kah-deh-nah*
chainsaw	**serrucho**	*seh-rroo-choh*
chair	**silla**	*see-yah*
champagne	**champaña** *(m.)*	*chahm-pah-nyah*
chandelier	**araña de luces**	*ah-rah-nyah deh loo-sehs*
change, to	**cambiar**	*kahm-bee-ahr*
changing table	**mesa de muda**	*meh-sah deh moo-dah*
check, to	**revisar**	*rreh-bee-sahr*
checkers	**damas**	*dah-mahs*
cheek	**mejilla**	*meh-hee-yah*
cheese (cream, Parmesan)	**queso (crema, parmesano)**	*keh-soh (kreh-mah, pahr-meh-sah-noh)*

continued

English	Spanish	Pronunciation
chemical	**compuesto químico**	kohm-poo-ehs-toh kee-mee-koh
cherry	**cereza**	seh-reh-sah
chess	**ajedrez** (m.)	ah-heh-drehs
chest	**pecho**	peh-choh
chestnut	**castaño**	kah-stah-nyoh
chicken	**pollo**	poh-yoh
chicken pox	**varicela**	bah-ree-seh-lah
chickpeas	**garbanzos**	gahr-bahn-sohs
children	**niños** (m., pl.)	nee-nyohs
chill, to	**enfriar**	ehn-free-ahr
chills	**escalofríos**	ehs-kah-loh-free-ohs
chin	**barbilla**	bahr-bee-yah
china	**porcelana**	pohr-seh-lah-nah
chisel	**cincel** (m.)	seen-sehl
chives	**cebollines**	seh-boh-yee-nehs
chlorine	**cloro**	kloh-roh
chocolate (dark, milk, semisweet, white)	**chocolate** (m.) **(oscuro, de leche, semi-dulce, blanco)**	choh-koh-lah-teh (oh-skoo-roh, deh leh-cheh, seh-mee-dool-seh, blahn-koh)
choke, to	**atragantar**	ah-trah-gahn-tahr
choose, to	**escoger**	ehs-koh-hehr
chop, to	**cortar en pedacitos**	kohr-tahr ehn peh-dah-see-tohs
chores	**quehaceres** (m., pl.)	keh-ah-seh-rehs
chrysanthemum	**crisantemo**	kree-sahn-teh-moh
cider	**cidra** (f.)	see-dreh
cinnamon	**canela**	kah-neh-lah
circuit breaker	**cortacircuito**	kohr-tah-seer-koo-ee-tohs
citizen	**ciudadano (ciudadana)**	see-oo-dah-dah-noh (see-oo-dah-dah-nah)
clam	**almeja**	ahl-meh-hah

English	Spanish	Pronunciation
clarinet	**clarinete** *(m.)*	*klah-ree-neh-teh*
clean	**limpio (limpia)**	*leem-pee-oh (leem-pee-ah)*
clean, to	**limpiar**	*leem-pee-ahr*
cleaner	**limpiador** *(m.)*	*leem-pee-ah-dohr*
clear	**claro (clara)**	*klah-roh (klah-rah)*
clip, to	**podar**	*poh-dahr*
clippers (hedge)	**tijeras podadoras**	*tee-heh-rahs poh-dah-doh-rahs*
close, to	**cerrar**	*seh-rrahr*
closet	**armario**	*ahr-mah-ree-oh*
closet, linen	**armario ropero**	*ahr-mah-ree-oh rroh-peh-roh*
clothespin	**pinza**	*peen-sah*
clothing	**ropa**	*rroh-pah*
cloves	**clavos**	*klah-bohs*
coat	**abrigo**	*ah-bree-goh*
cocktail	**coctél** *(m.)*	*kohk-tehl*
cocktail napkins	**servilletas de cóctel**	*sehr-bee-yeh-tahs deh kohk-tehl*
cocoa	**cacao**	*kah-kah-oh*
coconut	**coco**	*koh-koh*
cod	**bacalao**	*bah-kah-lah-oh*
coffee (decaffeinated, hot, iced)	**café** *(m.)* **(descafeinado, caliente, helado)**	*kah-feh (dehs kah-feh-ee-nah-doh, kah-lee-ehn-teh, eh-lah-doh)*
coffee filter	**filtro de café**	*feel-troh deh kah-feh*
coffee maker	**cafetera**	*kah-feh-teh-rah*
coil	**bobina**	*boh-bee-nah*
colander	**escurridor** *(m.)*	*ehs-koo-rree-dohr*
cold	**frío (fría)**	*free-oh (free-ah)*
cold (illness)	**catarro**	*kah-tah-rroh*
colic	**cólico**	*koh-lee-koh*

continued

English	Spanish	Pronunciation
collar	**collar** *(m.)*	*koh-yahr*
cologne	**colonia**	*koh-loh-nee-ah*
color, to	**colorear**	*loh-loh-reh-ahr*
comb	**peine** *(m.)*	*peh-ee-neh*
combine, to	**combinar**	*kohm-bee-nahr*
come, to	**venir**	*beh-neer*
comforter	**colcha**	*kohl-chah*
commit to, to	**comprometerse a**	*kohm-proh-meh-tehr-seh ah*
compost	**abono**	*ah-boh-noh*
computer	**computadora**	*kohm-poo-tah-doh-rah*
computer game	**juego de computadora**	*hoo-eh-goh deh kohm-poo-tah-doh-rah*
concentrate on something, to	**concentrarse**	*kohn-sehn-trahr-seh*
concussion	**conmoción** *(f.)* **cerebral**	*kohn-moh-see-ohn seh-reh-brahl*
condensed milk	**leche** *(f.)* **condensada**	*leh-cheh kohn-dehn-sah-dah*
condition	**condición** *(f.)*	*kohn-dee-see-ohn*
conditioner	**suavizador** *(m.)* **para el pelo**	*soo-ah-bee-sah-dohr pah-rah ehl peh-loh*
connection	**conexión** *(f.)*	*koh-nehk-see-ohn*
constipation	**estreñimiento**	*ehs-treh-nyee-mee-ehn-toh*
contact lenses	**lentes** *(m., pl.)* **de contacto**	*lehn-tehs deh kohn-tahk-toh*
contact, to	**contactar**	*kohn-tahk-tahr*
contagious	**contagioso (contagiosa)**	*kohn-tah-hee-oh-soh (kohn-tah-hee-oh-sah)*
container	**recipiente** *(m.)*	*rreh-see-pee-ehn-teh*
convulsions	**convulsiones** *(f., pl.)*	*kohn-bool-see-oh-nehs*
cook, to	**cocinar**	*koh-see-nahr*
cookie	**galleta**	*gah-yeh-tah*
cookie sheet	**hoja metálica para el horno**	*oh-hah meh-tah-lee-kah pah-rah ehl ohr-noh*

English	Spanish	Pronunciation
cool	**fresco (fresca)**	*frehs-koh (frehs-kah)*
copy machine	**fotocopiadora**	*foh-toh-koh-pee-ah-doh-rah*
cord	**cordón** *(m.)*	*kohr-dohn*
corduroy	**pana**	*pah-nah*
cork	**corcho**	*kohr-choh*
corkscrew	**sacacorchos** *(m., sing. and pl.)*	*sah-kah-kohr-chohs*
corn	**maíz** *(m.)*	*mah-ees*
cottage cheese	**requesón**	*rreh-keh-sohn*
cotton	**algodón** *(m.)*	*ahl-goh-dohn*
cotton ball	**bolita de algodón**	*boh-lee-tah deh ahl-goh-dohn*
cotton swab	**hisopo**	*ee-soh-poh*
couch	**sofá** *(m.)*	*soh-fah*
cough	**tos** *(f.)*	*tohs*
cough drop	**pastilla para la tos**	*pahs-tee-yah pah-rah lah tohs*
cough syrup	**jarabe** *(m.)* **para la tos**	*hah-rah-beh pah-rah lah tohs*
cough, to	**toser**	*toh-sehr*
counter	**mostrador** *(m.)*	*mohs-trah-dohr*
countertop	**encimera**	*ehn-see-meh-rah*
country	**país** *(m.)*	*pah-ees*
cousin	**primo (prima)**	*pree-moh (pree-mah)*
cover (for an area)	**cubierta**	*koo-bee-ehr-tah*
cover/lid	**tapa**	*tah-pah*
cover, to	**cubrir/tapar**	*koo-breer/tah-pahr*
CPU	**unidad** *(f.)* **central**	*oo-nee-dah sehn-trahl*
crabmeat	**carne** *(f.)* **de cangrejo**	*kahr-neh deh kahn-greh-hoh*
crab	**cangrejo**	*kahn-greh-hoh*
crack	**grieta**	*gree-eh-tah*

continued

English	Spanish	Pronunciation
cracker	galleta	gah-yeh-tah
cranberry	arándano	ah-rahn-dah-noh
cream	crema	kreh-mah
creamer	cremera	kreh-meh-rah
crib	cuna	koo-nah
crocus	azafrán *(m.)*	ah-sah-frahn
crowbar	palanca	pah-lahn-kah
crumb	miga	mee-gah
crutches	muletas	moo-leh-tahs
cry, to	llorar	yoh-rahr
crystal	cristal *(m.)*	krees-tahl
cucumber	pepino	peh-pee-noh
cup (paper, plastic)	taza (de papel, de plástico)	tah-sah (deh pah-pehl, deh plahs-tee-koh)
curfew	toque de queda *(m.)*	toh-keh deh keh-dah
curse, to	maldecir	mal-deh-seer
curtains	cortinas	kohr-tee-nahs
cushion	cojín *(m.)*	koh-heen
cut, to (oneself)	cortar (cortarse)	kohr-tahr (kohr-tahr-seh)
cutting board	tabla para cortar	tah-blah pah-rah kohr-tahr
cycle	ciclo	see-kloh
cypress	ciprés *(m.)*	see-prehs
cystic fibrosis	fibrosis cística *(f.)*	fee-broh-sees sees-tee-kah
daffodil	narciso	nahr-sees-oh
dahlia	dalia	dah-lee-ah
dairy products	productos lácteos	proh-dook-tohs lahk-teh-ohs
daisy	margarita	mahr-gah-ree-tah
dark	oscuro (oscura)	ohs-koo-roh (ohs-koo-rah)
date	fecha	feh-chah
date (fruit)	dátil *(m.)*	dah-teel
day	día *(m.)*	dee-ah
dead	muerto (muerta)	moo-ehr-toh (moo-ehr-tah)

English	Spanish	Pronunciation
deaf	**sordo (sorda)**	*sohr-doh (sohr-dah)*
December	**diciembre**	*dee-see-ehm-breh*
deck	**terraza**	*teh-rrah-sah*
defrost, to	**descongelar**	*dehs-kohn-heh-lahr*
delicatessen	**fiambrería**	*fee-ahm-breh-ree-ah*
delicious	**delicioso (deliciosa)**	*doh-loo-soo-oh-soh (deh-lee-see-oh-sah)*
denim	**dril**	*dreel*
dental floss	**hilo dental**	*ee-loh dehn-tahl*
dentist	**dentista (m. and f.)**	*dehn-tees-tah*
deodorant	**desodorante (m.)**	*deh-soh-doh-rahn-teh*
deodorizer	**desodorante (m.)**	*deh-soh-doh-rahn-teh*
depression	**depresión (f.)**	*deh-preh-see-ohn*
describe, to	**describir**	*dehs-kree-beer*
desk	**escritorio**	*ehs-kree-toh-ree-oh*
detergent	**detergente (m.)**	*deh-tehr-gehn-teh*
diabetes	**diabetes (f.)**	*dee-ah-beh-tehs*
dial	**marcador (m.)**	*mahr-kah-dohr*
diaper	**pañal (m.)**	*pah-nyahl*
diaper bag	**pañalera**	*pah-nyah-leh-rah*
diarrhea	**diarrea (f.)**	*dee-ah-rreh-ah*
dice, to	**cortar en tacos**	*kohr-tahr ehn tah-kohs*
dictionary	**diccionario**	*deek-see-oh-nah-ree-oh*
diffuser	**difusora**	*dee-foo-soh-rah*
dig, to	**excavar**	*ehks-kah-bahr*
dill	**eneldo**	*eh-nehl-doh*
dim, to	**bajar**	*bah-hahr*
dining room	**comedor (m.)**	*koh-meh-dohr*
dinner	**cena**	*seh-nah*
dirty	**sucio (sucia)**	*soo-see-oh (soo-see-ah)*
discipline, to	**castigar**	*kahs-tee-gahr*

continued

English	Spanish	Pronunciation
discuss, to	**discutir**	*dees-koo-teer*
dish	**plato**	*plah-toh*
dish rack	**escurreplatos** *(m.)*	*ehs-koo-rreh-plah-tohs*
dishwasher	**lavaplatos** *(m., sing. and pl.)*	*lah-bah-plah-tohs*
dishwashing detergent	**detergente** *(m.)* **para lavaplatos**	*deh-tehr-hehn-teh pah-rah lah-bah-plah-tohs*
disinfect, to	**desinfectar**	*dehs-een-fehk-tahr*
disinfectant	**desinfectante**	*dehs-een-fehk-tahn-teh*
dissolve, to	**disolver**	*dee-sohl-behr*
divide, to	**dividir**	*dee-bee-deer*
diving board	**trampolín** *(m.)*	*trahm-poh-leen*
dizziness	**mareo**	*mah-reh-oh*
do, to	**hacer**	*ah-sehr*
dog	**perro**	*peh-rroh*
doghouse	**casita de perro**	*kah-see-tah deh peh-rroh*
doll	**muñeca**	*moo-nyeh-kah*
dominoes	**dominós** *(m., pl.)*	*doh-mee-nohs*
door	**puerta**	*poo-ehr-tah*
doorknob	**pomo**	*poh-moh*
doorman	**portero**	*pohr-teh-roh*
double boiler	**olla de baño María**	*oh-yah deh bah-nyoh mah-ree-ah*
Down syndrome	**síndrome** *(m.)* **de Down**	*seen-droh-meh deh down*
dozen	**docena**	*doh-seh-nah*
drain	**desagüe** *(m.)*	*deh-sah-goo-eh*
drain board	**escurridero**	*ehs-koo-rree-deh-roh*
drape, to	**colgar**	*kohl-gahr*
draperies	**colgaduras**	*kohl-gah-doo-rahs*
drapes	**cortinas**	*kohr-tee-nahs*
draw, to	**dibujar**	*dee-boo-hahr*

English	Spanish	Pronunciation
drawer	**cajón** *(m.)*	*kah-hohn*
dress	**vestido**	*behs-tee-doh*
dress, to	**vestir**	*behs-teer*
dresser	**vestidor** *(m.)*	*behs-tee-dohr*
dressing area	**vestuario**	*behs-too-ah-ree-oh*
dressing table	**cómoda**	*koh-moh-dah*
drill	**taladro**	*tah-lah-droh*
drill bit	**broca**	*broh-kah*
drink	**bebida**	*beh-bee-dah*
drink, to	**beber**	*beh-behr*
drive, to	**manejar**	*mah-neh-hahr*
driver's license	**licencia de conducir**	*lee-sehn-see-ah deh kohn-doo-seer*
dropcloth	**lona protectora**	*loh-nah proh-tehk-toh-rah*
drug	**droga**	*droh-gah*
drum	**tambor** *(m.)*	*tahm-bohr*
dry	**seco (seca)**	*seh-koh (seh-kah)*
dry cleaner	**tintorería**	*teen-toh-reh-ree-ah*
dry, to	**secar**	*seh-kahr*
dryer	**secadora**	*seh-kah-doh-rah*
drying rack	**rejilla de secado**	*rreh-hee-yah deh seh-kah-doh*
duck	**pato**	*pah-toh*
during	**durante**	*doo-rahn-teh*
dust, to	**quitar el polvo**	*kee-tahr ehl pohl-boh*
dustpan	**pala de recoger basura**	*pah-lah deh rreh-koh-hehr bah-soo-rah*
Dutch oven	**horno holandés**	*ohr-noh oh-lahn-dehs*
duty	**responsabilidad** *(f.)*	*rrehs-pohn-sah-bee-lee-dahd*
DVD player	**reproductor** *(m.)* **de discos de video**	*rreh-proh-dook-tohr deh dees-kohs deh bee-deh-oh*
dyslexia	**dislexia**	*dees-lehks-ee-ah*

continued

English	Spanish	Pronunciation
ear	oído	oh-ee-doh
earache	dolor (m.) de oído	doh-lohr deh oh-ee-doh
early	temprano	tehm-prah-noh
earrings	aretes (m., pl.)	ah-reh-tehs
eat, to	comer	koh-mehr
edger	bordeadora	bohr-deh-ah-doh-rah
egg	huevo	oo-eh-boh
egg substitute	substituto de huevo	soobs-tee-too-toh deh oo-eh-boh
eggplant	berenjena	beh-rehn-heh-nah
eight	ocho	oh-choh
eighteen	dieciocho (diez y ocho)	dee-ehs-ee-oh-choh
eighth	octavo	ohk-tah-boh
eighty	ochenta	oh-chehn-tah
elbow	codo	koh-doh
elderly	personas mayores	pehr-soh-nahs mah-yoh-rehs
electric fry pan	sartén (f.) eléctrica	sahr-tehn eh-lehk-tree-kah
electric knife	cuchillo eléctrico	koo-chee-yoh eh-lehk-tree-koh
electric meter	contador (m.) de luz	kohn-tah-dohr deh loos
electric razor	rasuradora eléctrica	rah-soo-rah-doh-rah eh-lehk-tree-kah
electrical outlet	enchufe (m.)	ehn-choo-feh
electricity	electricidad (f.)	eh-lehk-tree-see-dahd
elevator	ascensor (m.)	ah-sehn-sohr
eleven	once	ohn-seh
elm	olmo	ohl-moh
emergency	emergencia	eh-mehr-hehn-see-ah
empty	vacío (vacía)	bah-see-oh (bah-see-ah)
empty, to	vaciar	bah-see-ahr
encyclopedia	enciclopedia	ehn-see-kloh-peh-dee-ah

English	Spanish	Pronunciation
endive	**endivia**	*ehn-dee-bee-ah*
enjoy, to	**divertirse**	*dee-behr-teer-seh*
enter, to	**entrar**	*ehn-trahr*
entertainment unit	**módulo de entretenimiento**	*moh-doo-loh deh ehn-treh-teh-nee-mee-ehn-toh*
envelope (legal, letter, manila)	**sobre** *(m.)* **(legal, regular, manila)**	*soh-bre (leh-gahl, rreh-goo-lahr, mah-nee-lah)*
epilepsy	**epilepsia**	*eh-pee-lehp-see-ah*
equipment	**equipo**	*eh-kee-poh*
eraser	**goma**	*goh-mah*
errand	**recado**	*rreh-kah-doh*
espresso	**espreso**	*ehs-preh-soh*
evaporated milk	**leche evaporada**	*leh-cheh eh-bah-poh-rah-dah*
eve	**víspera**	*bees-peh-rah*
evening	**noche** *(f.)*	*noh-cheh*
evening gown	**vestido de noche**	*behs-tee-doh deh noh-cheh*
every	**cada**	*kah-dah*
experience	**experiencia**	*ehks-peh-ree-ehn-see-ah*
explain, to	**explicar**	*ehks-plee-kahr*
express oneself, to	**expresarse**	*ehks-preh-sahr-seh*
eye	**ojo**	*oh-hoh*
eyedrops	**colirio**	*koh-lee-ree-oh*
fabric	**tela**	*teh-lah*
fabric softener	**suavizador** *(m.)*	*soo-ah-bee-sah-dohr*
face	**cara**	*kah-rah*
fall, to	**caer (caerse)**	*kah-ehr (kah-ehr-seh)*
fan (ceiling)	**ventilador** *(m.)* **(de techo)**	*behn-tee-lah-dohr (deh teh-choh)*
fat	**grasa**	*grah-sah*
father	**padre** *(m.)*	*pah-dreh*
fatigue	**fatiga**	*fah-tee-gah*

continued

English	Spanish	Pronunciation
faucet (cold, hot water)	grifo (agua fría, caliente)	gree-foh (ah-goo-ah free-ah, kah-lee-ehn-teh)
fax machine	máquina fax	mah-kee-nah fahks
feather duster	plumero	ploo-meh-roh
February	febrero	feh-breh-roh
feed, to	dar de comer	dahr deh koh-mehr
feeding dish	plato	plah-toh
female	hembra	ehm-brah
fence	cerca	sehr-kah
fertilize, to	abonar	ah-boh-nahr
fertilizer	abono	ah-boh-noh
fever	fiebre (f.)	fee-eh-breh
fifteen	quince	keen-seh
fifth	quinto (quinta)	keen-toh (keen-tah)
fifty	cincuenta	seen-koo-ehn-tah
fig	higo	ee-go
fight, to	pelear	peh-leh-ahr
fig tree	higo	ee-goh
figurine	figurita	fee-goo-ree-tah
file cabinet	fichero	fee-cheh-roh
fill out, to	llenar	yeh-nahr
filter	filtro	feel-troh
find, to	encontrar	ehn-kohn-trahr
finger	dedo	deh-doh
finish, to	terminar	tehr-mee-nahr
fir	pino noruego	pee-noh noh-roo-eh-goh
fire extinguisher	extinguidor (m.) de encendios	ehks-teen-gee-dohr deh ehn-sehn-dee-ohs
fireplace	chimenea	chee-meh-neh-ah
fireplace screen	pantalde (f.) de chimenea	pahn-tahl-deh deh chee-meh-neh-ah

English	Spanish	Pronunciation
fireplace tools	**herramientas de chimenea**	*eh-rrah-mee-ehn-tahs deh chee-meh-neh-ah*
firewood	**leña**	*leh-nyah*
first	**primero (primera)**	*pree-meh-roh (pree-meh-rah)*
first-aid kit	**botiquín (m.) de primeros auxilios**	*boh-tee-keen deh pree-meh-rohs ah-ook-see-lee-ohs*
fish (food)	**pescado**	*pehs-kah-doh*
fish (pet)	**pez (m.)**	*pehs*
fish store	**pescadería**	*pehs-kah-deh-ree-ah*
fish tank	**pecera**	*peh-seh-rah*
five	**cinco**	*seen-koh*
flannel	**franela**	*frah-neh-lah*
flexible	**flexible**	*flehk-see-bleh*
flip, to	**voltear**	*bohl-teh-ahr*
floor	**piso**	*pee-soh*
floor mat	**alfombrilla**	*ahl-fohm-bree-yah*
floor tile	**baldosa**	*bahl-doh-sah*
floral arrangement	**arreglo floral**	*ah-rreh-gloh floh-rahl*
flounder	**lenguado**	*lehn-goo-ah-doh*
flour	**harina**	*ah-ree-nah*
flour, to	**enharinar**	*ehn-ah-ree-nahr*
flower	**flor (f.)**	*flohr*
flower pot	**maceta**	*mah-seh-tah*
flowerbox	**cantero**	*kahn-teh-roh*
flu	**gripe (m.)**	*gree-peh*
fluff, to	**ahuecar**	*ah-oo-eh-kahr*
flute (glass)	**copa**	*koh-pah*
fly a kite, to	**volar una cometa**	*boh-lahr oo-nah koh-meh-tah*
foam	**espuma**	*ehs-poo-mah*
fold, to	**doblar**	*doh-blahr*

continued

English	Spanish	Pronunciation
folder	**carpeta**	*kahr-peh-tah*
folding chairs	**sillas plegables**	*see-yahs pleh-gah-blehs*
follow, to	**seguir**	*seh-geer*
food	**comida**	*koh-mee-dah*
food processor	**procesador** *(m.)* **de comida**	*proh-seh-sah-dohr deh koh-mee-dah*
foot	**pie** *(m.)*	*pee-eh*
footrest	**descanso para pies**	*dehs-kahn-soh pah-rah pee-ehs*
football	**fútbol americano** *(m.)*	*foot-bohl ah-meh-ree-kah-noh*
forehead	**frente** *(f.)*	*frehn-teh*
fork (plastic, silver, stainless steel)	**tenedor** *(m.)* **(plástico, de plata, de acero inoxidable)**	*teh-neh-dohr (plahs-tee-koh, deh plah-tah, deh ah-seh-roh een-ohk-see-dah-bleh)*
forsythia	**forsitia**	*fohr-see-tee-ah*
forty	**cuarenta**	*koo-ah-rehn-tah*
fountain	**fuente** *(f.)*	*foo-ehn-teh*
four	**cuatro**	*koo-ah-troh*
fourteen	**catorce**	*kah-tohr-seh*
fourth	**cuarto (cuarta)**	*koo-ahr-toh (koo-ahr-tah)*
fragile	**delicado (delicada)**	*deh-lee-kah-doh (deh-lee-kah-dah)*
freeze, to	**congelar**	*kohn-heh-lahr*
freezer	**congelador** *(m.)*	*kohn-heh-lah-dohr*
French toast	**tostada francesa**	*tohs-tah-dah frahn-seh-sah*
frequently	**frecuentemente**	*freh-koo-ehn-teh-mehn-teh*
fresh	**fresco (fresca)**	*frehs-koh (frehs-kah)*
Friday	**viernes**	*bee-ehr-nehs*
fried eggs	**huevos fritos**	*oo-eh-bohs free-tohs*
friendly	**amable**	*ah-mah-bleh*
from	**desde**	*dehs-deh*

English	Spanish	Pronunciation
frozen	**congelado (congelada)**	*kohn-heh-lah-doh (kohn-heh-lah-dah)*
fruit	**fruta**	*froo-tah*
fruit and vegetable market	**verdulería**	*behr-doo-leh-ree-ah*
fruit salad	**ensalada de fruta**	*ehn-sah-lah-dah de froo-tah*
fruit slices	**rodajas de frutas**	*rroh-dah-hahs deh froo-tahs*
fry, to	**freír**	*freh-eer*
frying pan	**sartén** *(f.)*	*sahr-tehn*
full	**lleno (llena)**	*yeh-noh (yeh-nah)*
funnel	**embudo**	*ehm-boo-doh*
fur	**piel** *(f.)*	*pee-ehl*
fur coat	**abrigo de piel**	*ah-bree-goh deh pee-ehl*
furniture	**muebles** *(m., pl.)*	*moo-eh-blehs*
fusebox	**caja de fusibles**	*kah-hah deh foo-see-blehs*
gallon	**galón** *(m.)*	*gah-lohn*
garage	**garaje** *(m.)*	*gah-rah-heh*
garbage bag	**bolsa para basura**	*bohl-sah pah-rah bah-soo-rah*
garbage disposal	**desechador** *(m.)*	*dehs-eh-chah-dohr*
garden	**jardín** *(m.)*	*hahr-deen*
garlic press	**prensa de ajo**	*prehn-sah deh ah-hoh*
gas meter	**contador** *(m.)* **de gas**	*kohn-tah-dohr deh gahs*
gasp for air, to	**jadear**	*hah-deh-ahr*
gathering	**reunión** *(f.)*	*rreh-oo-nee-ohn*
gauze	**gasa**	*gah-sah*
gel	**gel** *(m.)*	*hehl*
gelatin (such as Jell-O brand)	**gelatina**	*heh-lah-tee-nah*
genetic disease	**enfermedad** *(f.)* **genética**	*ehn-fehr-meh-dahd heh-neh-tee-kah*
geranium	**geranio**	*heh-rah-nee-oh*

continued

English	Spanish	Pronunciation
gerbil	**jerbo**	*hehr-boh*
gin	**ginebra**	*hee-neh-brah*
ginger	**jengibre** *(m.)*	*hehn-hee-breh*
give, to	**dar**	*dahr*
gladiolus	**gladiolo**	*glah-dee-oh-loh*
glass (plastic)	**vaso (plástico)**	*bah-soh (plahs-tee-koh)*
glasses (for vision)	**espejuelos**	*ehs-peh-hoo-eh-lohs*
gloves (rubber)	**guantes (de goma)**	*goo-ahn-tehs deh goh-mah*
go, to	**ir**	*eer*
go to bed, to	**acostarse**	*ah-kohs-tahr-seh*
godfather	**padrino**	*pah-dree-noh*
godmother	**madrina**	*mah-dree-nah*
gold	**oro**	*oh-roh*
goldfish	**pez** *(m.)* **de colores**	*pehs deh koh-loh-rehs*
golf	**golf** *(m.)*	*gohlf*
gout	**gota**	*goh-tah*
grain	**grano**	*grah-noh*
gram	**gramo** *(m.)*	*grah-moh*
grandfather	**abuelo**	*ah-boo-eh-loh*
grandmother	**abuela**	*ah-boo-eh-lah*
grape	**uva**	*oo-bah*
grapefruit	**toronja**	*toh-rohn-hah*
grass	**hierba**	*ee-ehr-bah*
grate	**rejilla**	*rreh-hee-yah*
grate, to	**rallar**	*rrah-yahr*
grater	**rallador** *(m.)*	*rrah-yah-dohr*
gravy	**salsa**	*sahl-sah*
gray	**gris**	*grees*
grease, to	**engrasar**	*ehn-grah-sahr*
greasy	**grasoso (grasosa)**	*grah-soh-soh (grah-soh-sah)*
green	**verde**	*behr-deh*

English	Spanish	Pronunciation
greenhouse	**invernadero**	*een-behr-nah-deh-roh*
griddle	**comal** *(m.)*	*koh-mahl*
grill	**parrilla**	*pah-rree-yah*
grill, to	**asar a la parrilla**	*ah-sahr ah lah pah-ree-yah*
grimy	**mugriento** **(mugrienta)**	*moo-gree-ehn-toh (moo-gree-ehn-tah)*
grind, to	**moler**	*moh-lehr*
grinder	**molino**	*moh-lee-noh*
grocery store	**bodega**	*boh-deh-gah*
groomer	**peluquero canino**	*peh-loo-keh-roh kah-nee-noh*
grouper	**mero**	*meh-roh*
grout	**lechada**	*leh-chah-dah*
guest	**huésped**	*oo-ehs-pehd*
guinea pig	**cobaya**	*koh-bah-yah*
guitar	**guitarra**	*gee-tah-rrah*
gum	**chicle** *m.*	*chee-kleh*
hair	**pelo**	*peh-loh*
hairdryer	**secador** *(m).* **de pelo**	*seh-kah-dohr deh peh-loh*
hair gel	**gomina**	*goh-mee-nah*
hair pin	**horquilla**	*ohr-kee-yah*
hair spray	**laca**	*lah-kah*
half hour	**media hora**	*meh-dee-ah oh-rah*
half pound	**media libra**	*meh-dee-ah lee-brah*
ham	**jamón** *(m.)*	*hah-mohn*
hamburger	**hamburguesa**	*ahm-boor-geh-sah*
hammer	**martillo**	*mahr-tee-yoh*
hammock	**hamaca**	*ah-mah-kah*
hamper	**canasta**	*kah-nahs-tah*
hamster	**hámster** *(m.)*	*ahm-stehr*
hand	**mano** *(f.)*	*mah-noh*

continued

English	Spanish	Pronunciation
hand lotion	**crema para las manos**	*kreh-mah pah-rah lahs mah-nohs*
handkerchief	**pañuelo**	*pah-nyoo-eh-loh*
handyman	**mecánico**	*meh-kah-nee-koh*
hang, to	**colgar**	*kohl-gahr*
hanger	**percha**	*pehr-chah*
hard	**duro (dura)**	*doo-roh (doo-rah)*
hard-boiled eggs	**huevos duros**	*oo-eh-bohs doo-rohs*
hat	**sombrero**	*sohm-breh-roh*
hatchet	**hacha**	*ah-chah*
have just, to	**acabar de**	*ah-kah-bahr deh*
hay fever	**fiebre (f.) de heno**	*fee-eh-breh deh eh-noh*
hazelnut	**avellana**	*ah-beh-yah-nah*
head	**cabeza**	*kah-beh-sah*
headache	**dolor (m.) de cabeza**	*doh-lohr deh kah-beh-sah*
headboard	**cabecera**	*kah-beh-seh-rah*
health	**salud (f.)**	*sah-lood*
hear, to	**oír**	*oh-eer*
hearing aid	**audífono**	*ah-oo-dee-foh-noh*
heart	**corazón (m.)**	*koh-rah-sohn*
heat, to	**calentar**	*kah-lehn-tahr*
heater	**calentador (m.)**	*kah-lehn-tah-dohr*
heating pad	**placa de calentamiento**	*plah-kah deh kah-lehn-tah-mee-ehn-toh*
heating unit	**calentador (m.)**	*kah-lehn-tah-dohr*
hedge	**seto**	*seh-toh*
heirloom	**reliquia**	*rreh-lee-kee-ah*
helmet	**casco**	*kahs-koh*
help	**ayuda**	*ah-yoo-dah*
help, to	**ayudar**	*ah-yoo-dahr*
hem	**dobladillo**	*doh-blah-dee-yoh*
hen	**gallina**	*gah-yee-nah*

English	Spanish	Pronunciation
hepatitis	**hepatitis** *(f.)*	*eh-pah-tee-tees*
herb	**hierba**	*ee-ehr-bah*
herring	**arenque** *(m.)*	*ah-rehn-keh*
hibiscus	**hibisco**	*ee-bees-koh*
highchair	**silla alta para niños**	*see-yah ahl-tah pah-rah nee-nyohs*
high hat	**luz de techo**	*loos deh teh-choh*
highlighter	**marcador** *(m.)*	*mahr-kah-dohr*
hip	**cadera**	*kah-deh-rah*
hit, to	**golpear**	*gohl-peh-ahr*
hoe	**azadón** *(m.)*	*ah-sah-dohn*
hold, to	**abrazar**	*ah-brah-sahr*
hole	**hoyo**	*oh-yoh*
home care	**cuidado doméstico**	*koo-ee-dah-doh doh-mehs-tee-koh*
homework	**tarea**	*tah-reh-ah*
honey	**miel** *(m.)*	*mee-ehl*
horse	**caballo**	*kah-bah-yoh*
horseradish	**rábano picante**	*rrah-bah-noh pee-kahn-teh*
hose	**manguera**	*mahn-geh-rah*
hot	**caliente**	*kah-lee-ehn-teh*
hot chocolate	**chocolate** *(m.)* **caliente**	*choh-koh-lah-teh kah-lee-ehn-teh*
hot dog	**perro caliente**	*peh-rroh kah-lee-ehn-teh*
hot tub	**bañera de hidromasaje**	*bah-nyeh-rah deh ee-droh-mah-sah-heh*
hot-water bag	**bolsa de agua caliente**	*bohl-sah deh ah-goo-ah kah-lee-ehn-teh*
hour	**hora**	*oh-rah*
housekeeping	**limpieza**	*leem-pee-eh-sah*
how?	**¿cómo?**	*koh-moh*

continued

English	Spanish	Pronunciation
how much/ how many?	**¿cuánto (cuánta, cuántos, cuántas)?**	*koo-ahn-toh (koo-ahn-tah, koo-ahn-tohs, koo-ahn-tahs)*
hubcap	**tapacubo**	*tah-pah-koo-boh*
humid	**húmedo (húmeda)**	*oo-meh-doh (oo-meh-dah)*
hundred	**ciento (cien)**	*see-ehn-toh (see-ehn)*
hurry, to	**apurarse**	*ah-poo-rahr-seh*
hurt (oneself) to	**dañarse**	*dah-nyahr-seh*
hyacinth	**jacinto**	*hah-seen-toh*
hydrangea	**hortensia**	*ohr-tehn-see-ah*
hyperactivity	**hiperactividad** *(f.)*	*ee-pehr-ahk-tee-bee-dahd*
ice (cubes, crushed)	**hielo (en cubitos, molido)**	*ee-eh-loh (ehn koo-bee-tohs, moh-lee-doh)*
ice bucket	**cubitera**	*koo-bee-teh-rah*
ice cream (low-fat)	**helado (bajo en grasa)**	*eh-lah-doh (bah-hoh ehn grah-sah)*
ice-cream scoop	**heladera**	*eh-lah-deh-rah*
icemaker	**hielera**	*ee-eh-leh-rah*
ice pack	**bolsa de hielo**	*bohl-sah deh ee-eh-loh*
identification	**identificación** *(f.)*	*ee-dehn-tee-fee-kah-see-ohn*
ill	**enfermo (enferma)**	*ehn-fehr-moh (ehn-fehr-mah)*
illness	**enfermedad** *(f.)*	*ehn-fehr-meh-dahd*
immediately	**inmediatamente**	*een-meh-dee-ah-tah-mehn-teh*
immersion blender	**licuadora de immersion**	*lee-koo-ah-doh-rah deh ee-mehr-see-ohn*
immobile	**inmóvil**	*een-moh-beel*
in	**en**	*ehn*
index card	**ficha**	*fee-chah*
indigestion	**indigestión** *(f.)*	*een-dee-behs-tee-ohn*
infection	**infección** *(f.)*	*een-fehk-see-ohn*
inhaler	**inhalador** *(m.)*	*een-ah-lah-dohr*

English	Spanish	Pronunciation
insect	**insecto**	*een-sehk-toh*
insect repellent	**repelente** *(m.)* **para insectos**	*rreh-peh-lehn-teh pah-rah een-sehk-tohs*
insecticide	**insecticida**	*een-sehk-tee-see-dah*
insert, to	**meter**	*meh-tehr*
inside	**adentro**	*ah-dehn-troh*
invite, to	**invitar**	*een-bee-tahr*
iris	**lirio**	*lee-ree-oh*
iron	**plancha**	*plahn-chah*
iron, to	**planchar**	*plahn-chahr*
ironing board	**tabla de planchar**	*tah-blah deh plahn-chahr*
ironing-board cover	**tapa de la tabla de planchar**	*tah-pah deh lah tah-blah deh plahn-chahr*
jacket	**chaqueta**	*chah-keh-tah*
Jacuzzi	**jacuzzi** *(m.)*	*yah-koo-see*
jam/jelly	**mermelada**	*mehr-meh-lah-dah*
January	**enero**	*eh-neh-roh*
jar	**frasco**	*frahs-koh*
jeans	**vaqueros**	*bah-keh-rohs*
job	**trabajo**	*trah-bah-hoh*
juice (apple, cranberry, grape, grapefruit, lemon, lime, orange, pineapple)	**jugo (de manzana, de arándano agrio, de uva, de toronja, de limón, de lima, de naranja, de piña)**	*hoo-goh (deh mahn-sah-nah, deh ah-rahn-dah-noh ah-gree-oh, deh oo-bah, deh toh-rohn-hah, deh lee-mohn, deh lee-mah, deh nah-rahn-hah, deh pee-nyah)*
July	**julio**	*hoo-lee-oh*
jumprope	**cuerda de saltar**	*koo-ehr-dah deh sahl-tahr*
jump, to	**saltar**	*sahl-tahr*
June	**junio**	*hoo-nee-oh*
keep, to	**guardar**	*goo-ahr-dahr*
ketchup	**salsa de tomate**	*sahl-sah deh toh-mah-teh*

continued

English	Spanish	Pronunciation
key	**llave**	*yah-beh*
keyboard	**teclado**	*teh-klah-doh*
kick, to	**dar patadas**	*dahr pah-tah-dahs*
kilogram	**kilo**	*kee-loh*
kiwi	**kiwi**	*kee-wee*
knee	**rodilla**	*rroh-dee-yah*
knickknacks	**cachivache** *(m.)*	*kah-chee-bah-cheh*
knife (electric, plastic, silver, stainless steel)	**cuchillo (eléctrico, plástico, de plata, de acero inoxidable)**	*koo-chee-yoh (ch lchk tree-koh, plahs-tee-koh, deh plah-tah, deh ah-seh-roh een-ohk-see-dah-bleh)*
knife sharpener	**afilador** *(m.)* **de cuchillos**	*ah-fee-lah-dohr deh koo-chee-yohs*
know, to (a fact)	**saber**	*sah-behr*
know, to (a person)	**conocer**	*koh-noh-sehr*
kosher	**kosher**	*koh-shehr*
label	**etiqueta**	*eh-tee-keh-tah*
label, to	**etiquetar**	*eh-tee-keh-tahr*
lace	**encaje** *(m.)*	*ehn-kah-heh*
lacrosse	**lacrosse** *(m.)*	*lah-krohs*
ladder	**escalera**	*ehs-kah-leh-rah*
ladle	**cucharón** *(m.)*	*koo-chah-rohn*
lamb	**cordero**	*kohr-deh-roh*
lamp (desk, floor)	**lámpara (de escritorio, de piso)**	*lahm-pah-rah (deh ehs-kree-toh-ree-oh, deh pee-soh)*
lampshade	**pantalla**	*pahn-tah-yah*
last (in a series)	**último (última)**	*ool-tee-moh (ool-tee-mah)*
last (most recent)	**pasado (pasada)**	*pah-sah-doh (pah-sah-dah)*
late (in arriving)	**tarde**	*tahr-deh*
later	**más tarde**	*mahs tahr-deh*
laundry	**ropa sucia**	*rroh-pah soo-see-ah*

English	Spanish	Pronunciation
laundry basket	**cesta para la ropa sucia**	*sehs-tah pah-rah lah rroh-pah soo-see-ah*
laundry room	**lavandería**	*lah-bahn-deh-ree-ah*
lawn	**césped** *(m.)*	*sehs-pehd*
lawnmower	**cortacésped** *(m.)*	*kohr-tah-sehs-pehd*
laxative	**laxante** *(m.)*	*lahk-sahn-teh*
leaf	**hoja**	*oh-hah*
leash	**traílla**	*trah-ee-yah*
leather	**cuero**	*koo-eh-roh*
leaf	**hoja**	*oh-hah*
leave behind, to	**dejar**	*deh-hahr*
leave, to (go out)	**salir**	*sah-leer*
leek	**puerro**	*poo-eh-rroh*
leg	**pierna**	*pee-ehr-nah*
lemon	**limón**	*lee-mohn*
lemonade	**limonada**	*lee-moh-nah-dah*
lentils	**lentejas**	*lehn-teh-hahs*
letter	**carta**	*kahr-tah*
lettuce	**lechuga**	*leh-choo-gah*
leukemia	**leucemia**	*leh-oo-seh-mee-ah*
level	**nivel** *(m.)*	*nee-behl*
lid	**tapa**	*tah-pah*
light	**luz** *(f.)*	*loos*
light switch	**interruptor** *(m.)*	*een-teh-roop-tohr*
light, to	**encender**	*ehn-sehn-dehr*
lilac	**lila**	*lee-lah*
lily	**lirio**	*lee-ree-oh*
lima beans	**frijoles** *(m., pl.)* **de lima**	*free-hoh-lehs deh lee-mah*
lime	**lima**	*lee-mah*
linen	**lino**	*lee-noh*

continued

English	Spanish	Pronunciation
linens	**ropa blanca**	*rroh-pah blahn-kah*
lingerie	**lencería**	*lehn-seh-ree-ah*
linoleum	**linóleo**	*lee-noh-leh-oh*
lip	**labio**	*lah-bee-oh*
liquefy, to	**licuar**	*lee-koo-ahr*
liqueur	**licor**	*lee-kohr*
liquid	**líquido**	*lee-kee-doh*
liquor store	**licorería**	*lee-koh-reh-ree-ah*
listen, to	**escuchar**	*ehs-koo-chahr*
liter	**litro**	*lee-troh*
live, to	**vivir**	*bee-beer*
liver	**hígado**	*ee-gah-doh*
lizard	**lagartija**	*lah-gahr-tee-hah*
load, to	**cargar**	*kahr-gahr*
loaf pan	**molde** *(m.)* **para pan**	*mohl-deh pah-rah pahn*
lobster	**langosta**	*lahn-gohs-tah*
lock, to	**cerrar con llave**	*seh-rrahr kohn yah-beh*
log	**tronco**	*trohn-koh*
look at, to	**mirar**	*mee-rahr*
look for, to	**buscar**	*boos-kahr*
lotion	**loción** *(f.)*	*loh-see-ohn*
lounge chair	**sillón** *(m.)*	*see-yohn*
loveseat	**sofá de dos plazas**	*soh-fah deh dohs plah-sahs*
lower, to	**bajar**	*bah-hahr*
lozenge	**pastilla**	*pahs-tee-yah*
lukewarm	**tibio (tibia)**	*tee-bee-oh (tee-bee-ah)*
lunch	**almuerzo**	*ahl-moo-ehr-soh*
lunchbox	**fiambrera**	*fee-ahm-breh-rah*
macaroni	**macarrones** *(m., pl.)*	*mah-kah-rroh-nehs*
machine	**máquina**	*mah-kee-nah*
mackerel	**caballa**	*kah-bah-yah*

English	Spanish	Pronunciation
magazine	**revista**	*rreh-bees-tah*
magazine rack	**revistero**	*rreh-bees-teh-roh*
magnolia	**magnolia**	*mahg-noh-lee-ah*
mailbox	**buzón** *(m.)*	*boo-sohn*
maintain, to	**mantener**	*mahn-teh-nehr*
make, to	**hacer**	*ah-sehr*
make a mess, to	**ensuciar**	*ehn-soo-see-ahr*
makeup	**maquillaje** *(m.)*	*mah-kee-yah-heh*
male	**varón**	*bah-rohn*
mango	**mango**	*mahn-goh*
manicure set	**estuche** *(m.)* **de** **manicura**	*ehs-too-cheh deh mah-nee-koo-rah*
manners	**modales** *(m., pl.)*	*moh-dah-lehs*
mantel	**repisa**	*rreh-pree-sah*
manure	**estiércol** *(m.)*	*ehs-tee-ehr-kohl*
maple	**arce** *(m.)*	*ahr-seh*
maple syrup	**jarabe** *(m.)* **de arce**	*hah-rah-beh deh ahr-seh*
March	**marzo**	*mahr-soh*
margarine	**margarina**	*mahr-gah-ree-nah*
marigold	**maravilla**	*mah-rah-bee-yah*
market	**mercado**	*mehr-kah-doh*
mash, to	**machacar**	*mah-chah-kahr*
mask	**máscara**	*mahs-kah-rah*
matches	**fósforos**	*fohs-foh-rohs*
mattress	**colchón** *(m.)*	*kohl-chohn*
mattress pad/ cover	**cobertor** *(m.)*	*koh-behr-tohr*
May	**mayo**	*mah-yoh*
mayonnaise	**mayonesa**	*mah-yoh-neh-sah*
meal	**comida**	*koh-mee-dah*

continued

English	Spanish	Pronunciation
measles	**sarampión**	*sah-rahm-pee-ohn*
measure (tape)	**cinta de medir**	*seen-tah deh meh-deer*
measure, to	**medir**	*meh-deer*
measuring cup	**taza de medir**	*tah-sah deh meh-deer*
measuring spoons	**cucharas de medir**	*koo-chah-rahs deh meh-deer*
meat	**carne** *(f.)*	*kahr-neh*
meatballs	**albóndigas**	*ahl-bohn-dee-gahs*
medicine cabinet	**botiquín** *(m.)*	*boh-tee-keen*
medium	**mediano (mediana)**	*meh-dee-ah-noh (meh-dee-ah-nah)*
medium rare	**término medio**	*tehr-mee-noh meh-dee-oh*
melon	**melón**	*meh-lohn*
melt, to	**derretirse**	*deh-rreh-teer-seh*
member	**miembro**	*mee-ehm-broh*
mend	**arreglar**	*ah-rreh-glahr*
meter	**contador** *(m.)*	*kohn-tah-dohr*
microplane	**microplano**	*mee-kroh-plah-noh*
microwave oven	**microondas** *(m.)*	*mee-kroh-ohn-dahs*
midnight	**medianoche** *(f.)*	*meh-dee-ah-noh-cheh*
mildew	**moho**	*moh-oh*
milk (skim)	**leche** *(f.)* **(desnatada)**	*leh-cheh (dehs-nah-tah-dah)*
milkshake	**batido**	*bah-tee-doh*
million	**millón**	*mee-yohn*
mineral water (carbonated, noncarbonated)	**agua** *(m.)* **mineral (gaseosa, sin gas)**	*ah-goo-ah mee-neh-rahl (gah-seh-oh-sah, seen gahs)*
mint	**menta**	*mehn-tah*
minute	**minuto**	*mee-noo-toh*
mirror (magnifying)	**espejo (de amplificación)**	*ehs-peh-hoh (deh ahm-plee-fee-kah-see-ohn)*
misbehave, to	**portarse mal**	*pohr-tahr-seh mahl*
mittens	**mitones** *(m., pl.)*	*mee-toh-nehs*

English	Spanish	Pronunciation
mix, to	**mezclar**	*mehs-klahr*
mixer	**batidora**	*bah-tee-doh-rah*
moist	**húmedo (húmeda)**	*oo-meh-doh (oo-meh-dah)*
moisturizer	**crema hidratante**	*kreh-mah ee-drah-tahn-teh*
mold	**moho**	*moh-oh*
moldings	**moldaduras**	*mohl-dah-doo-rahs*
Monday	**lunes**	*loo-nehs*
monitor	**pantalla monitor**	*pahn-tah-yah moh-nee-tohr*
monkfish	**rape** *(m.)*	*rrah-peh*
mononucleosis	**mononucleosis** *(f.)*	*moh-noh-noo-kleh-oh-sees*
month	**mes** *(m.)*	*mehs*
mop	**trapeador** *(m.)*	*trah-peh-ah-dohr*
mop, to	**trapear**	*trah-peh-ahr*
morning	**mañana**	*mah-nyah-nah*
mother	**madre** *(f.)*	*mah-dreh*
mouse	**ratón** *(m.)*	*rrah-tohn*
mouth	**boca**	*boh-kah*
mouthwash	**enjuague** *(m.)* **bucal**	*ehn-hoo-ah-geh boo-kahl*
move, to	**mover**	*moh-behr*
movie	**película**	*peh-lee-koo-lah*
muffin tin	**molde** *(m.)* **metálico para hacer molletes en el horno**	*mohl-deh meh-tah-lee-koh pah-rah ah-sehr moh-yeh-tehs ehn ehl ohr-noh*
mulch	**mantillo**	*mahn-tee-yoh*
multiple sclerosis	**esclerosis** *(f.)* **múltiple**	*ehs-kleh-roh-sees mool-tee-pleh*
mumps	**paperas**	*pah-peh-rahs*
muscular dystrophy	**distrofia muscular**	*dees-troh-fee-ah moos-koo-lahr*
mushroom	**champiñón** *(m.)*	*cham-pee-nyohn*
mussels	**mejillones** *(m., pl.)*	*meh-hee-yoh-nehs*
mustard	**mostaza**	*mohs-tah-sah*

continued

English	Spanish	Pronunciation
mute	**mudo (muda)**	*moo-doh (moo-dah)*
nail	**clavo**	*klah-boh*
nail clippers	**cortauñas**	*kohr-tah-oo-nyahs*
nail file	**lima de uñas**	*lee-mah deh oo-nyahs*
nail polish	**esmalte *(m.)* de uñas**	*ehs-mahl-teh deh oo-nyahs*
nail polish remover	**quitaesmalte *(m.)***	*kee-tah-ehs-mahl-teh*
napkin	**servilleta**	*sehr-bee-yeh-tah*
napkin holder	**servilletero**	*sehr-bee-yeh-teh-roh*
nausea	**náusea**	*nah-oo-seh-ah*
neat	**en orden**	*ehn ohr-dehn*
neck	**cuello**	*koo-eh-yoh*
necklace	**collar *(m.)***	*koh-yahr*
nectarine	**nectarina**	*nehk-tah-ree-nah*
need	**necesidad *(f.)***	*neh-seh-see-dahd*
need, to	**necesitar**	*neh-seh-see-tahr*
needle	**aguja**	*ah-goo-hah*
neurological disease	**enfermedad *(f.)* neurológica**	*ehn-fehr-meh-dahd neh-oo-roh-loh-hee-kah*
never	**nunca**	*noon-kah*
newspaper	**periódico**	*peh-ree-oh-dee-koh*
next	**próximo (próxima)**	*prohk-see-moh (prohk-see-mah)*
nightgown	**ropa de dormir**	*rroh-pah deh dohr-meer*
nightlight	**luz *(f.)* de noche**	*loos deh noh-cheh*
nightshirt	**camisa de dormir**	*kah-mee-sah deh dohr-meer*
night table	**mesa de noche**	*meh-sah deh noh-cheh*
nine	**nueve**	*noo-eh-beh*
nineteen	**diecinueve (diez y nueve)**	*dee-ehs-ee-noo-eh-beh*
ninety	**noventa**	*noh-behn-tah*
ninth	**noveno (novena)**	*noh-beh-noh (noh-beh-nah)*

English	Spanish	Pronunciation
nonabrasive	**no-abrasivo** (no-abrasiva)	*noh-ah-brah-see-boh* (*noh-ah-brah-see-bah*)
noodles	**fideos**	*fee-deh-ohs*
noon	**mediodía**	*meh-dee-oh-dee-ah*
nose	**nariz** *(f.)*	*nah-rees*
nose drops	**gotas para la nariz**	*goh-tahs pah-rah lah nah-rees*
notepad (notepads)	**bloc** *(m.)* (bloques)	*blohk (bloh-kehs)*
notice, to	**notar**	*noh-tahr*
notify, to	**notificar**	*noh-tee-fee-kahr*
novel	**novela**	*noh-beh-lah*
November	**noviembre**	*noh-bee-ehm-breh*
nozzle	**boquilla**	*boh-kee-yah*
nut	**nuez** *(f.)*	*noo-ehs*
nut (tool)	**tuerca**	*too-ehr-kah*
nutmeg	**nuez** *(f.)* **moscada**	*noo-ehs mohs-kah-dah*
nylon	**nilón** *(m.)*	*nee-lohn*
oak	**roble** *(m.)*	*rroh-bleh*
oatmeal	**avena**	*ah-beh-nah*
object	**objeto**	*ohb-beh-toh*
oboe	**oboe** *(m.)*	*oh-boh-eh*
October	**octubre**	*ohk-too-breh*
odds and ends	**artículos misceláneos**	*ahr-tee-koo-lohs mee-seh-lah-neh-ohs*
often	**a menudo**	*ah meh-noo-doh*
oil (olive, virgin olive oil, vegetable, canola, corn)	**aceite** *(m.)* (de oliva, de oliva virgen, vegetal, de canola, de maíz)	*ah-seh-ee-teh (deh oh-lee-bah, deh oh-lee-bah beer-hehn, beh-heh-tahl, deh kah-noh-lah, deh mah-ees)*
oil burner	**quemador** *(m.)* **de petróleo**	*keh-mah-dohr deh peh-troh-leh-oh*

continued

English	Spanish	Pronunciation
ointment	**pomada**	*poh-mah-dah*
olive	**aceituna**	*ah-seh-ee-too-nah*
omelet	**tortilla**	*tohr-tee-yah*
on	**sobre**	*soh-breh*
on top of	**encima de**	*ehn-see-mah deh*
one	**uno (una)**	*oo-noh (oo-nah)*
onion	**cebolla**	*seh-boh-yah*
open, to	**abrir**	*ah-breer*
orange (the fruit)	**naranja**	*nah-rahn-hah*
orange (the color)	**anaranjado (anaranjada)**	*ah-nah-rahn-hah-doh (ah-nah-rahn-hah-dah)*
orchid	**orquídea**	*ohr-kee-deh-ah*
order, to	**ordenar**	*ohr-deh-nahr*
oregano	**orégano**	*oh-reh-gah-noh*
organic	**orgánico (orgánica)**	*ohr-gah-nee-koh (ohr-gah-nee-kah)*
organize, to	**organizar**	*ohr-gah-nee-sahr*
ounce	**onza**	*ohn-sah*
outside	**afuera**	*ah-foo-eh-rah*
oven	**horno**	*ohr-noh*
oven mitt	**guante (m.) del horno**	*goo-ahn-teh dehl ohr-noh*
overalls	**overol (m.)**	*oh-beh-rohl*
oyster	**ostra**	*ohs-trah*
pacifier	**chupete (m.)**	*choo-peh-teh*
pack, to	**empaquetar**	*ehm-pah-keh-tahr*
package	**paquete (m.)**	*pah-keh-teh*
pail	**cubo**	*koo-boh*
pain	**dolor (m.)**	*doh-lohr*
paint	**pintura**	*peen-too-rah*
paint pan	**bandeja para pintura**	*bahn-deh-hah pah-rah peen-too-rah*

English	Spanish	Pronunciation
paint remover	**quitapintura** *(m.)*	*kee-tah-peen-too-rah*
paint roller	**rodillo para pintar**	*rroh-dee-yoh pah-rah peen-tahr*
paint stirrer	**agitador** *(m.)* **de pintura**	*ah-hee-tah-dohr deh peen too-rah*
paint, to	**pintar**	*peen tahr*
pajamas	**pijamas**	*pee-hah-mahs*
palm (tree)	**palmera**	*pahl-meh-rah*
pan	**sartén** *(f.)*	*sahr-tehn*
pancake	**panqueque** *(m.)*	*pahn keh keh*
pansy	**pensamiento**	*pehn-sah-mee-ehn-toh*
pantry	**despensa**	*dehs-pehn-sah*
pants	**pantalones** *(m., pl.)*	*pahn-tah-loh-nehs*
pantsuit	**traje** *(m.)* **pantalón**	*trah-heh pahn-tah-lohn*
pantyhose	**medias**	*meh-dee-ahs*
paper	**papel** *(m.)*	*pah-pehl*
paper clip	**sujetapapel** *(m.)*	*soo-heh-tah-pah-pehl*
paper goods	**comestibles** *(m., pl.)* **de papel**	*koh-mehs-tee-blehs deh pah-pehl*
paper towel	**toalla de papel**	*toh-ah-yah deh pah-pehl*
paperweight	**pisapapeles** *(m., sing. and pl.)*	*pee-sah-pah-peh-lehs*
paprika	**pimentón** *(m.)* **dulce**	*pee-mehn-tohn dool-seh*
parakeet	**perico**	*peh-ree-koh*
paralyzed	**paralizado** **(paralizada)**	*pah-rah-lee-sah-doh (pah rah lee-sah-dah)*
parchment paper	**papel** *(m.)* **de pergamino**	*pah-pehl deh pehr-gah-mee-noh*
park	**parque** *(m.)*	*pahr-keh*
park, to	**aparcar**	*ah-pahr-kahr*
parrot	**loro**	*loh-roh*
parsley	**perejil** *(m.)*	*peh-reh-heel*

continued

English	Spanish	Pronunciation
party	**fiesta**	*fee-ehs-tah*
pass, to	**pasar**	*pah-sahr*
pasta	**pasta**	*pahs-tah*
pastry brush	**cepillo para los pasteles**	*seh-pee-yoh pah-rah lohs pahs-teh-lehs*
pay attention, to	**prestar atención**	*prehs-tahr ah-tehn-see-ohn*
pay, to	**pagar**	*pah-gahr*
peach	**melocotón**	*meh-loh-koh-tohn*
peanut	**cacahuate** *(m.)*	*kah-kah-oo-ah-teh*
peanut butter	**crema de maní**	*kreh-mah deh mah-nee*
pear	**pera**	*peh-rah*
pear tree	**peral** *(m.)*	*peh-rahl*
peas	**guisantes** *(m., pl.)*	*gee-sahn-tehs*
peel, to	**pelar**	*peh-lahr*
pen, ballpoint	**bolígrafo**	*boh-lee-grah-foh*
pencil (pencils)	**lápiz** *(m.)* **(lapices)**	*lah-pees (lah-pee-sehs)*
pencil sharpener	**sacapuntas** *(m., sing. and pl.)*	*sah-kah-poon-tahs*
penicillin	**penicilina**	*peh-nee-see-lee-nah*
peony	**peonía**	*peh-oh-nee-ah*
pepper, black	**pimienta**	*pee-mee-ehn-tah*
pepper (green, orange, red, yellow)	**pimiento (verde, naranja, rojo, amarillo)**	*pee-mee-ehn-toh (behr-deh, nah-rahn-hah, rroh-hoh ah-mah-ree-yoh)*
pepper shaker	**pimentero**	*pee-mehn-teh-roh*
perennials	**perennes** *(f., pl.)*	*peh-reh-nehs*
perfume	**perfume**	*pehr-foo-meh*
permanent press	**planchado permanente**	*plahn-chah-doh pehr-mah-nehn-teh*
permission	**permiso**	*pehr-mee-soh*
permit, to	**permitir**	*pehr-mee-teer*
personality disorder	**trastorno de la personalidad**	*trahs-tohr-noh deh lah pehr-soh-nah-lee-dahd*

English	Spanish	Pronunciation
pet, to	**acariciar**	*ah-kah-ree-see-ahr*
petroleum jelly	**vaselina**	*bah-seh-lee-nah*
phlegm	**flema**	*fleh-mah*
phone number	**número de teléfono**	*noo-meh-roh deh teh-leh-foh-noh*
photograph	**fotografía**	*foh-toh-grah-fee-ah*
physical therapy	**fisioterapia**	*fee-see-oh-teh-rah-pee-ah*
piano	**piano**	*pee-ah-noh*
pick	**pico**	*pee-koh*
pick up, to	**recoger**	*rreh-koh-hehr*
pickle	**encurtido**	*ehn-koor-tee-doh*
picture	**cuadro**	*koo-ah-droh*
picture frame	**marco**	*mahr-koh*
pie	**tarta**	*tahr-tah*
piece	**pedazo**	*peh-dah-soh*
pill	**píldora**	*peel-doh-rah*
pillow	**almohada** *(m.)*	*ahl-moh-ah-dah*
pillow sham	**funda de almohada**	*foon-dah deh ahl-moh-ah-dah*
pillowcase	**funda de almohada**	*foon-dah deh ahl-moh-ah-dah*
pin (type of jewelry)	**broche** *(m.)*	*broh-cheh*
pin (clothes, hair)	**pinza**	*peen-sah*
pinch	**pizca**	*pees-kah*
pine	**pino**	*pee-noh*
pineapple	**piña**	*pee-nyah*
pink	**rosado (rosada)**	*rroh-sah-doh (rroh-sah-dah)*
pint	**pinta**	*peen-tah*
pitcher	**jarra**	*hah-rah*
pizza	**pizza**	*pee-sah*
place	**lugar** *(m.)*	*loo-gahr*

continued

English	Spanish	Pronunciation
placemat	mantel (m.) individual	mahn-tehl een-dee-bee-doo-ahl
plane (tool)	cepillo	seh-pee-yoh
plant	planta	plahn-tah
plant, to	plantar	plahn-tahr
plantain	plátano	plah-tah-noh
plaster	yeso	yeh-soh
plastic container	envase (m.) plástico	ehn-bah-seh plahs-tee-koh
plastic pants	pantalones (m., pl.) plásticos	pahm-tah-loh-nehs plahs-tee-kohs
plastic silverware	cubiertos de plástico	koo-bee-ehr-tohs deh plahs-tee-koh
plastic wrap	papel (m.) de plástico	pah-pehl deh plahs-tee-koh
plate (dinner, paper, plastic)	plato (de cena, de papel, de plástico)	plah-toh (deh seh-nah, deh pah-pehl, deh plahs-tee-koh)
play, to	jugar	hoo-gahr
playground	patio de recreo	pah-tee-oh deh rreh-kreh-oh
playpen	corral (m.)	koh-rrahl
please	favor de	fah-bohr deh
pliers	pinzas	peen-sahs
plug in, to	enchufar	ehn-choo-fahr
plum	ciruela	see-roo-eh-lah
pneumonia	pulmonía	pool-moh-nee-ah
poached eggs	huevos escalfados	oo-eh-bohs ehs-kahl-fah-dohs
pocketbook	cartera	kahr-teh-rah
polish	lustrador (m.)	loos-trah-dohr
polish, to	lustrar	loos-trar
pollen	polen (m.)	poh-lehn
polyester	poliéster	poh-lee-ehs-tehr
pomegranate	granada	grah-nah-dah
pool	piscina	pee-see-nah

English	Spanish	Pronunciation
poplar	**álamo**	*ah-lah-moh*
poppy	**petunia**	*peh-too-nee-ah*
porkchop	**chuleta**	*choo-leh-tah*
port	**oporto**	*oh-pohr-toh*
pot	**olla**	*oh-yah*
potato	**papa**	*pah-pah*
potholder	**portaollas** (m., sing. and pl.)	*pohr-tah-oh-yahs*
potpourri	**popurrí** (m.)	*poh-poo-rree*
pottery	**cerámica**	*seh-rah-mee-kah*
potting soil	**tierra abonada**	*tee-eh-rrah ah-boh-nah-dah*
potty (for child)	**orinal de niño** (m.)	*oh-ree-nahl deh nee-nyoh*
pound	**libra**	*lee-brah*
pour, to	**verter**	*behr-tehr*
powder	**polvo**	*pohl-boh*
preheat, to	**precalentar**	*preh-kah-lehn-tahr*
prepare, to	**preparar**	*preh-pah-rahr*
prescription medicine	**medicamento recetado**	*meh-dee-kah-mehn-toh rreh-seh-tah-doh*
press, to	**oprimir**	*oh-pree-meer*
pressure	**presión**	*preh-see-ohn*
pressure cooker	**olla de presión**	*oh-yah deh preh-see-ohn*
printer	**impresora**	*eem-preh-soh-rah*
problem	**problema** (m.)	*proh-bleh-mah*
product	**producto**	*proh-dook-toh*
protector	**protector** (m.)	*proh-tehk-tohr*
prune	**ciruela pasa**	*see-roo-eh-lah pah-sah*
prune, to	**podar**	*poh-dahr*
pruner	**podadora**	*poh-dah-doh-rah*
pudding	**pudín**	*poo-deen*
pull out, to	**arrancar**	*ah-rrahn-kahr*

continued

English	Spanish	Pronunciation
pull, to	**jalar**	*hah-lahr*
pullover	**jersey** *(m.)*	*hehr-seh*
pump	**bomba**	*bohm-bah*
pumpkin	**calabaza**	*kah-lah-bah-sah*
punch	**ponche** *(m.)*	*pohn-cheh*
purifier	**depurador** *(m.)*	*deh-poo-rah-dohr*
purple	**púrpura**	*poor-poo-rah*
push, to	**empujar**	*ehm-poo-hahr*
put, to	**poner**	*poh-nehr*
put away, to	**guardar**	*goo-ahr-dahr*
put in, to	**meter**	*meh-tehr*
put on, to	**ponerse**	*poh-nehr-seh*
put on a burner, to	**prender**	*prehn-dehr*
put to bed, to	**acostar**	*ah-kohs-tahr*
puzzle	**rompecabeza**	*rrohm-peh-kah-beh-sah*
quart	**cuarto**	*koo-ahr-toh*
quarter	**cuarto**	*koo-ahr-toh*
quietly	**tranquilamente**	*trahn-kee-lah-mehn-teh*
quilt	**colcha**	*kohl-chah*
rabbit	**conejo**	*koh-neh-hoh*
rabies	**rabia**	*rrah-bee-ah*
raccoon	**mapache** *(m.)*	*mah-pah-cheh*
rack	**estante** *(m.)*	*ehs-tahn-teh*
radio (clock)	**radio** *(m.)* **(reloj)**	*rrah-dee-oh (rreh-loh)*
radish	**rábano**	*rrah-bah-noh*
rag	**trapo**	*trah-poh*
rain, to	**llover**	*yoh-behr*
raincoat	**impermeable** *(m.)*	*eem-pehr-meh-ah-bleh*
raise, to	**levantar (levatarse)**	*leh-bahn-tahr (leh-bahn-tahr-seh)*
raisin	**pasa**	*pah-sah*
rake	**rastrillo**	*rrahs-tree-yoh*

English	Spanish	Pronunciation
rake, to	**rastrillar**	*rrahs-tree-yahr*
range	**fogón** *(m.)*	*foh-gohn*
range hood	**cubierta del fogón**	*koo-bee-ehr-tah dehl foh-gohn*
rare	**poco hecho (poca hecha)**	*poh-koh eh-choh (poh-kah eh chah)*
rash	**erupción** *(f.)*	*eh-roop-see-ohn*
raspberry	**frambuesa**	*frahm-boo-eh-sah*
rattle	**sonajero**	*soh-nah-heh-roh*
raw	**crudo (cruda)**	*kroo-doh (kroo dah)*
razor	**rasuradora**	*rrah-soo-rah-doh-rah*
razor blade	**hoja de afeitar**	*oh-hah deh ah-feh-ee-tahr*
reach	**alcance** *(m.)*	*ahl-kahn-seh*
read, to	**leer**	*leh-ehr*
reason	**razón** *(f.)*	*rrah-sohn*
recipe	**receta**	*rreh-seh-tah*
recliner	**sillón** *(m.)* **reclinable**	*see-yohn rreh-klee-nah-bleh*
recycle, to	**reciclar**	*rreh-see-klahr*
red	**rojo (roja)**	*rroh-hoh (rroh-hah)*
red snapper	**pargo del golfo**	*pahr-goh dehl gohl-foh*
reduce, to	**reducir**	*rreh-doo-seer*
reference book	**libro de referencias**	*lee-broh deh rreh-feh-rehn-see-ahs*
references	**referencias**	*rreh-feh-rehn-see-ahs*
refrigerator	**refrigerador** *(m.)*	*rreh-free-heh-rah-dohr*
reheat, to	**recalentar**	*rreh-kah-lehn-tahr*
remain, to	**quedar (quedarse)**	*keh-dahr (keh-dahr-seh)*
remember, to	**recordar**	*rreh-kohr-dahr*
remote	**remoto**	*rreh-moh-toh*
remove, to	**quitar**	*kee-tahr*

continued

English	Spanish	Pronunciation
repair person	**mecánico (mecánica)**	*meh-kah-nee-koh (meh-kah-nee-kah)*
replenish, to	**rellenar**	*rreh-yeh-nahr*
resident	**residente**	*rreh-see-dehn-teh*
respect	**respeto**	*rrehs-peh-toh*
restricted	**restringido (restringida)**	*rrehs-treen-gee-doh (rrehs-treen-gee-dah)*
return (come back), to	**regresar**	*rreh-greh-sahr*
return (something somewhere), to	**devolver**	*deh-bohl-behr*
rhododendron	**rododendro**	*rroh-doh-dehn-droh*
rhubarb	**ruibarbo**	*rroo-ee-bahr-boh*
rice	**arroz** *(m.)*	*ah-rrohs*
rice pudding	**pudín** *(m.)* **de arroz**	*poo-deen deh ah-rrohs*
ride a bicycle, to	**montar en bicicleta**	*mohn-tahr ehn bee-see-kleh-tah*
ring (jewelry)	**anillo**	*ah-nee-yoh*
rinse, to	**enjuagar**	*ehn-hoo-ah-gahr*
ripe	**maduro (madura)**	*mah-doo-roh (mah-doo-rah)*
roast beef	**rosbif** *(m.)*	*rrohs-beef*
roast, to	**asar**	*ah-sahr*
roasting pan	**asador** *(m.)*	*ah-sah-dohr*
robe	**bata**	*bah-tah*
roll	**panecillo**	*pah-neh-see-yoh*
rolling pin	**rodillo**	*rroh-dee-yoh*
room	**habitación** *(f.)*	*ah-bee-tah-see-ohn*
rope	**soga**	*soh-gah*
rosemary	**romero**	*rroh-meh-roh*
rose	**rosa**	*rroh-sah*
rotate, to	**dar vueltas a**	*dahr boo-ehl-tahs ah*
rotisserie	**asador** *(m.)*	*ah-sah-dohr*

English	Spanish	Pronunciation
rototiller	**rototiller** *(m.)*	*rroh-toh-tee-yehr*
rub	**restregar**	*rrehs-treh-gahr*
rubber	**goma**	*goh-mah*
rubber band	**goma elástica**	*goh-mah eh-lahs-tee-kah*
rubber gloves	**guantes de goma** *(m., pl.)*	*goo-ahn-tehs deh goh-mah*
rubber sheet	**sábana de plástico**	*sah-bah-nah deh plahs-tee-koh*
rubella	**rubiola**	*rroo-bee-oh-lah*
rug	**alfombra**	*ahl-fohm-brah*
ruler	**regla**	*rreh-glah*
rum	**ron** *(m.)*	*rrohn*
run, to	**correr**	*koh-rrehr*
rye	**whisky de centeno**	*oo-ees-kee deh sehn-teh-noh*
sachet	**sobrecito**	*soh-breh-see-toh*
safety pin	**imperdible**	*eem-pehr-dee-bleh*
saffron	**azafrán** *(m.)*	*ah-sah-frahn*
sage	**salvia**	*sahl-bee-ah*
salad bowl	**ensaladera**	*ehn-sah-lah-deh-rah*
salad dressing	**aderezo**	*ah-deh-reh-soh*
salmon	**salmón** *(m.)*	*sahl-mohn*
salt	**sal** *(f.)*	*sahl*
salt shaker	**salero**	*sah-leh-roh*
sandals	**sandalias**	*sahn-dah-lee-ahs*
sandpaper	**papel** *(m.)* **de lija**	*pah-pehl deh lee-hah*
sanitary napkin	**toalla sanitaria**	*toh-ah-yah sah-nee-tah-ree-ah*
sardine	**sardina**	*sahr-dee-nah*
satin	**raso**	*rrah-soh*
Saturday	**sábado**	*sah-bah-doh*
sauce	**salsa**	*sahl-sah*

continued

English	Spanish	Pronunciation
saucepan	**cacerola**	*kah-seh-roh-lah*
saucer	**platillo**	*plah-tee-yoh*
sausage	**salchicha**	*sahl-chee-chah*
sauté, to	**sofreír**	*soh-freh-eer*
saw	**sierra**	*see-eh-rah*
saxophone	**saxofón**	*sahk-soh-fohn*
scale	**pesa**	*peh-sah*
scallops	**vieiras**	*bee-eh-ee-rahs*
scanner	**escáner** *(m.)*	*ehs-kah-nehr*
scarf	**bufanda**	*boo-fahn-dah*
schedule	**horario**	*oh-rah-ree-oh*
school night	**noche** *(f.)* **escolar**	*noh-cheh ehs-koh-lahr*
scissors	**tijeras**	*tee-heh-rahs*
Scotch (whiskey)	**whisky escocés**	*ooees-kee ehs-koh-sehs*
scouring pad	**estropajo**	*ehs-troh-pah-hoh*
scrambled eggs	**huevos revueltos**	*oo-eh-bohs rreh-boo-ehl-tohs*
scrap paper	**hojas de papel** *(m.)* **suelto**	*oh-hahs deh pah-pehl soo-ehl-toh*
scrape, to	**rallar**	*rrah-yahr*
scraper	**raspador** *(m.)*	*rrahs-pah-dohr*
scream, to	**gritar**	*gree-tahr*
screen (decorative, folding)	**biombo**	*bee-ohm-boh*
screen (for computer, TV, movies)	**pantalla**	*pahn-tah-yah*
screen (outdoor)	**tamiz** *(m.)* **metálico**	*tah-mees meh-tah-lee-koh*
screen door	**puerta con tela metálica**	*poo-ehr-tah kohn teh-lah meh-tah-lee-kah*
screw	**tornillo**	*tohr-nee-yoh*
screwdriver	**destornillador** *(m.)*	*dehs-tohr-nee-yah-dohr*
scrub, to	**fregar**	*freh-gahr*
sculpture	**escultura**	*ehs-kool-too-rah*

English	Spanish	Pronunciation
season, to	**sazonar**	*sah-soh-nahr*
second	**segundo (segunda)**	*seh-goon-doh (seh-goon-dah)*
see, to	**ver**	*behr*
seed	**semilla**	*seh-mee-yah*
Seeing Eye dog	**perro guía**	*peh-rroh gee-ah*
send, to	**mandar**	*mahn-dahr*
separate, to	**separar**	*seh-pah-rahr*
September	**septiembre**	*sehp-tee-ehm-breh*
serve, to	**servir**	*sehr-beer*
set the table, to	**poner la mesa**	*poh-nehr lah meh-sah*
seven	**siete**	*see-eh-teh*
seventeen	**diecisiete**	*dee-ehs-ee-see-eh-teh*
seventh	**séptimo (séptima)**	*sehp-tee-moh (sehp-tee-mah)*
seventy	**setenta**	*seh-tehn-tah*
sew, to	**coser**	*koh-sehr*
sewing kit	**costurero**	*kohs-too-reh-roh*
shade (window)	**persiana**	*pehr-see-ah-nah*
shade (of tree)	**sombra**	*sohm-brah*
shake, to	**agitar**	*ah-hee-tahr*
shaker	**coctelera**	*kohk-teh-leh-rah*
shampoo	**champú**	*chahm-poo*
sharpen	**afilar**	*ah-fee-lahr*
shaving cream	**crema de afeitar**	*kreh-mah deh ah-feh-ee-tahr*
sheet (flat, fitted)	**sábana (encimera, ajustable)**	*sah-bah-nah (ehn-see-meh-rah, ah-hoos-tah-bleh)*
shelf	**estante** *(m.)*	*ehs-tahn-teh*
shellfish	**mariscos**	*mah-rees-kohs*
sherry	**jerez**	*heh-rehs*
shirt	**camisa**	*kah-mee-sah*
shock	**choque** *(m.)*	*choh-keh*

continued

English	Spanish	Pronunciation
shoe	zapato	sah-pah-toh
shoe rack	zapatero	sah-pah-teh-roh
shorts	pantalones (m., pl.) cortos	pahn-tah-loh-nehs kohr-tohs
shot glass	vasito de tragos	bah-see-toh deh trah-gohs
shoulder	hombro	ohm-broh
shovel	pala	pah-lah
show, to	mostrar	mohs-trahr
shower	ducha	doo-chah
shower curtain	cortina de ducha	kohr-tee-nah deh doo-chah
shower door	puerta de la ducha	poo-ehr-tah deh lah doo-chah
shower tile	azulejo	ah-soo-leh-hoh
shred, to	cortar en tiras	kohr-tahr ehn tee-rahs
shredder	trituradora	tree-too-rah-doh-rah
shrimp	camarón (m.)	kah-mah-rohn
shrub	arbusto	ahr-boos-toh
shutter	contraventana	kohn-trah-behn-tah-nah
sick	enfermo (enferma)	ehn-fehr-moh (ehn-fehr-mah)
sift, to	tamizar	tah-mee-sahr
sign language	lenguaje (m.) de señas	lehn-goo-ah-heh deh seh-nyahs
sign, to	firmar	feer-mahr
silk	seda	seh-dah
silver	plata	plah-tah
silverware	cubiertos	koo-bee-ehr-tohs
simmer, to	hervir a fuego lento	ehr-beer ah foo-eh-goh lehn-toh
since	desde	dehs-deh
sink	lavabo (m.)	lah-bah-boh
sister	hermana	ehr-mah-nah
six	seis	seh-ees

English	Spanish	Pronunciation
sixteen	**dieciséis**	*dee-ehs-ee-seh-ees*
sixth	**sexto (sexta)**	*sehks-toh (sehks-tah)*
sixty	**sesenta**	*seh-sehn-tah*
skate, to	**patinar**	*pah-tee-nahr*
skewer	**pincho**	*peen-choh*
skillet	**sartén** *(f.)*	*sahr-tehn*
skim, to	**espumar**	*ehs-poo-mahr*
skin	**piel** *(m.)*	*pee-ehl*
skirt	**falda**	*fahl-dah*
sleep, to	**dormir**	*dohr-meer*
slice	**tajada**	*tah-hah-dah*
slice, to	**cortar en tajadas**	*kohr-tahr ehn tah-hah-dahs*
sliding door	**puerta corrediza**	*poo-ehr-tah koh-rreh-dee-sah*
slip (half, full)	**combinación** *(f.)* **(corta, larga)**	*kohm-bee-nah-see-ohn (kohr-tah, lahr-gah)*
slipcover	**funda removible**	*foon-dah rreh-moh-bee-bleh*
slippers	**chancletas**	*chahn-kleh-tahs*
slow cooker	**vasija de barro**	*bah-see-hah deh bah-rroh*
smoke, to	**fumar**	*foo-mahr*
snack	**merienda**	*meh-ree-ehn-dah*
snail	**caracol** *(m.)*	*kah-rah-kohl*
snake	**serpiente** *(m.)*	*sehr-pee-ehn-teh*
sneakers	**tenis** *(m., pl.)*	*teh-nees*
sneeze, to	**estornudar**	*ehs-tohr-noo-dahr*
snow, to	**nevar**	*neh-bahr*
snow shovel	**pala de nieve**	*pah-lah deh nee-eh-beh*
soak, to	**remojar**	*rreh-moh-hahr*
soap	**jabón** *(m.)*	*hah-bohn*
soap dish	**jabonera**	*hah-boh-neh-rah*
soap scum	**desecho**	*deh-seh-choh*

continued

English	Spanish	Pronunciation
soccer	fútbol *(m.)*	*foot-bohl*
socket	enchufe	*ehn-choo-feh*
socks	calcetines *(m., pl.)*	*kahl-seh-tee-nehs*
soda (diet, decaffeinated)	gaseosa (de dieta, descafeinado)	*gah-seh-oh-sah (deh dee-eh-tah, dehs-kah-feh-ee-nah-doh)*
sofa (couch)	sofá *(m.)*	*soh-fah*
sofa bed	sofá-cama *(m.)*	*soh-fah-kah-mah*
soft	suave	*soo-ah-beh*
soft-boiled eggs	huevos pasados por agua	*oo-eh-bohs pah-sah-dohs pohr ah-goo-ah*
softener	suavizador	*soo-ah-bee-sah-dohr*
soil	tierra	*tee-eh-rah*
solarium	solario	*soh-lah-ree-oh*
sole	lenguado	*lehn-goo-ah-doh*
sometimes	a veces	*ah beh-sehs*
sore throat	dolor *(m.)* de garganta	*doh-lohr deh gahr-gahn-tah*
soup	sopa	*soh-pah*
sour	agrio (agria)	*ah-gree-oh (ah-gree-ah)*
sour cream	crema agria	*kreh-mah ah-gree-ah*
soy sauce	salsa de soja	*sahl-sah deh soh-hah*
spade	pala	*pah-lah*
spaghetti	espagueti *(m.)*	*ehs-pah-geh-tee*
spare tire	neumático de repuesto	*neh-oo-mah-tee-koh deh rreh-poo-ehs-toh*
spatula	espátula	*ehs-pah-too-lah*
speak, to	hablar	*ah-blahr*
speaker	altavoz *(m.)*	*ahl-tah-bohs*
special	especial	*ehs-peh-see-ahl*
spell, to	deletrear	*deh-leh-treh-ahr*
spice	especia	*ehs-peh-see-ah*
spicy	picante	*pee-kahn-teh*

English	Spanish	Pronunciation
spill, to	**derramar**	*deh-rrah-mahr*
spinach	**espinaca**	*ehs-pee-nah-kah*
spine	**espina dorsal**	*chs pcc nah dohr sahl*
spit	**asador** *(m.)*	*ah-sah-dohr*
sponge	**esponja**	*ehs-pohn-hah*
sponge cake	**pastel** *(m.)* **esponjoso**	*pahs-tehl ehs-pohn-hoh-soh*
spoon (plastic, silver, stainless steel, wooden)	**cuchara (de plástico, de plata, de acero inoxidable, de madera)**	*koo-chah-rah (deh plahs-tee-koh, deh plah-tah, deh ah-seh-roh een-ohk-see-dah-bleh, deh mah-deh-rah)*
sport	**deporte** *(m.)*	*deh-pohr-teh*
sports coat	**americana**	*ah-meh-ree-kah-nah*
spot	**mancha**	*mahn-chah*
spot remover	**quitamanchas**	*kee-tah-mahn-chahs*
sprain, to	**torcerse**	*tohr-sehr-seh*
spray	**atomizador**	*ah-toh-mee-sah-dohr*
spray, to	**rociar**	*rroh-see-ahr*
spray gun	**atomizador**	*ah-toh-mee-sah-dohr*
sprayer	**rociador** *(m.)*	*rroh-see-ah-dohr*
spreader	**esparcidor** *(m.)*	*ehs-pahr-see-dohr*
spring	**primavera**	*pree-mah-beh-rah*
springform pan (9 inch)	**caserola de springform (de nueve pulgadas)**	*kah-seh-roh-lah deh spreeng-fohrm (deh noo-eh-beh pool-gah-dahs)*
sprinkle, to	**rociar**	*rroh-see-ahr*
spruce	**abeto**	*ah-beh-toh*
squash	**calabaza**	*kah-lah-bah-sah*
squeegee	**enjugador de goma para limpiar cristales**	*ehn-hoo-gah-dohr deh goh-mah pah-rah leem-pee-ahr krees-tah-lehs*
squeeze, to	**apretar**	*ah-preh-tahr*

continued

English	Spanish	Pronunciation
squid	**calamar** *(m.)*	*kah-lah-mahr*
stack, to	**colocar**	*koh-loh-kahr*
stain remover	**quitamanchas** *(m.)*	*kee-tah-mahn-chahs*
stainless steel	**acero inoxidable**	*ah-seh-roh een-ohk-see-dah-bleh*
stamp	**sello**	*seh-yoh*
staple remover	**quitagrapas** *(m.)*	*kee-tah-grah-pahs*
stapler	**grapadora**	*grah-pah-doh-rah*
staples	**grapas**	*grah-pahs*
starch	**almidón** *(m.)*	*ahl-mee-dohn*
start, to	**empezar**	*ehm-peh-sahr*
stationery	**artículos de papelería**	*ahr-tee-koo-lohs deh pah-peh-leh-ree-ah*
stay, to	**quedar (quedarse)**	*keh-dahr (keh-dahr-seh)*
steak	**bistec** *(m.)*	*bees-tehk*
steam, to	**cocer al vapor**	*koh-sehr ahl bah-pohr*
steamer	**olla de vapor**	*oh-yah deh bah-pohr*
stepbrother	**hermanastro**	*ehr-mah-nahs-troh*
stepfather	**padrastro**	*pah-dahs-troh*
stepladder	**escalera de mano**	*ehs-kah-leh-rah deh mah-noh*
stepmother	**madrastra**	*mah-drahs-trah*
stepsister	**hermanastra**	*ehr-mah-nahs-trah*
stereo	**estéreo**	*ehs-teh-reh-oh*
stew	**cocido**	*koh-see-doh*
stickpin	**alfiler** *(m.)*	*ahl-fee-lehr*
sticky	**pegajoso (pegajosa)**	*peh-gah-hoh-soh (peh-gah-hoh-sah)*
still	**todavía**	*toh-dah-bee-ah*
stir, to	**revolver**	*rreh-bohl-behr*
stirrer	**agitador** *(m.)*	*ah-hee-tah-dohr*
stitches	**puntos**	*poon-tohs*

English	Spanish	Pronunciation
stockings	**medias**	*meh-dee-ahs*
stomach	**estómago**	*ehs-toh-mah-goh*
stomachache	**dolor (m.) de estómago**	*doh-lohr deh ehs-toh-mah-goh*
stop, to	**parar**	*pah-rahr*
storage	**almacenamiento**	*ahl-mah-seh-nah-mee-ehn-toh*
storage room	**depósito**	*deh-poh-see-toh*
store	**tienda**	*tee-ehn-dah*
store, to	**guardar**	*goo-ahr-dahr*
stove	**estufa**	*ehs-too-fah*
strain, to	**colar**	*koh-lahr*
strainer	**colador (m.)**	*koh-lah-dohr*
stranger	**desconocido (desconocida)**	*dehs-koh-noh-see-doh (dehs-koh-noh-see-dah)*
strawberry	**fresa**	*freh-sah*
stroke	**apoplejía**	*ah-poh-pleh-hee-ah*
stroller	**cochecillo**	*koh-cheh-see-yoh*
stuff, to	**rellenar**	*rreh-yeh-nahr*
stuffed animal	**animal (m.) de peluche**	*ah-nee-mahl deh peh-loo-cheh*
suck, to	**chupar**	*choo-pahr*
suede	**gamuza**	*gah-moo-sah*
sugar	**azúcar m.**	*ah-soo-kahr*
sugar bowl	**azucarera**	*ah-soo-kah-reh-rah*
suit	**traje m.**	*trah-heh*
summer	**verano**	*beh-rah-noh*
Sunday	**domingo**	*doh-meen-goh*
sunflower	**girasol (m.)**	*hee-rah-sohl*
suntan lotion (with sun block)	**crema protectora**	*kreh-mah proh-tehk-toh-rah*
supermarket	**supermercado**	*soo-pehr-mehr-kah-doh*

continued

English	Spanish	Pronunciation
supervise, to	**supervisar**	*soo-pehr-bee-sahr*
surgeon	**cirujano (cirujana)**	*see-roo-hah-noh (see-roo-hah-nah)*
surgery	**cirugía**	*see-roo-hee-ah*
surprise	**sorpresa**	*sohr-preh-sah*
suspenders	**tirantes** *(m., pl.)*	*tee-rahn-tehs*
swallow	**tragar**	*trah-gahr*
sweater	**suéter** *(m.)*	*soo-eh-tehr*
sweatsuit	**chándal** *(m.)*	*chahn-dahl*
sweep, to	**barrer**	*bah-rrehr*
sweetener (artificial)	**dulcificante** *(m.)* **(artificial)**	*dool-see-fee-kahn-teh (ahr-tee-fee-see-ahl)*
swim, to	**nadar**	*nah-dahr*
swing	**columpio**	*koh-loom-pee-oh*
swordfish	**pez** *(m.)* **espada**	*pehs ehs-pah-dah*
syrup	**jarabe** *(m.)*	*hah-rah-beh*
table (coffee, end, Ping Pong, pool)	**mesa (de café, mesita auxiliaria de salón, de pimpón, de billar)**	*meh-sah (deh kah-feh, meh-see-tah ah-oo-see-lee-ah-ree-ah, deh sah-lohn, deh peem-pohm, deh bee-yahr)*
table leaves	**extensiones de mesa**	*ehks-tehn-see-oh-nehs deh meh-sah*
table pads	**almohadillas de mesa**	*ahl-moh-ah-dee-yahs deh meh-sah*
table runner	**salvamanteles**	*sahl-bah-mahn-teh-lehs*
tablecloth (linen, paper, plastic)	**mantel** *(m.)* **(de lino, de papel, de plástico)**	*mahn-tehl (deh lee-noh, deh pah-pehl, deh plahs-tee-koh)*
tablespoon	**cuchara**	*koo-chah-rah*
tablespoonful	**cucharada**	*koo-chah-rah-dah*
tablet	**pastilla**	*pahs-tee-yah*
tailor	**sastre** *(m.)*	*sahs-treh*
take care of, to	**cuidar**	*koo-ee-dahr*

English	Spanish	Pronunciation
take out, to	**sacar**	*sah-kahr*
take, to	**tomar**	*toh-mahr*
talcum powder	**talco**	*tahl-koh*
tame	**domesticado (domesticada)**	*doh-mehs-tee-kah-doh (doh-mehs-tee-kah-dah)*
tampon	**tampón**	*tahm-pohn*
tangerine	**mandarina**	*mahn-dah-ree-nah*
tape (adhesive, such as Scotch brand)	**cinta adhesiva**	*seen-tah ahd-eh-see-bah*
tape measure	**cinta métrica**	*seen-tah meh-tree-kah*
tart	**tarta**	*tahr-tah*
tasty	**sabroso (sabrosa)**	*sah-broh-soh (sah-broh-sah)*
tea (herbal, decaffeinated, iced, hot)	**té (m.) (de hierba, descafeinado, helado, caliente)**	*teh (deh ee-ehr-bah, dehs-kah-feh-ee-nah-doh, eh-lah-doh, kah-lee-ehn-tch)*
tea cart	**carrito de té**	*kah-rree-toh deh teh*
tea service (silver)	**servicio de té (de plata)**	*sehr-bee-see-oh deh teh (deh plah-tah)*
teapot	**tetera**	*teh-teh-rah*
teaspoon	**cucharita**	*koo-chah-ree-tah*
teaspoonful	**cucharadita**	*koo-chah-rah-dee-tah*
T-shirt	**camiseta**	*kah-mee-seh-tah*
telephone	**teléfono**	*teh-leh-foh-noh*
television (large-screen television)	**televisión (f.) (televisor [m.] de pantalla grande)**	*teh-leh-bee-see-ohn (teh-leh-bee-sohr deh pahn-tah-yah grahn-deh)*
tell, to	**decir**	*deh-seer*
temperature	**temperatura**	*tehm-peh-rah-too-rah*
ten	**diez**	*dee-ehs*
tender	**tierno (tierna)**	*tee-ehr-noh (tee-ehr-nah)*
tennis	**tenis (m.)**	*teh-nees*
tennis court	**cancha de tenis**	*kahn-chah deh teh-nees*

continued

English	Spanish	Pronunciation
tenth	**décimo (décima)**	*deh-see-moh (deh-see-mah)*
teriyaki sauce	**salsa japonesa**	*sahl-sah hah-poh-neh-sah*
terrarium	**terrario**	*teh-rrah-ree-oh*
tetanus	**tétano**	*teh-tah-noh*
thank you	**gracias**	*grah-see-ahs*
there is/are	**hay**	*ah-ee*
thermometer (instant read, oven)	**termómetro (instantáneo, de horno)**	*tehr-moh-meh-troh (een-stahn-tah-neh-oh, deh ohr-noh)*
Thermos	**termo**	*tehr-moh*
thesaurus	**tesauro**	*teh-sah-oo-roh*
thicken, to	**espesar**	*ehs-peh-sahr*
thing	**cosa**	*koh-sah*
think, to	**pensar**	*pehn-sahr*
third	**tercero (tercera)**	*tehr-seh-roh (tehr-seh-rah)*
thirteen	**trece**	*treh-seh*
thirty	**treinta**	*treh-een-tah*
thousand	**mil**	*meel*
thread	**hilo**	*ee-loh*
three	**tres**	*trehs*
throat	**garganta**	*gahr-gahn-tah*
throw away, to	**botar**	*boh-tahr*
thumb tack	**tachuela**	*tah-choo-eh-lah*
Thursday	**jueves** *(m., sing. and pl.)*	*hoo-eh-behs*
thyme	**tomillo**	*toh-mee-yoh*
tie	**corbata**	*kohr-bah-tah*
tie rack	**estirador** *(m.)* **de corbatas**	*ehs-tee-rah-dor deh kohr-bah-tahs*
tie, to	**atar**	*ah-tahr*
tights	**leotardo**	*leh-oh-tahr-doh*
tile	**loceta**	*loh-seh-tah*

English	Spanish	Pronunciation
time (in series)	**vez** *(f.)*	*behs*
timer	**reloj** *(m.)* **de cocina**	*rreh-loh deh koh-see-nah*
tin	**lata**	*lah-tah*
tip	**propina**	*proh-pee-nah*
tire	**goma**	*goh-mah*
tissue	**kleenex** *(m.)*	*klee-nehks*
toast (in a toaster/oven), to	**tostar**	*tohs-tahr*
toaster/toaster oven	**tostador** *(m.)*	*tohs-tah-dohr*
today	**hoy**	*oh-ee*
toe	**dedo del pie**	*deh-doh dehl pee-eh*
toilet	**inodoro**	*een-oh-doh-roh*
toilet paper	**papel** *(m.)* **higiénico**	*pah-pehl ee-hee-eh-nee-koh*
toilet paper holder	**soporte** *(m.)* **del papel higiénico**	*soh-pohr-teh dehl pah-pehl ee-hee-eh-nee-koh*
tomato	**tomate** *(m.)*	*toh-mah-teh*
tomorrow	**mañana**	*mah-nyah-nah*
tongs	**pinzas**	*peen-sahs*
tongue	**lengua**	*lehn-goo-ah*
tonic	**tónico**	*toh-nee-koh*
tonsilitis	**amigdalitis** *(f.)*	*ah-meeg-dah-lee-tees*
too much/many	**demasiado**	*deh-mah-see-ah-doh*
tool	**herramienta**	*eh-rrah-mee-ehn-tah*
toolbox	**caja de herramientas**	*kah-hah deh eh-rrah-mee-ehn-tahs*
tooth	**diente** *(m.)*	*dee-ehn-teh*
toothache	**dolor** *(m.)* **de muelas**	*doh-lohr deh moo-eh-lahs*
toothbrush	**cepillo de dientes**	*seh-pee-yoh deh dee-ehn-tehs*
toothbrush holder	**soporte** *(m.)* **del cepillo de dientes**	*soh-pohr-teh dehl seh-pee-yoh deh dee-ehn-tehs*
toothpaste	**pasta de dientes**	*pahs-tah deh dee-ehn-tehs*

continued

English	Spanish	Pronunciation
toothpicks	**palillos de dientes**	*pah-lee-yohs deh dee-ehn-tehns*
touch, to	**tocar**	*toh-kahr*
tough	**duro (dura)**	*doo-roh (doo-rah)*
towel (beach)	**toalla (playera)**	*toh-ah-yah (plah-yeh-rah)*
towel (face/hand)	**toalla (de mano)**	*toh-ah-yah (deh mah-noh)*
towel rack	**toallero**	*toh-ah-yeh-roh*
toy	**juguete** *(m.)*	*hoo-geh-teh*
toy cars (trains, trucks)	**coches (trenes, camiones) de juguete**	*koh-chehs (treh-nehs, kah-mee-oh-nehs) deh hoo-geh-teh*
trained	**entrenado (entrenada)**	*ehn-treh-nah-doh (ehn-treh-nah-dah)*
training	**entrenamiento**	*ehn-treh-nah-mee-ehn-toh*
training pants	**calzones** *(m.)* **para entrenar**	*kahl-soh-nehs pah-rah ehn-treh-nahr*
trash bag	**bolsa para basura**	*bohl-sah pah-rah bah-soo-rah*
trash can	**cesto de basura**	*sehs-toh deh bah-soo-rah*
trash compactor	**comprimidor** *(m.)* **de basura**	*kohm-pree-mee-dohr deh bah-soo-rah*
tray	**bandeja**	*bahn-deh-hah*
treat, to	**tratar**	*trah-tahr*
trim, to	**recortar**	*rreh-kohr-tahr*
trimmer	**podador** *(m.)*	*poh-dah-dohr*
trombone	**trombón** *(m.)*	*trohm-bohn*
trout	**trucha**	*troo-chah*
trowel	**paleta**	*pah-leh-tah*
trumpet	**trompeta**	*trohm-peh-tah*
try to, to	**tratar de**	*trah-tahr deh*
tube pan	**caserola de tubo**	*kah-seh-roh-lah deh too-boh*
Tuesday	**martes** *(m., sing. and pl.)*	*mahr-tehs*

English	Spanish	Pronunciation
tulip	**tulipán** *(m.)*	*too-lee-pahn*
tumor	**tumor** *(m.)*	*too-mohr*
tuna	**atún** *(m.)*	*ah-toon*
turkey	**pavo**	*pah-boh*
turn off, to	**apagar**	*ah-pah-gahr*
turn on, to	**prender (prenderse)**	*prehn-dehr (prehn-dehr-seh)*
turn, to	**doblar**	*doh-blahr*
turnip	**nabo**	*nah-boh*
turtle	**tortuga**	*tohr-too-gah*
tweezers	**pinzas**	*peen-sahs*
twelve	**doce**	*doh-seh*
twenty	**veinte**	*beh-een-teh*
twine	**bramante**	*brah-mahn-teh*
two	**dos**	*dohs*
ulcer	**úlcera**	*ool-seh-rah*
umbrella	**paraguas** *(m., sing. and pl.)*	*pah-rah-goo-ahs*
unattended	**desatendido (desatendida)**	*dehs-ah-tehn-dee-doh (dehs-ah-tehn-dee-dah)*
uncle	**tío**	*tee-oh*
unconscious	**inconsciente**	*een-kohn-see-ehn-teh*
uncover, to	**destapar**	*dehs-tah-pahr*
undercooked	**poco cocinado (poca cocinada)**	*poh-koh koh-see-nah-doh (poh-kah koh-see-nah-dah)*
underneath	**debajo de**	*deh-bah-hoh deh*
understand, to	**comprender**	*kohm-prehn-dehr*
underwear	**ropa interior**	*rroh-pah een-teh-ree-ohr*
undress, to	**desvestir (desvestirse)**	*dehs-behs-teer (dehs-behs-teer-seh)*
uniform	**uniforme** *(m.)*	*oo-nee-fohr-meh*
United States	**Estados Unidos**	*ehs-tah-dohs oo-nee-dohs*

continued

English	Spanish	Pronunciation
unmold, to	desmoldear	dehs-mohl-deh-ahr
unplug, to	desenchufar	dehs-ehn-choo-fahr
until	hasta	ahs-tah
use, to	usar	oo-sahr
utensil	utensilio	oo-tehn-see-lee-oh
vaccination	vacuna	bah-koo-nah
vacuum cleaner	aspiradora	ah-spee-rah-doh-rah
vacuum cleaner bag	bolsa para la aspiradora	bohl-sah pah-rah lah ahs-pee-rah-doh-rah
vacuum, to	pasar la aspiradora	pah-sahr lah ahs-pee-rah-doh-rah
vanilla	vainilla	bah-ee-nee-yah
vanity	tocador (m.)	toh-kah-dohr
vase	florero	floh-reh-roh
veal roast	ternera asada	tehr-neh-rah ah-sah-dah
vegetable	legumbre (m.)	leh-goom-breh
vegetable peeler	pelador (m.)	peh-lah-dohr
vegetarian	vegetariano (vegerariana)	beh-heh-tah-ree-ah-noh (beh-heh-tah-ree-ah-nah)
velvet	terciopelo	tehr-see-oh-peh-loh
vermouth	vermut	behr-moot
very	muy	moo-ee
vest	chaleco	chah-leh-koh
veterinarian	veterinario (veterinaria)	beh-teh-ree-nah-ree-oh (beh-teh-ree-nah-ree-ah)
video game	juego de vídeo	hoo-eh-goh deh bee-deh-oh
video recorder (digital)	aparato de vídeo (digital)	ah-pah-rah-toh deh bee-deh-oh (dee-hee-tahl)
vinegar (balsamic)	vinagre (m.) (balsámico)	bee-nah-greh (bahl-sah-mee-koh)
vinyl	vinilo	bee-nee-loh
violet	violeta	bee-oh-leh-tah
violin	violín (m.)	bee-oh-leen

English	Spanish	Pronunciation
virus	**virus** (*m.*)	*bee-roos*
vitamin	**vitamina**	*bee-tah-mee-nah*
vodka	**vodca**	*bohd-kah*
volleyball	**voleibol** (*m.*)	*boh-leh-ee-bohl*
vomit, to	**vomitar**	*boh-mee-tahr*
waffle	**gofre** (*m.*)	*goh-freh*
waffle iron	**plancha para gofres**	*plahn-chah pah-rah goh-frehs*
wait, to	**esperar**	*ehs-peh-rahr*
wake up, to	**despertar** (**despertarse**)	*dehs-pehr-tahr (dehs-pehr-tahr seh)*
walk, to	**caminar**	*kah-mee-nahr*
walker (used by babies)	**andador**	*ahn-dah-dohr*
walker (used by adults)	**andador** (*m.*)	*ahn-dah-dohr*
wall	**pared** (*f.*)	*pah-rehd*
wall unit	**unidad** (*f.*) **de pared**	*oo-nee-dahd deh pah-rehd*
wallet	**cartera**	*kahr-teh-rah*
walnut	**nuez** (*f.*)	*noo-ehs*
wardrobe	**armario**	*ahr-mah-ree-oh*
warm	**tibio** (**tibia**)	*tee-bee-oh (tee-bee-ah)*
warm, to	**calentar**	*kah-lehn-tahr*
wash, to	**lavar**	*lah-bahr*
washcloth	**toallita**	*toh-ah-yee-tah*
washing machine	**lavadora**	*lah-bah-doh-rah*
wastepaper basket	**papelero**	*pah-peh-leh-roh*
watch/wristwatch	**reloj** (*m.*)	*rreh-loh*
watch, to	**mirar**	*mee-rahr*
water	**agua** (*f., but takes m. article*)	*ah-goo-ah*
water, to	**regar**	*rreh-gahr*

continued

English	Spanish	Pronunciation
water heater	calentador (m.) para agua	kah-lehn-tah-dohr pah-rah ah-goo-ah
watering can	regadera	rreh-gah-deh-rah
watermelon	sandía	sahn-dee-ah
wax paper	papel (m.) encerado	pah-pehl ehn-seh-rah-doh
wax, to	encerar	ehn-seh-rahr
weak	débil	deh-beel
wear, to	llevar	yeh-bahr
weather	tiempo	tee-ehm-poh
Wednesday	miércoles (m., sing and pl.)	mee-ehr-koh-lehs
weed	mala hierba	mah-lah ee-ehr-bah
weed killer	herbicida (m.)	ehr-bee-see-dah
week	semana	seh-mah-nah
weeping willow	sauce (m.) llorón	sah-oo-seh yoh-rohn
well done	bien hecho	bee-ehn eh-choh
wet	mojado (mojada)	moh-hah-doh (moh-hah-dah)
what?	¿qué?	keh
wheelbarrow	carretilla	kah-rreh-tee-yah
wheelchair	silla de ruedas	see-yah deh rroo-eh-dahs
wheeze	resollar	rreh-soh-yahr
when?	¿cuándo?	koo-ahn-doh
where?	¿dónde?	dohn-deh
which?	¿cuál?	koo-ahl
which ones?	¿cuáles?	koo-ah-lehs
while	rato	rrah-toh
whip, to	batir	bah-teer
whisk	batidor (m.)	bah-tee-dohr
whisky	whisky	oo-ees-kee
white	blanco (blanca)	blahn-koh (blahn-kah)
who/whom?	¿quién?	kee-ehn

English	Spanish	Pronunciation
why?	¿por qué?	pohr keh
windbreaker	cazadora	kah-sah-doh-rah
window	ventana	behn-tah-nah
window sill	alféizar (m.)	ahl-feh-ee-sahr
window treatment	decoración de la ventana	deh-koh-rah-see-ohn deh lah behn-tah-nah
windshield	parabrisas (m., sing. and pl.)	pah-rah-bree-sahs
wine (red, rosé, sparkling, white)	vino (tinto, rosado, espumoso, blanco)	bee-noh (teen-toh, rroh-sah-doh, ehs-poo-moh-soh, blahn-koh)
wine decanter	licorera de vino	lee-koh-reh-rah deh bee-noh
winter	invierno	een-bee-ehr-noh
wipe, disposable	toallita desechable	toh-ah-yee-tah deh-seh-chah-bleh
wipe, to	pasarle un trapo a	pah-sahr-leh oon trah-poh ah
wire	alambre (m.)	ah-lahm-breh
wire cutters	cortaalambres (m.)	kohr-tah-ah-lahm-brehs
with	con	kohn
without	sin	seen
wok	wok (m.)	wohk
wood	madera	mah-deh-rah
wool	lana	lah-nah
Worchestershire sauce	salsa inglesa	sahl-sah een-gleh-sah
work, to	trabajar	trah-bah-hahr
workbench	banco de trabajo	bahn-koh deh trah-bah-hoh
workstation	terminal (m.)	tehr-mee-nahl
wound	herida	eh-ree-dah
wrap, to	envolver	ehn-bohl-behr

continued

English	Spanish	Pronunciation
wrapping paper	**papel para envolver**	*pah-pehl pah-rah ehn-bohl-behr*
wrench	**llave** *(f.)* **inglesa**	*yah-beh een-gleh-sah*
wrist	**muñeca**	*moo-nyeh-kah*
write, to	**escribir**	*ehs-kree-beer*
wrong	**equivocado (equivocada)**	*eh-kee-boh-kah-doh (eh-kee-boh-kah-dah)*
yam	**batata**	*bah-tah-tah*
yardstick	**regla**	*rreh-glah*
year	**año**	*ah-nyoh*
yellow	**amarillo (amarilla)**	*ah-mah-ree-yoh (ah-mah-ree-yah)*
yes	**sí**	*see*
yesterday	**ayer**	*ah-yehr*
yogurt	**yogur** *(m.)*	*yoh-goor*
you're welcome	**de nada**	*deh nah-dah*
zero	**cero**	*seh-roh*
zipper	**cremallera**	*kreh-mah-yeh-rah*
zucchini	**calabacín** *(m.)*	*kah-lah-bah-seen*